Social Work with
Autistic People

of related interest

A Practical Guide to the Mental Capacity Act 2005, Second Edition
Putting the Principles of the Act into Practice
Matthew Graham and Jakki Cowley
ISBN 978 1 78775 452 2
eISBN 978 1 78775 453 9

The Straightforward Guide to Safeguarding Adults
From Getting the Basics Right to Applying the
Care Act and Criminal Investigations
Deborah Barnett
ISBN 978 1 78592 327 2
eISBN 978 1 78450 640 7

A Practical Guide to Happiness in Adults on the Autism Spectrum
A Positive Psychology Approach
Victoria Honeybourne
ISBN 978 1 78592 577 1
eISBN 978 1 78450 988 0

Safeguarding Adults and the Law, Third Edition
An A–Z of Law and Practice
Michael Mandelstam
ISBN 978 1 78592 225 1
eISBN 978 1 78450 499 1

Overcoming Challenges in the Mental Capacity Act 2005
Practical Guidance for Working with Complex Issues
Camillia Kong and Alex Ruck Keene
Foreword by Anselm Eldergill
ISBN 978 1 78592 259 6
eISBN 978 1 78450 548 6

Autism and Enablement
Occupational Therapy Approaches to Promote
Independence for Adults with Autism
Matt Bushell, Sandra Gasson and Ute Vann
ISBN 978 1 78592 087 5
eISBN 978 1 78450 348 2

The Guide to Good Mental Health on the Autism Spectrum
Jeanette Purkis, Emma Goodall and Jane Nugent
Forewords by Wenn Lawson and Kirsty Dempster-Rivett
ISBN 978 1 84905 670 0
eISBN 978 1 78450 195 2

Social Work with Autistic People

Essential Knowledge, Skills and the Law for Working with Children and Adults

Yo Dunn

Forewords by Alex Ruck Keene
and Ruth Allen

Jessica Kingsley Publishers
London and Philadelphia

First published in Great Britain in 2020 by Jessica Kingsley Publishers

An Hachette Company

1

Copyright © Yo Dunn 2020

Lists on pp100–1 and pp.230–1 reproduced with kind
permission from the National Autistic Taskforce.

A CIP catalogue record for this title is available from the
British Library and the Library of Congress

ISBN 978 1 78592 079 0
eISBN 978 1 78450 339 0

Printed and bound in Great Britain by Clays

Jessica Kingsley Publishers policy is to use papers that are natural,
renewable and recyclable products and made from wood grown in
sustainable forests. The logging and manufacturing processes are expected
to conform to the environmental regulations of the country of origin.

Jessica Kingsley Publishers
73 Collier Street
London N1 9BE, UK

www.jkp.com

For 'the other half': those autistic people
who are less able to advocate for themselves

Contents

Foreword

Alex Ruck Keene

With Yo, you get precisely what she promises. I remember this vividly from a discussion we had shortly before we went on stage to share a session at a conference, when she told me that she had timed her speech and it would last a specific amount of time. True enough, her careful but passionate presentation lasted exactly that length of time, and delivered exactly what she had promised it would. Having shared the platform with many speakers over the years, I only wish that this was something that I could say more often.

Likewise, this book promises to cover essential knowledge, skills and the law for working with autistic children and adults.[1] And it does precisely that. With precision, patience, flashes of humour and, where necessary, quiet fury, the book provides all those who work with autistic people with the knowledge of the condition in all of its extraordinary spectrum of manifestations, the skills that they require then to respond to the needs which might arise in consequence, and a fantastically clear and detailed exegesis of the legal frameworks that are engaged, and how they are engaged.

From my perspective as a self-avowed mental capacity nerd, I would single out for specific attention the chapters on assessing mental capacity and autism, and supporting decision-making and autism. They should be required reading not only for the social workers who are the target audience of the book, but also for lawyers seeking to meet and responds to the needs of autistic people, in

---

1   I use the term 'autistic children and adults' because that is the term that Yo uses. I am conscious that others might use the term 'person with autism,' but I take my lead here from Yo.

particular in the context of potential or actual proceedings before the Court of Protection. Questions of capacity in the context of autism are, from my experience, so often poorly addressed; anyone who reads this book could have no sensible excuse not to do better in future.

Yo is to be congratulated on this work, and I welcome its publication.

Foreword

Ruth Allen

This is a much-needed book and an excellent resource for social workers and social work educators. It is clear, well-evidenced and uses case examples throughout that bring its principles and ideas to life. BASW has worked with the Department of Health and Social Care in England to produce a Capabilities Statement for social work with Autistic People and learning pathways (BASW 2019). We did this because there is a great gap in literature and professional guidance. Yo's book, which reflects her wide professional knowledge as well as her experiences as an autistic person, is a vital and timely resource that I hope is part of sea change in recognising what social workers can offer in this field.

Social work celebrates diversity and is rooted in commitment to removing barriers to inclusion, helping all people thrive, progress, achieve. As a unified profession with common aims of promoting rights, justice and wellbeing, social workers in the UK are most often trained in generic, holistic skills, values, ethics and knowledge. This is a foundation for practice in any setting and from there we often specialise and deepen our practice in particular fields. Throughout our careers we must embrace new knowledge and constantly reflect and learn – and this includes recognising our need to deepen skills and knowledge of sub-specialisms complementary to our main field.

Social work with autistic people has been largely uncharted until recently. Yet, as Yo describes, autism inevitably threads through all areas of social work with children and adults. Social workers encounter autistic people in all other fields of practice – but have often not even realised it or, having realised it, have not been able to access good training and guidance relevant to their roles.

Autism was largely invisible in policy and services until the 1970s and has only developed its own policy and practice fields across different professions in the last 20 years. Despite legislation (Autism Act 2009) and policy initiatives, practice by all professionals, and provision of specialist services particularly for adults has developed very slowly, not least hindered in social care by austerity and swinging cuts in local authorities. There are still very few specialist social care or integrated services for autistic adults and adults struggle to get recognition and support.

Where services for autistic people have developed, this has most often been in a diagnostic and clinical paradigm for people with the most disabling needs, perhaps co-existing with learning disabilities or mental distress.

Yo's book clearly lays out the vital importance of a social approaches to autism being integrated with other helpful perspectives, and highlights social workers' key roles in promoting and addressing barriers to services, stigma, lack of adjustments for instance in appropriate communication, care planning and relationships with professionals.

This is an important, thoughtful and thought provoking book that provides both practical and conceptual frameworks to improve practice, and ultimately to improve the lives of autistic people.

Acknowledgements

A book is never solely the work of an individual. So many people have contributed in various ways. I would like to especially acknowledge and say a very big thank you to:

- my children, Jamie and Aaron, for providing emotional support and encouragement; Richard, for providing a steadying hand; and to William Gadsby for patiently listening

- a team of very special support workers – Janet Regan, Melody Boughton, Nicky Stephenson and Mish Liddle – for essential and much-valued practical and logistical support (without which I would not be able to live the life I choose)

- my friends K. Leneh Buckle, Martijn Dekker, Kabie Brook and Josh Hennessy, and all those who have attended Autscape, for developing my understanding of autism, listening and debating ideas over many years

- Claire Wright, Paul Hollingdale and, especially, Clare Brown for giving up their valuable time to read drafts of chapters and contributing their insightful comments from a practice perspective

- some truly exceptional and memorable social workers I have met who have inspired me over the years: Anne Rigby, Paul Chandelaney and Stephanie Holmes

- an equally exceptional advocate: Pauline Needham

- all the individuals who have willingly allowed me to use their stories throughout this book

- David S. (a very patient proof-reader)

- finally, Steve Jones, my editor, for his patience over a substantial period and endless faith that I would, eventually, get it written.

CHAPTER 1

Where Does Autism Fit from a Social Work Perspective?

1.1 Autism in the context of social work

1.1.1 A very brief history

Autism was largely invisible in social work until the 1970s. Autistic adults and children of earlier generations mostly existed, alongside others rejected by mainstream society, amongst the vaguely labelled 'mentally handicapped' accommodated in long-stay hospitals. Some 'higher-functioning' individuals survived in the community, considered merely 'eccentric'.

As the community care movement of the 1970s and 1980s led to the closure of long-stay institutions, so understanding of autism developed into recognition of it as a neurodevelopmental disability. Care and support decisions increasingly moved away from health and into social care and the importance of social work to the lives of autistic children and adults grew.

During the 1990s, recognition of autism in adults without accompanying learning disabilities led to the broadening of diagnostic criteria to cover the full range of the autistic spectrum. The important role of informal carers in 'community care' and their resulting needs began to be acknowledged. Disability equality and human rights enjoyed a prominent place on the political agenda and, for a brief period, the future of social work with autistic people looked bright.

In the new century, however, new challenges and strains have emerged. Broadly, adult social work has focused on person-centred and strengths-based work, but in a context marked by ever increasing need and significantly diminishing resources. At the same time, social work in the child protection context has been high-profile and, at times, defensive in a climate of media-driven crises.

It is against the backdrop of this climate that autism has begun to attract a policy focus of its own, distinct from those of other (sometimes overlapping) disabilities. The Autism Act 2009, related statutory guidance and resulting Autism Strategy documents (Fulfilling and Rewarding Lives in 2010, Think Autism in 2014 and the forthcoming strategy refresh 2019/2020) emphasize the importance of recognizing autism holistically and as distinct from other conditions.

However, this autism-specific recognition struggles to impact significantly on frontline social work practice and there is considerable variation in practice in different parts of the country. Historical divisions between children and adult services and between physical disabilities, learning disabilities, mental health and older adults continue to mean that social work with autistic people rarely forms part of a holistic service. Social workers can find themselves working with autistic individuals in a variety of services and contexts, very few of them autism-specific. And autistic people, families and carers may experience difficult transitions, poorly co-ordinated services and limited understanding of our particular needs and perspectives. Many other autistic individuals remain on the outside of social care services: some because they are able to manage adequately without formal support, others because they are unable to access social care at all or are only able to do so when they have reached a crisis point.

1.1.2 Autism and models of disability

The social model of disability, which defines disability in terms of the barriers created by the way society is organized, rather than by a person's impairment or difference, is undoubtedly valuable in recognizing the lack of equality disabled people (including autistic people) experience in society. The dominant medical model, which sees autism in terms of deficit in the individual, has had some negative consequences for autistic people (Milton 2019). On occasion, however, the social model can be used in a way which risks minimizing, avoiding or trivializing real and valid experience of impairment in disability (such as chronic pain). Many autistic adults and children do experience difficulties – such as getting 'stuck' (Shah 2019) – which cause functional impairment even in the absence of a social context. Views differ considerably within the autistic community (that is, amongst autistic people ourselves), as well as the wider autism community (including families and professionals), on the 'right' balance between social model and medical model views of autism (Milton 2019; Woods 2017). I do not intend to debate the issue here but I will draw on both models at different times to the extent that they are useful in making sense of autistic experience.

1.1.3 Autism and organizational structures in social care

'Teams' and structures in social care vary between local authorities and over time. There are many different models: the 'traditional' divisions – older adults, child protection, learning disability, mental health, children with disabilities; transition teams crossing over children and adult services; increasingly generic, place-based all-age disabilities teams, remodelling teams and a bewildering array of other terms. Pure 'autism' teams are rare, although not entirely unknown. Autistic children are most commonly subsumed under 'children with disabilities' or, more broadly, 'child in need' groupings. Where generic teams are not in use, autistic adults are most commonly subsumed under learning disabilities (LD), now often becoming learning disability and autism teams, but LD social workers may have limited experience working with autistic adults without learning disabilities and be provided with little or no useful training. At the same time and in parallel, mental health social workers encounter autistic adults with mental health diagnoses both with and without learning disabilities. Autistic adults without a learning disability and who do not have severe and enduring mental health issues rarely receive social care services and it is sometimes assumed they will not meet eligibility criteria. Older adults' social workers, in all probability, encounter autistic older adults regularly but lack of an autism diagnosis means that neither social worker nor client may recognize their autism.

In some authorities, structures have refocused on process stages rather than client group. Preventive and 'wellbeing' coaching, advice and information, self-commissioning from micro-providers, self-help and self-assessment processes and (sometimes essentially compulsory) reablement/enablement services, whilst providing useful support for some, can also act as 'gatekeeping' to discourage access to statutory services at all. Initial screening tends to rely heavily on one or more telephone conversations, with face-to-face contact only occurring at the point of a full assessment for those who are referred further into the system. Those who do receive social care support, once a care package is in place, now commonly find that their case is 'closed' and contact ceases with any social worker involved, apart from infrequent reviews – often carried out by different staff in a separate 'review team'.

In all types of structures, case holding, once the norm, is now a rarity. Whatever view is taken about the pros and cons of this development for social work generally, the impact is disproportionately negative for autistic people, who find change difficult, need more time to become comfortable with new people and new situations, require additional time to take decisions and struggle with communication (see Chapters 2 and 5 particularly).

Similarly, in all types of structures, social care has become much more reliant on staff who are not qualified social workers in frontline roles: in ongoing work with children and families, in reablement/ enablement, in initial screening, many assessments, and in reviewing cases. Some unqualified individuals excel in their roles, but negative consequences for clients can result where there is insufficient access to advice, supervision and support from qualified social workers. Local authorities have also been encouraged to outsource many functions which may include services such as: assessment and support for carers; care planning; and direct payments support. Again, such outsourcing can be successful, but negative consequences for clients can result where insufficient responsibility is taken by local authorities for the delegated service or there is poor liaison between the outsourced services and council staff with related responsibilities (such as social care assessment). These are broad issues within social care which affect all client groups. But here, again, autistic people may be disproportionately affected. Effective assessment, support and work with autistic people takes time, autism-specific skills and knowledge, and clear and honest communication (see Chapter 2).

1.2 Why do I need to do anything differently for autism?

'Good social work is good social work. Diagnosis should not matter' is a common social work view. Some practitioners see such an 'anti-labelling' view as essential for non-discriminatory practice. However, in the same way that the importance of considering aspects of identity, such as ethnicity and culture (Thoburn, Norford and Rashid 2000), has been recognized in social work theory and practice, it is important that the different perceptions and experience of the world which are encapsulated in a diagnosis of autism are fully acknowledged.

Modern understandings of autism increasingly recognize that the autistic view of the world is a fundamentally different one (Silberman 2015). That view is not automatically or necessarily wrong or deficient, but distinctly different. Just as it is possible for well-meaning professionals to inadvertently discriminate against minority ethnic or cultural groups through lack of knowledge of a range of cultures, similarly there is a constant risk for professionals of doing more harm than good by wading into the lives of autistic clients without sufficient understanding and awareness of neurodivergent ways of seeing the world.

Some common examples of thinking which may inadvertently discriminate by treating autistic people as if they were the same as non-autistic people include:

- Seeking to comfort and reassure, a gentle touch on the hand or shoulder will help.

- The client who turns away and says 'No' is choosing not to engage with me.

- Someone who speaks fluently and has a good vocabulary is capable of telling me their needs and views.

- He spends so much time alone and rarely goes out, so he is lonely and needs support to go to groups and make friends.

- She keeps saying that she wants to clear up all this clutter but it never happens. That must mean she doesn't really want to do it. I need to motivate and persuade her.

- He can tell me all the reasons why that behaviour would be dangerous, so he clearly understands the risks.

- The psychology report says her global IQ score is below 50, so of course she doesn't have the capacity to decide which is the most appropriate placement for her.

- He won't look at me so he isn't engaging with what I am saying and doesn't understand.

None of these are safe conclusions where a client is autistic. Touch may cause pain and distress (see Chapter 3). Lack of eye contact does not mean an autistic person is not listening and is not a reliable guide to comprehension. Verbal utterances may be scripted or echolalic and not entirely voluntary. Those with fluent speech can have profound difficulties communicating effectively and actually achieving mutual understanding of words and concepts (see Chapter 2). This can often include the ability to recite learned information (such as why something is dangerous) without actually understanding how the information might apply in a range of circumstances (see Chapters 2 and 6). Some of us find social interaction distressing and much prefer to be alone. Many of us struggle with executive function and/ or inertia and are unable to initiate or sustain tasks despite being motivated to do so (Buckle 2019). Global IQ is woefully meaningless in autism because autistic individuals invariably have a 'spiky profile' and can be highly able in some areas, whilst being profoundly disabled in other areas (Dawson *et al.* 2007).

I could go on. And on. And on.

Recognizing and seeking to avoid indirect discrimination is a requirement on public services under the Equality Act 2010. Equality does not mean treating everyone the same way. It means recognizing and responding to individual needs to avoid substantial disadvantage in accessing services.

Recognizing and accepting differences between your own perspective and that of the client is also good relationship-based practice (Wilson *et al.* 2011). It is important that discomfort with the *potential* for discrimination in 'grouping' or 'labelling' does not become an unwillingness to accept the importance and relevance to good social work of an individual's diagnosis of autism.

Social workers do not, generally, need to become expert in the diagnosis of autism, nor in the various academic theories about the causation of autism. However, just as with cultural awareness, it is vital to gain sufficient knowledge and understanding of a fundamentally different way of being so as to be able to avoid doing harm through ignorance (Health Education England 2019).

Nevertheless, however much you learn about autism, there will always be more that you do not know. Avoiding defensiveness about inevitable gaps in knowledge and sustaining an open-minded attitude are elements of professional and respectful practice. As Wilson notes, acknowledging what you do not know is an essential reflective capability (Wilson *et al.* 2011).

Acknowledging and accepting difference, adjusting and adapting your practice and being open to learning are the building blocks of positive relationships with autistic clients.

1.3 Autism and co-occurring conditions

Autistic individuals may also have a range of other conditions and are at increased risk of some health issues. It is useful, therefore, to be aware of the most common co-occurring conditions.

Broadly speaking, autistic people are more likely than the general population to have physical health conditions, including hearing and visual impairments and physical disabilities (Rydzewska *et al.* 2018). Some conditions are particularly common. Autistic people are significantly more likely to have (or to develop) epilepsy than non-autistic people (Thomas *et al.* 2017). Rates of epilepsy are between 20% and 40% amongst autistic people, compared to a rate of just 1% in the general population (Cusack *et al.* 2018). Sleep difficulties and disturbances, including diagnosable sleep disorders, appear to be much more common amongst autistic people than in the general population (Aitken 2012; Devnani and Hegde 2015). Autistic people seem to experience more gastrointestinal symptoms than non-autistic people, although the reasons why appear complex and are still being researched (Rose *et al.* 2018). Joint hypermobility and related disorders also appear to be more common in autistic people than the general population, potentially resulting in pain and mobility difficulties (Baeza-Velasco *et al.* 2018). Immune-mediated conditions, including allergies and auto-immune conditions, also occur more commonly in autistic people than non-autistic people (Fortuna *et al.* 2016; Zerbo *et al.* 2015). There are also a wide variety of rarer neurological and other health conditions which commonly co-occur with autism (Research Autism 2019).

Learning disabilities are another significant area of overlap. Roughly speaking, about one-third of autistic people have a learning disability and about one-third of people with a learning disability have autism. Learning disabilities in autistic people may be similar to or quite different from learning disabilities in people who are not autistic. In autism, it is common for individuals to have a 'spiky profile', which may include strong abilities in some areas alongside significant difficulties in others (Dawson *et al.* 2007; Scheuffgen *et al.* 2000).

Motor abnormalities are also frequently seen in autistic people. Dyspraxia (difficulties with co-ordination, motor planning and balance) is much more common in autistic people than non-autistic people (Cassidy *et al.* 2016). Autistic people are also at significantly increased risk of catatonia (Shah 2019).

It is generally considered that both dyslexia and dyscalculia (difficulties with numbers, maths, timetables, etc.) occur more commonly in autistic people than in the general population because of their shared neurodevelopmental basis. However, studies of prevalence are complicated due to disputed diagnostic thresholds for these conditions and the prevalence of learning disability in autism, so it is difficult to obtain reliable figures.

Similarly, experts do not entirely agree on the relationship between attention-deficit hyperactivity disorder (ADHD) and autism. There are a number of related and overlapping features between the two conditions. Some individuals have both ADHD and autism and, again, it is likely that ADHD occurs more often in autistic people than the general population because of the shared neurodevelopmental basis of both conditions. How common that overlap is though is not well understood (Leitner 2014). Executive function difficulties (issues with organization, sequencing, planning and executing actions) are common in both conditions (Craig *et al.* 2016). On the other hand, however, ADHD is characterized by impulsive behaviour, whilst rigidity is a core characteristic of autism. How can sense be made of this by practitioners?

Experience suggests that it is not uncommon to encounter children who present significant behavioural difficulties and who have collected a motley 'alphabet soup' of diagnoses: ADHD, autistic spectrum disorder (ASD), pathological demand avoidance (PDA), attachment disorder, oppositional defiant disorder (ODD) and more. I am not convinced of the usefulness of such multiple and varied diagnoses – especially in young children. Sometimes it seems as if some clinicians (often those who do not have the benefit of working in experienced multi-disciplinary teams) tend to resort to multi-diagnoses when presented with children with complex and challenging needs. It may not be possible, and, even then, can be extremely difficult, to fully appreciate which diagnoses are most relevant and meaningful for an individual until they are much older. That said, however, it does appear that ADHD occurs more commonly in autistic people than in the general population (Leitner 2014).

Mental health conditions are also more common in autistic people than in the general population. Estimates of prevalence vary widely, but a recent meta-analysis of studies produced prevalence estimates of 28% for ADHD; 20% for anxiety disorders; 13% for sleep–wake disorders; 12% for disruptive, impulse-control, and conduct disorders; 11% for depressive disorders; 9% for obsessive-compulsive disorder (OCD); 5% for bipolar disorders; and 4% for schizophrenia spectrum disorders in the autistic population (Rydzewska *et al.* 2018). Eating disorders are also believed to be significantly more common amongst autistic people than in the general population (Shea 2015). Some of the potential causes and consequences of mental health conditions in autism in terms of their implications for social work practice will be discussed in Chapter 3.

A final, and significant, complexity for practitioners is found in the experience and consequences of trauma amongst the autistic population (Fuld 2018). As I will discuss further in Chapter 5, trauma-related symptoms, such as attachment difficulties, can have superficial similarities to autistic traits and, at the same time, autistic people are (throughout the lifespan) more likely to experience trauma. This can result both in difficulty distinguishing between, and in co-occurrence with autism of, post-traumatic stress disorder (PTSD), complex PTSD, attachment disorders and, in some cases, personality disorders (Haruvi-Lamdan, Horesh and Golan 2018).

1.4 Undiagnosed autism

It is likely that, especially amongst older adults, there are autistic people who have yet to be diagnosed (O'Regan 2014; Wright 2015). Autism in individuals without intellectual disability has only been recognized since the early 1990s and full understanding and recognition of the varied range of presentations of autism is still developing (Hull *et al.* 2019). Many such individuals may have come into contact with health or social services during their lives and are, perhaps, particularly likely to be found amongst those with other diagnoses, such as learning disabilities, mental health conditions and/or substance misuse, and amongst the prison and homeless populations.

Consequently, social workers may well encounter older adults who have autistic traits in contexts outside of autism services. The potential benefits of recognition and understanding of autism are significant. Adults who have been diagnosed late in life often say they find it helpful to know they are autistic (see, for example, Harris 2016). While most social workers are not trained diagnosticians, practitioners can play a significant role in identifying and facilitating referral to a diagnostic service for adults who may need to be assessed for a potential autism diagnosis.

I would also encourage practitioners not to be hesitant in using strategies suggested in this book with any of their clients, whether or not they have an autism diagnosis. Fortunately, strategies that help autistic people are often quite helpful (and rarely do any harm) to non-autistic people.

1.5 How can this book help social workers?

In this book I will try to bring together up-to-date knowledge and understanding of autism with the realities of social work practice (primarily in the context of England, although with relevance to social work elsewhere). Increasing legal requirements in relation to autism-specific training for social care assessors and practitioners with primary responsibility for autistic clients (see Chapter 2) mean that there is growing appetite for improved autism knowledge within social work. I hope this book contributes to addressing that need by applying autism-specific knowledge to social work contexts and offering strategies and practical suggestions for practice.

Most social workers will have had or been offered 'autism awareness training'. Such training may be of limited usefulness if (as is often the case) it merely provides an overview of the diagnostic criteria and a few simple (and not social care specific) examples of autistic behaviour (e.g. an autistic person is likely to take what you say literally so don't tell them to 'pull their socks up'). Busy practitioners typically lack the time to read vast amounts of up-to-date autism research to find the bits relevant to their practice.

This book seeks to provide social workers with useful information by:

- focusing on realistic examples and good practice tips written in the language of social work

- starting from initial referral situations and the demands of disentangling autism from other complex social and family factors in day-to-day practice

- working through examples of adaptations and adjustments to assessment practice which facilitate access whilst also producing the key information needed for decision making

- discussing how autistic characteristics relate to the areas covered in assessments and eligibility criteria and issues around access to social care services

- addressing the benefits and pitfalls of person-centred planning with autistic clients

- grappling with the interaction between a neurodevelopmental disability and the age-related criteria and transitions of the social care system

- considering the relationships between autism, intellectual disability and mental capacity and the practical implications for capacity assessment

- providing autism-specific strategies for supporting decision making in line with Mental Capacity Act 2005 (MCA) principles

- looking at specific issues around safeguarding work with autistic children and adults

- demonstrating how autism-specific knowledge can transform behaviour management

- providing practical strategies to prevent and minimize placement breakdown for autistic individuals.

In Chapter 2, I will discuss the implications of autism for practitioners carrying out assessments of various types: providing practical suggestions for reasonable adjustments, highlighting potential pitfalls and illustrating how high-quality person-centred assessments can be carried out with autistic people. In Chapter 3, I turn to the issue of social care eligibility in autism, challenging assumptions and recognizing the barriers. This chapter also sets out an overview of the impact of autism on daily life and illustrates the breadth of social care needs which autistic people may have. Chapter 4 focuses on person-centred care planning, including a wide-ranging discussion of what a 'good life' with autism looks like and encouraging practitioners to discuss and reflect with clients about the goals (outcomes) of social care provision. I also set out a framework, based on the National Autistic Taskforce's (NAT) *Independent Guide to Quality Care for Autistic People* (National Autistic Taskforce 2019), for assessing whether an autistic person's care plan, and the resulting care provision, represent good practice. In Chapter 5, I discuss the risk of adverse experiences which autistic people face and the complexities of distinguishing between autism and attachment difficulties. Also covered are autistic development and transition experiences and processes throughout the lifespan: from children's to adults' services; moving out of the parental home; and transitions to older adult services. Inevitably, transitions raise issues around housing, which is also discussed in this chapter. In Chapter 6, I turn to the issue of assessing the mental capacity of autistic people, focusing primarily on elements of the functional test set out in the MCA 2005 and how these may or may not be affected by autism. Perhaps surprisingly, I consider this chapter just as relevant to social work with children and families as to work with adults and the chapter includes discussion of the impact of lack of experience and developmental delay on the development of decision-making skills. Chapter 7 sets out ways to support autistic people with decision making, offering practical strategies to maximize the ability of autistic people of all ages to take, communicate and execute our own decisions. Importantly, Chapter 8 focuses on safeguarding autistic people, highlighting how the vulnerability of autistic people to abuse and exploitation lead to high rates of victimization, but also offering strategies to increase skills and autonomy and support autistic people to better protect ourselves. Also discussed are autistic people encountering the criminal justice system and ways to prevent and address offending behaviour. Finally, in Chapter 9, I turn to the difficult issue of behaviour which may challenge in autism. While recognizing the complex and difficult situations practitioners encounter, I challenge established approaches to behaviour which may challenge, arguing that we can do much better. I set out a radically different approach, based on empathy with autistic perspectives: recognizing sources of stress; understanding and preventing distress; planning to prevent and manage crises; and empowering self-management strategies.

Throughout the book I will use examples to illustrate some key concepts and issues. Many of the examples are from social care contexts. Some are from contexts outside of social care, but nevertheless provide useful illustration of issues which are relevant for social work. Each example is drawn from one of three sources. Some draw on publicly available information such as: case law; published Safeguarding Adults Reviews; or, in one case, a published account of an autistic person's lived experience. Some are anonymized examples from the lived experience of autistic people. Others are composite examples which draw both on my own experience and on the practice experiences of the many social workers I talk with and listen to. Each example is followed by some questions for reflection.

Sometimes I will seek to challenge assumptions and beliefs, but always it is with the aim of supporting and encouraging reflective practice. I am autistic[2] and have wide experience of a range of autistic people right across the spectrum, as well as familiarity with research on autism. I am not a practising social worker. However, in my day-to-day work providing training for social workers on both autism and social care law, I spend much of my time talking with practitioners at all levels of experience and across many different local authorities about real practice situations they encounter. In addition to specialist courses on autism for social workers, I also create and deliver training to social workers at all levels on the practical applications of mental capacity and mental health law; adult safeguarding enquiries and legal literacy for adult safeguarding; the Care Act 2014; and a range of other areas. I greatly admire and value the role and commitment of the many social workers I encounter. So, I have set about writing this book with the aim of supporting dedicated and overworked social workers to develop and enhance their practice with autistic people.

---

2   I choose to use the identity-first terminology 'autistic' because I do not feel that I am a separate person from my autism, it is part of who I am. I also use this terminology because person-first terminology is only used for identities that are considered negative (I have never heard anyone refer to themselves as a 'person with Englishness' or a 'person with femaleness') and I don't consider being autistic to be inherently entirely negative or positive. My choice of terminology also reflects research published in the Autism journal in 2015 which looked at the preferences of autistic people in the UK (and also parents and professionals) around the language used to describe autism.

CHAPTER 2

Social Care Assessment and Autism

To achieve an effective assessment of an autistic child or adult's needs, it is vital to consider adaptations and adjustments to the process of assessment. Reasonable adjustments under the Equality Act should be considered (and made) alongside and in addition to other types of help or support such as advocacy. Effective adjustments will not just benefit the autistic person, but will also increase the quality and reliability of the assessment.

A range of different types of assessments may be needed (across health and social care) for an autistic child or adult, such as:

- Child in Need assessment

- s.47 investigation

- Education, Health and Care Plan assessment

- transition assessment

- Care Act assessment

- Mental Health Act assessment

- Social Circumstances Report

- s.117 needs assessment

- Continuing Health Care (CHC) checklisting

- Full Decision Support Tool assessment for CHC.

Most of the adaptations and adjustments which can help autistic people will be the same across all types of assessment.[1]

2.1 Before the assessment

2.1.1 Assessment format

Making effective adjustments to the assessment process for an autistic person begins in advance of the assessment itself. Review information previously known about the person and/or communicate with them in order to consider:

- who should conduct the assessment

- format of the assessment (face to face, phone, email/paper, supported self-assessment)

- location of the assessment

- who should be involved in the assessment and how

- timing and length of the overall assessment process and individual conversations

- communication aids and/or support

- preparing yourself for the assessment

- preparing the autistic person for the assessment.

It is important that the person carrying out the assessment has sufficient autism-specific knowledge to carry out an effective assessment and sometimes it will be necessary to involve another professional with greater expertise.[2]

Due to time and case load pressures, more and more initial screening (which may, legally speaking, effectively be an assessment) is being conducted entirely over the phone. Telephone conversations are highly likely to substantially disadvantage autistic people and result in poor-quality decision making, including crucial decisions around whether or not to offer a face-to-face assessment. This is because a significant proportion of autistic people find communicating by phone particularly difficult (Doherty, O'Sullivan and Neilson 2020). This is largely because communication by phone relies entirely on communicating through speech and processing auditory information, one or both of which many autistic people struggle with.

EXAMPLE

James, who is autistic, has fluent speech but is slow to process information he hears. He finds communication by phone difficult and prefers email, but manages to call his local council's Social Care Single Point of Access phone number to ask for an assessment. The Single Point of Access worker tells him that he can clearly communicate just fine because he can speak and has a good vocabulary. So, she carries out an initial screening assessment over the phone, referring to council policy stating that employees must not communicate with clients by email because of data protection.

James does not really have time to process much of what he is asked and gives brief, literal answers that fail to include relevant information. For example, when he is asked if he needs help to wash, he simply says 'No'. It does not occur to him that this question might include other personal care tasks such as brushing his teeth and shaving, which he does struggle with.

The conversation feels extremely fast to James and he struggles to keep up. He tries to say that he is overwhelmed, but the assessor just reassures him not to worry and carries on asking questions. Several times he just agrees with things she says, even though he does not really understand. By the time the call is over James is not too sure what has just happened.

What decision do you think would be likely to result from the interaction above?

What could the worker have done differently?

Would the outcome have been any different if those changes had been made?

Under the Care Act 2014, local authorities must offer adults the option of a supported self-assessment.[3] The Children and Families Act 2014 encourages co-production for Education, Health and

Care Plans.[4] These options can offer useful and person-centred flexibility to how an assessment is carried out. However, they are not without their pitfalls for autistic people. Even if an autistic person seems confident that they can undertake part or all of their assessment themselves, it is important to ensure they have sufficient support to do so and to follow up in case the person may be running into difficulties. Many autistic people (including 'high-functioning' individuals) struggle markedly with aspects of initiative and organization (Buckle 2019) and may be entirely unable to reliably complete assessment paperwork without external support such as prompting. Even where the bulk of an assessment is carried out at a distance (such as by email), in most cases at least one face-to-face encounter will be needed to ensure sufficiently robust information is obtained to support a good quality assessment.

For face-to-face assessments, it is worth giving some thought to the location of an assessment. Many autistic people would be most comfortable at home, but others would find an assessment at home intrusive and find a neutral location more comfortable. Whether the location is familiar or unfamiliar to the autistic person may also be a relevant consideration, as, of course, is confidentiality. However, the most important consideration in location is likely to be ensuring a communication-friendly environment, with a minimum of noise, people and distractions.

Who should be involved in an assessment will be determined on a case-by-case basis. On the professionals' side, it is important to consider who is already known to the autistic person and who has the most effective communication with them. Family, carers and/ or friends should be involved if the autistic person wants them to be (or is a child) and should not be excluded against the autistic person's wishes (unless there are safeguarding concerns). However, it is important that the autistic person's own voice is heard in the assessment process and that the views of their family do not become an automatic substitute (important as they are in their own right). This is particularly important, and particularly likely to be overlooked, where an autistic person has a learning disability and/ or does not communicate by speaking. In some situations, it may be appropriate to meet the autistic person with family members present on one occasion, but see them alone on another occasion.

Timing and length of assessment sessions and the overall process should be planned whenever possible, considering whether, for example, it may be helpful to agree a finish time for each session and arrange additional sessions as needed to make the process more predictable. It is not uncommon for it to take additional time to achieve a good quality assessment with an autistic person. Given the typical workload and scheduling pressures frontline social workers are under, it is vital to acknowledge that this is not just 'nice to have'. Where additional time is needed, as will often be the case, to make adaptations like processing time and adjustments to communication for an autistic person, the provision of that time is likely to be a reasonable adjustment under the Equality Act 2010.

2.1.2 Communication adaptations and support

Consider whether any communication support is needed to enable the autistic person to be fully involved in their assessment. If the autistic person uses an alternative mode of communication, such as Makaton or the Picture Exchange Communication System (PECS), and the assessor is not trained in that mode of communication, then someone who is should be present throughout the assessment. It may often be that there is someone already known to the autistic person who can interpret for them, but the appropriateness of this should be considered on a case-by-case basis. The use of an interpreter who is already known to the autistic person may not be appropriate where a conflict of interest may arise or there are safeguarding concerns.

It is also important to consider what resources can be prepared in advance to support communication with an autistic person during an assessment. If they have a communication passport, ensure you adapt to the needs set out. Consider whether a speech and language therapy (SALT) referral or input may be needed to assist the person in communicating during the assessment.

So, for example, it might be useful to have photographs of people in the autistic person's life for a discussion about support or a collection of symbols and a 'first–then'[5] frame (see Figure 2.1) for a discussion of risks. 'Talking mats' can also be a helpful tool, as can using objects of reference. For literate autistic people, it may well be helpful to take with you and/or (preferably) send in advance written/typed versions of any forms, information or draft documents you intend to discuss. A brief agenda or list of topics might also be useful to have prepared in advance. A basic adaptation is to have pen and paper available for either the assessor or the autistic person to write down information or draw diagrams during the assessment.

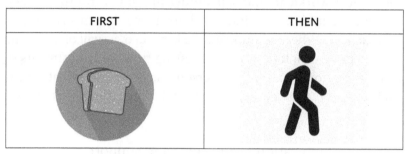

FIRST	THEN

Figure 2.1 A 'first–then' frame to communicate a sequence of first, breakfast, then go for a walk

EXAMPLE

Tuxcia wants to explore with her client, Toby (22, autism, learning disability), who is largely non-verbal, his understanding of the importance of consent in sexual relationships.[6] Tuxcia knows that Toby has completed a course, run by an LD nurse, about sex and relationships and that the course used visual illustrations and clear, simple language to explain consent. She also finds out, from Toby's family members and care workers who interact with him daily, that Toby is accustomed to making day-to-day choices by pointing to line drawings of objects and activities and that staff use a 'first–then' frame with line drawings and symbols to show Toby what will happen next.

Tuxcia uses specialist resources which set out common scenarios using line drawings of people, speech and thought bubbles to prepare simple examples of situations where a person can choose whether to engage in sex. She also prepares a selection of options for Toby to choose from, such as thought bubbles with things he might be thinking and illustrations of actions he could take.

Tuxcia spends some time familiarizing Toby with these resources, before beginning to use them, in conjunction with a 'first–then' frame, to offer Toby choices about his actions in various scenarios.

Do you think any particular adaptations are more important than others?

Can you think of any other ways of adapting communication which might help in a similar situation?

2.1.3 Advocacy

Prior to an assessment, and in addition to any support with communication, consideration should be given to whether the autistic person needs an advocate. Potentially relevant statutory advocacy duties include appointing an Independent Mental Capacity Advocate (IMCA) for decisions about serious medical treatment or moving into or changing hospital or residential accommodation when an adult lacks capacity (s.37–39 Mental Capacity Act 2005) and the Care Act advocacy duties (s.67 and s.68 Care Act 2014) which apply to adults who may have substantial difficulty being involved in their assessment, care planning or safeguarding enquiry. In the case of autism, it is extremely important to note that 'substantial difficulty' goes wider than just adults who may lack the capacity to make relevant decisions. This means that it should not be assumed that an autistic person does not need an advocate because they have a high IQ and wide vocabulary and sound like they 'can communicate just fine'. So-called 'high-functioning' autistic people often have sophisticated strategies to mask our communication problems. Fluent speech does not equate to an absence of difficulties with communication and, similarly, absence of or limited speech does not equate to a complete inability to communicate. An autism diagnosis indicates a fundamentally different approach to communicating. Difficulties may be subtle and not obvious to strangers but still serious. The Care Act guidance (Department of Health 2014, Para. 7.15) specifically mentions Asperger's syndrome (as it was then) as an example of a condition where someone may have capacity but nevertheless have substantial difficulty communicating effectively without the additional support of an advocate.

Throughout the assessment process, it is likely to be helpful to bear in mind that we, as autistic people, may:

- have limited communication skills and understanding

- feel uncomfortable having a conversation with a stranger

- not understand who you are and what you want

- not be able to define what our own needs are

- not be able to talk about or explain our needs very easily, and so risk misrepresenting them

- be able to speak fluently, but this may mask difficulties with actual understanding

- try to say the 'right' thing in response to your questions rather than stating what our actual needs are

- find it hard to plan for the future or to think about change, and be uncomfortable talking about support that involves changes to an established routine or a move to a different service

- not understand what you are asking and take things very literally, so if you ask, 'Are you able to wash yourself on your own?' a person might reply, 'Yes' – when in fact they can only do it with verbal prompting at every stage (Saeki and Powell 2008).

All the statutory advocacy duties apply only where the person does not have a suitable family member or friend who can represent them and support their involvement. However, it is important that proper consideration is given on a case-by-case basis to the question of whether a friend or family member is suitable. They must be willing and able to support the adult's own voice to be heard, not merely put forward their own views (which may differ from those of the adult). The adult must also be comfortable with the choice and want their friend or family member to support them. If you consider there is or may be a conflict of interest then an independent advocate must be appointed.

There are also numerous other situations in which advocacy should be considered, even if family members are involved. It is important to consider whether the decisions to be taken are likely to engage the autistic person's human rights and whether the involvement of a family member or friend is sufficient to safeguard their human rights.

However, involvement of an advocate does not replace the need for the assessor to adapt to an autistic person's communication needs. Many advocates will have had little or no training on autism and may well struggle themselves to communicate effectively with an autistic person. Even where a family member or friend is supporting the autistic person's involvement, they may vary in their own communication skills and understanding of autism and may find it difficult to distinguish between their own views and those of the autistic person, so it is always important for the assessor to consider and adapt to communication needs.

2.1.4 Preparation

Another important step is to prepare yourself in advance of the assessment. Ensure that you have read the relevant background information, especially any information about the autistic person's communication needs and preferences. Whilst keeping an open mind and avoiding assumptions is important, it is also important to try to avoid the autistic person and their family having to repeat the same information over and over to different professionals. As a result, it is important to consider reading previous assessments and information already on file and/or (with the autistic person's consent) gathering information from other professionals, family and friends in advance of an assessment. This can assist in making effective adaptations to communication and focusing assessment questions to avoid an autistic person having to start from scratch in explaining their needs to you.

Consider any available information about the autistic person's sensory needs and preferences and make adaptations to your personal presentation and behaviour accordingly. If relevant information is not available, then it is sensible to follow these basic rules to try to avoid common autistic sensory issues:

- Do not wear perfume or too much deodorant. Good personal hygiene and neutral, scent-free products are less likely to cause distress.

- Avoid clothing or jewellery which jangles, dangles or billows.

- Do not touch an autistic person unless you already know their sensory preferences around touch.

Being organized and honest in your communication are also important aspects of preparation: 'Simple things like arriving on time, having the necessary paperwork and not making promises unless you are sure they can be kept, will help the person to develop trust in you. Inconsistent and unreliable support can be worse than no support at all' (Saeki and Powell 2008, p.15).

It is also likely to be helpful to take steps to prepare an autistic person in advance of the assessment whenever possible. A basic, but useful, step is to send out (by post or email) clear, factual information about any visit or meeting in advance. Consider sending in advance:

- a photograph of yourself

- clear, accurate information about the time, date and location of an appointment and how long it is likely to last

- photographs of the assessment location if it is not the autistic person's own home

- clear, specific information about the purpose and format of the assessment (e.g. 'I am coming to ask questions about the types of help you need in everyday life, so that I can work out whether any changes are needed to your support')

- if appropriate, a simple, direct explanation that social workers/social care assessors sometimes have to deal with emergencies; warn that it is possible for you to be interrupted/called away and that you will try to avoid this if at all possible but you cannot guarantee it.

An adjustment which is particularly likely to be helpful to autistic people is to provide the questions, or, at least, information in written/visual form about the areas which will be asked about in advance of the assessment. This enables the autistic person to have time to properly process the questions, think through their answers and identify (sometimes by asking friends/family/support workers) relevant examples. This can greatly improve the quality of an assessment. Even in a short-notice or urgent situation, providing a written/visual version of the questions and a few minutes of quiet thinking time can be immensely helpful. In summary, try to avoid springing surprises on an autistic person and, whenever possible, provide quiet thinking time between giving information and expecting an autistic person to respond.

2.1.5 Predictability

Finally, consider the timing of an assessment. Autistic people may struggle to cope with you arriving late (or early) or a sudden, last-minute cancellation. Of course, it is not always possible to avoid these things, but it makes sense to try to arrange any assessment for a date and time when last-minute hiccups are less likely to occur. Consider arranging the assessment for the first appointment of the day (when you are less likely to run late from other meetings) and for a day when you are not on duty and do not have a case in court. If possible, also factor in any information about the autistic person's schedule and preferences. Sleeping difficulties are common in autistic people, so there may be a time of day which is better for them, or perhaps they have a regular activity scheduled which they would find distressing to miss. If you can't be sure of your exact arrival time, it may be helpful to offer a time window within which you will arrive, but limit this to a maximum of an hour, because the autistic person may be constantly checking for your arrival for the entire period.

EXAMPLE

Abigail (who is autistic) has been screened by phone and referred to a locality team, where she is allocated to Sophie. The notes say she can communicate perfectly well, so Sophie concludes an advocate is not required. She arranges by phone to meet Abigail at her home for an assessment. Due to an emergency on another case, Sophie has to cancel at the last minute and rearrange for another day. Unfortunately, there is a miscommunication about the date and the assessment turns out to have been scheduled when Sophie was away on annual leave. A third date is arranged and Sophie arrives for the assessment, though unfortunately she is 50 minutes late due to dealing with a phone call about a safeguarding matter and experiencing difficulty finding the address.

> What impact would you expect the above combination of events to have on Abigail?

> Could Sophie still carry out an assessment during this visit? Should she do so?

> Is there anything Sophie could have done differently?

> Is there anything she could do at this point to improve the situation for Abigail?

2.2 During the assessment

2.2.1 Establishing rapport

Typically, practitioners undertaking an assessment seek to establish rapport in the early stages of a meeting, prior to beginning their assessment. The concept of rapport is just as valid when working with an autistic person. However, natural autistic approaches to establishing rapport are very different from typical approaches. So, it may be appropriate to rethink your approach.

It is particularly important to avoid overwhelming an autistic person the moment you arrive. Launching into cheery 'small talk', chatting non-stop or asking lots of banal, social questions (which may seem entirely irrelevant to an autistic person) the moment you arrive are not likely to be good ways to start the interaction.

Autistic people do not necessarily feel compelled to greet or interact with others as soon as we enter the space they are in. Consider whether it may be appropriate to simply spend time being present in a space with an autistic person before initiating interaction with them. It may then be appropriate to consider the autistic person's current focus (which may not be where they are looking). If an autistic person is already focused on something else, it may be respectful and helpful to acknowledge that focus and join the person in their focus or interest for a short period before shifting the focus to the assessment you need to carry out.

Autistic people generally see communication and interaction as a process of exchanging information. So, reframing rapport in that context, consider starting with a clear, direct explanation of who you are and what the purpose of the conversation is (avoiding jargon!).

EXAMPLE

Lucinda entered the room where Mark was. She was there to carry out an assessment. At first, she just stood still near the door and breathed slowly and calmly in silence. She didn't stare at Mark. She noticed that Mark's body was orientated towards the window. After a while, she moved to a position nearer Mark where she could also see the window. It was raining outside. She joined Mark in silently watching the raindrops running down the glass for several minutes.

After a while, she slowly shifted her focus from the window and started speaking to Mark:

'My name is Lucinda. I am a social worker. I have come to talk to you to find out what help and support you might need in everyday life. I am going to ask you some questions and write down some of the things you say. It will take about an hour and then I will leave.'

How do you think Lucinda felt when she was standing in silence?

Do you think Lucinda's approach would have made any difference to Mark's experience of the situation (compared to past experiences he may have had)?

What techniques do you use to establish rapport with new clients? How might you consider adapting those with autistic clients?

2.2.2 Creating a communication-friendly environment

It is also important, before and during an assessment, to consider the environment in which you are expecting an autistic person to communicate. Whenever possible, try to eliminate or minimize any sources of background noise, such as TV, other people speaking, traffic, etc. Turning off sources of noise (such as mobile phones, radios, etc.), closing doors or windows, moving away from the source of any noise may all be potentially helpful. Many autistic people find it difficult to 'screen out' background noise, so ensuring a quiet environment is likely to be helpful. If the assessment is taking place away from the autistic person's own home, also consider their sensory needs around issues such as smells and lighting.

It may also help to try to ensure that you are only expecting an autistic person to deal with one thing at a time. Many autistic people find multi-tasking extremely difficult. So it can help to try to avoid situations such as:

- talking whilst walking along

- continuing to speak whilst the autistic person is searching for a pen or writing something down

- asking an autistic person to demonstrate how they carry out a task and talking to them while they are doing so

- handing an autistic person a document to read and then talking to them while they are trying to read it.

For many autistic people right across the spectrum, slowing down is also likely to help. At all levels of cognitive ability, many of us are relatively slow at processing information and often find it impossible to think and communicate at the same time. Typically, non-autistic people allow only a fraction of a second (200 milliseconds on average) for a conversation partner to respond (Holler *et al.* 2015). It often feels awkward to leave a longer gap, but this can be very helpful for an autistic person who may need time to think before responding. It also helps to try to avoid staring at the autistic person whilst waiting, since many autistic people find eye contact overwhelming and may be very sensitive to someone gazing at them (Williams 2002).

2.2.3 Building a communication bridge

People (including non-autistic people) vary enormously in their natural styles of communication. On the whole, autistic people are most likely to find communication a little easier with individuals who tend towards blunt, honest, direct communication than with those whose communication is focused largely on adaptation to social and emotional concerns (such as worrying about offending or upsetting others). Autistic perspectives on communication are more likely to focus on information exchange than on social content. So, it is likely to be helpful to try to focus on providing and seeking detailed, specific, concrete information and avoid vagueness, generalizations and reassurance.

Honesty is often very important to autistic people and our perspective on honesty can be quite black and white. As a result, it is important to be cautious about making promises which you cannot or may not be able to keep, such as:

'I will get back to you later today.'

'We will talk about that on Thursday.'

'I'm sure we will be able to help you.'

Explaining the reasons behind things and making implied information explicit are likely to help. For example:

'I will do my best to get back to you later today if I don't get interrupted by any emergencies.'

'We will have an opportunity to talk about that on Thursday. I will write myself a note and try to remember to come back to it then.'

'I would really like to be able to help you and will do my best, but I can't be sure yet what support you will be offered.'

Effective communication also requires guarding against assumptions and keeping an open mind. It is often difficult to identify unconscious biases and assumptions but they are often present. As I will discuss at more length in Chapter 3, the most pervasive but hazardous assumption autistic people face is that 'functioning' is a broadly stable level throughout different skills and aspects of a person's life. So, an autistic person who has a learning disability and is non-verbal may be assumed to function poorly across the board when, in fact, they may have above average skills in navigating and using maps. Conversely, a highly educated autistic person may be assumed to be capable of basic self-care tasks when, in fact, they are highly dependent on prompting from others and at high risk of self-neglect.

So, to achieve a good quality assessment, it is vital to be aware of autism-specific communication issues and to adapt questioning technique (including wording on forms if relevant).

2.2.4 Four key points to adapt questioning

1. INFERENCE IS DIFFICULT

Autistic people may struggle to work out what is relevant to a question and make connections to other information. This can lead to not volunteering important information. We are particularly likely to answer literally the exact question asked and fail to recognize wider implications and context. So, for example, if an assessor was to ask a question like: 'Do you need any help to cook your meals?' an autistic person may answer, 'No' because no one hands them saucepans or physically helps them chop vegetables. But, perhaps, they need help to decide what to cook and to get all the ingredients in one place. As these types of 'help' are not literally or obviously help in the sense of actually carrying out the immediate task of cooking itself, it may well not occur to an autistic person that this information may be relevant and they are unlikely to volunteer it.

Very broad, open questions are particularly difficult. This poses a challenge to person-centred approaches to assessment, which often depend heavily on open questions to avoid limiting or presupposing a person's answers. There are three techniques which may help. Firstly, it is likely to be helpful to explain the reasons behind your questions and the type of information you are seeking. So, for example, in relation to the question above, it would probably be helpful to have first explained that you are asking questions in order to work out what support the person might need from other people in order to be able to eat adequately and that includes considering the whole process, from obtaining food, planning meals and preparing them.

EXAMPLE

Melanie (an autistic parent) had to take her daughter, Bella, to regular appointments with a consultant rheumatologist throughout her childhood. The consultant began each appointment by asking 'How's things?'

On different occasions both Melanie and her support worker tried explaining to the consultant that Melanie's autism meant that she found such open questions difficult to answer and tried to persuade the consultant to reword the question to be more specific. Despite this, every appointment began with 'How's things?' Over several years, Melanie read up on doctor–patient interactions, developed a number of theories about what the consultant might mean and tried out a variety of types of answer. Initially, these didn't seem to be successful and communication between Melanie and her daughter's consultant continued to be poor. Eventually, Melanie worked out that, in this particular context, what the consultant was actually asking when he said 'How's things?' was 'What has changed in the past year in the symptoms of the condition for which I am treating your daughter?'!

> What similar difficulties could arise in your interaction with an autistic client?
>
> What changes might you consider to the wording of common questions you might ask?

The second technique which may help is to ask more closed questions, but to include an explicit open option. For example:

What help do you need with meals? Do you need:

1. Someone to help you cook, chop or prepare food?
2. Someone to help you think or plan?
3. Reminders or prompting?
4. No help at all?
5. Something else?

This style of questioning provides an autistic person with concrete examples of the types of answer which you consider relevant to the question. Even if none of the closed options are correct, the additional information may well enable an autistic person to then be able to identify additional options or other relevant information.

A third approach is to reverse the typical order of questioning and ask more specific questions about an area of need first, and only then move to one or more open questions to explore further. By the time you are asking the open question, the autistic person is more likely to have an idea of the type of information you need as a result of the more specific questions.

It is therefore important to be very cautious of taking answers at face value without checking and verifying with the person that your understanding is complete and accurate. It is vital to go beyond general, open questions and to ask more specific questions to probe each issue. Specific questions may be needed to consider less obvious types of help that the person may need such as prompting, supervision, using aids, adaptations or special ways of doing things. It can also help to look for and consider alternative sources of information, avoiding assumptions. For example, if the person's home is clean and tidy, you might ask how it got that way and whether it is always like that.

Of course, one difficulty with asking more specific questions is that you may inadvertently lead the person's responses and, no matter how many questions you ask, there is a risk of missing crucial information. There is also a risk of overwhelming an autistic person with too many questions and too much interaction. All of these things need to be considered and balanced within the assessment.

2. GENERALIZATION IS DIFFICULT

Autistics may struggle to identify specific examples of a general concept. So, for example, if an assessor asks:

'Do you need someone with you when you go to places in the community?'

An autistic person may struggle to identify specific examples of what is meant by 'places'. This may cause them to respond with 'I don't know' or 'No'. It can help to provide specific examples of what you mean. So, a better question would be:

'Do you need someone with you when you go to places in the community, like the sports centre?'

However, this may not completely resolve the problem. Some autistic people may still struggle to generalize the concept and may focus just on the specific example given. As a result, this question might produce the response:

'My friend comes with me to the sports centre when I go swimming.'

This could indicate that the autistic person has considered only the sports centre. Perhaps it has not occurred to them to add:

'I am able to go to other places more independently, including the library, GP surgery and my favourite café because they are less busy.'

There is no simple answer to these types of communication difficulties, so it is important to be aware that they may occur and to work with the autistic person to overcome them.

3. AUTISTIC PEOPLE TEND TO TAKE THINGS LITERALLY

Many people are aware that autistic people tend to take things literally. However, the impact of this is not straightforward to overcome. Simply trying to avoid using idioms or metaphors, while helpful for some, does not adequately compensate for this difficulty. Metaphor is pervasive throughout our use of language (Lakoff and Johnson 1980).

An illuminating example of this is to be found in the heart of the Care Act eligibility criteria for adult social care. All the eligibility criteria focus on whether an adult is 'unable' to achieve an outcome. However, the Care Act[7] defines an adult as 'unable' to achieve an outcome if that adult:

- is unable to achieve it without assistance

- is able to achieve it without assistance but doing so causes the adult significant pain, distress or anxiety

- is able to achieve it without assistance but doing so endangers or is likely to endanger the health or safety of the adult, or of others

- is able to achieve it without assistance but takes significantly longer than would normally be expected.

Only the first of these is a literal definition of the word 'unable' in normal English usage. All the others are not at all literal and, therefore, not at all obvious to an autistic person being assessed and who, when asked if they are 'unable' to do something, is unlikely to identify the additional non-literal definitions and volunteer relevant information. So, for example, an assessor might ask:

'Are you able to brush your teeth?'

An autistic person might answer simply, 'Yes.'

However, perhaps it has not occurred to them to volunteer that they rely on their mother prompting them to do it. Or an exchange might go like this:

'Are you able to walk to the shop?'

'Yes.'

But perhaps the autistic person means that they can physically walk. However, they do not ever actually go to the shop due to agoraphobia.

Another example might be:

'Can you manage your own money?'

'Yes.'

Perhaps the autistic person's answer indicates that they can count coins and have some budgeting skills, but they may not have considered that their poor social understanding, limited understanding of risk and the fact that they have regularly been a victim of financial abuse from people they know may be relevant.

Finally, consider this exchange:

'Can you do the cleaning yourself?'

'Yes.'

This dialogue might fail to pick up that the autistic person has obsessive-compulsive issues about germs and spends three hours every day cleaning their bathroom.[8]

All of the above examples meet the Care Act definition of unable, but could easily be missed due to an autistic person taking language literally.

4. DIFFERENCES IN BODY LANGUAGE AND FACIAL EXPRESSION

Practitioners are often aware from autism training that autistic people may struggle to 'read' another person's body language or facial expression. But the impact of this is rarely considered in the other direction. An autistic person's body language and facial expression may or may not portray conventional expressions of emotions. So, an autistic person may present with 'flat affect' (lack of expression), which is conventionally considered potentially indicative of depression, whilst feeling entirely happy. Conversely, an autistic person may be extremely distressed, but give little or no outward indication of this through facial expression or body language.

Non-verbal communication is an important aspect of assessment. So, it can be very helpful to reflect cautiously on any unconscious impressions you may have 'read into' an autistic person's body language or facial expression and whether this might pose risks of drawing inaccurate conclusions.

EXAMPLE

Assessor: 'How do you get to college?'

Ed: 'On the bus.'

Assessor: 'Do you do that by yourself?'

Ed: 'Yes.'

Ed started at college last September. For the first three weeks his mother took him in her car. Ed's mother then started taking him on the bus and showing him what to do. After another month of practising with his mother, he began to do parts of the journey by himself, gradually increasing this until he could do the whole journey by himself. Now (in February) he is making the journey independently most days. However, twice in the last fortnight something has gone wrong. Once the bus did not come and once a person on the bus shouted at him. Both times Ed got distressed and sat rocking until his mother came and picked him up.

Ed would like to travel to his friend's house and to the local swimming pool independently, but he finds it hard to generalize skills and has not yet managed to learn these specific journeys. So, he still relies on his mother to take him in her car. Ed tries to smile throughout his assessment because in social skills lessons at school he was taught that it is polite and friendly to smile at people.

The assessor notes that Ed is smiling and assumes this reinforces the verbal answers and indicates absence of difficulty. So, the assessor ticks the category 'can travel independently, no support needed' on the assessment paperwork.

Do you think the assessor developed a clear understanding of Ed's needs for care and support around travelling?

How do you think Ed experienced this section of his assessment?

What adaptations could the assessor have made that might have enabled Ed to communicate his experiences more fully?

There is therefore a great deal that can be done to adapt your communication. However, it is crucial to understand that difficulties in communication are inevitable and that it is important to go into an assessment with an attitude of working collaboratively with the autistic person to try to achieve mutual understanding. Communication is a two-way process. It is important to consider both transmission and reception of communication in both directions.

Carrying out an initial assessment or review is, of course, only one aspect of the potential involvement of social workers in the lives of autistic people. In the following chapter, I turn to look at how decisions around eligibility for support or services may be made and affect autistic people's lives.

2.3 Chapter summary and key points

- Reasonable adjustments are likely to include providing information in advance and allowing more time for the assessment.

- Being prepared and organized yourself is likely to help.

- Avoid small talk and get to the point: who are you and why are you there?

- Ensure a communication-friendly environment, free from distractions and background noise.

- Guard against assumptions and keep an open mind.

- Work collaboratively with an autistic person to achieve mutual communication, remembering:

  - Inference is difficult.

  - Generalization is difficult.

  - Autistic people tend to take things literally.

  - There may be differences in body language and facial expression.

Recommended resources

St Clement's Practical Autism Video Guides (available on YouTube):

- *Communication – Pre-Verbal*

- *Communication – Verbal*

- *Diagnosis and Identity*

- *Coping with Change*

National Autistic Taskforce (2019) *An Independent Guide to Quality Care for Autistic People*. London: National Autistic Taskforce.

■ CHAPTER 3 ■

Social Care Eligibility and Autism

3.1 Assumptions

In discussing eligibility for autistic people, it is vital to examine and challenge some pervasive assumptions.

3.1.1 The idea of 'functioning'

Research has demonstrated that autism is autism is autism, in all its various guises, right across the autistic spectrum. Autistic traits, intellectual abilities, speech and language issues can be found in an infinite number of combinations in autistic people. The term 'spectrum' was coined by Lorna Wing, who chose the term specifically to illustrate the variety and variability of abilities and disabilities found in autistic individuals (Happé and Baron-Cohen 2014).

Unfortunately, despite this, the autistic spectrum is often assumed to be a more or less straight line from 'mild' to 'severe', with 'high-functioning' individuals being those with higher IQ and more verbal communication skills at one end, and 'low-functioning' individuals being those with learning disabilities and less verbal communication skills at the other. Although such assumptions are not evidence-based, they are pervasive and often impact on eligibility for support.

In reality, the autistic spectrum is more like a scatter graph than it is a straight line (see Figure 3.1).

As a result, support needs can vary widely between autistic individuals and are not automatically directly related to someone else's perception (usually based largely on intellectual ability) of 'functioning level'. It is not unusual for autistic people to be 'book smart' but not 'street smart': to be intellectually capable of complex learning but lack the functional adaptive ability to apply our theoretical knowledge in everyday life. So it is possible for a highly intelligent autistic individual to struggle with severe inertia and rigidity and need a lot of support and prompting to adequately achieve basic self-care, while, on the other hand, another autistic individual may have strong intellectual skills (in particular with less language-based areas) despite having been diagnosed with a learning disability (Courchesne *et al.* 2015; Scheuffgen *et al.* 2000). In short, it is common for autistic people to have a 'spiky profile' of uneven skills and difficulties.

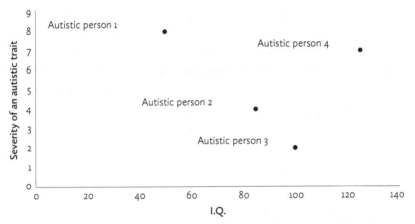

Figure 3.1 A scatter graph illustrating the varied, unique combinations of IQ and 'severity' of autistic traits which can occur in autistic people

Similarly, the vulnerability of autistic people is often underestimated, particularly where an autistic person is verbal and/or has an advanced education. Even highly educated autistic people often struggle to identify exploitation. Additionally, autistic people who are lonely may choose (with capacity) to accept abusive behaviour, believing it is the only way they can find and keep friends or maintain an intimate relationship (see Chapter 8).

3.1.2 Developmental delay and the speed of change

Autism is a neurodevelopmental disorder. Consequently, autistic people often acquire skills more slowly and over longer periods of time than non-autistic people. This results in a particularly high likelihood of encountering difficulties during periods of transition and change (Anderson *et al.* 2018). Many autistic people may need to take transitions more slowly, later and/or one at a time, and may require additional support to achieve positive outcomes. Due to autistic communication difficulties and difficulty coping with change, it may take time and consistency for an autistic person to become sufficiently comfortable with a new person or situation and be able to benefit effectively from that support.

These needs do not always sit comfortably with the specific age and/or time-limited nature of much of the support available. Employment support services are frequently only available to people within a specified age group (often under 25). Transition from children's to adults' services still often happens fairly abruptly at 18, despite the flexibility available in the statutory framework.[9] Transitions from a parental home to independent living can occur at any age, but often transition planning does not take place with older adults, leading to crises when parents/carers die or become unable to care due to age or ill health. Within health and social care, many services are time-limited and of quite short duration, for instance reablement or enablement support and Improving Access to Psychological Therapies (IAPT).

3.1.3 Over-focus on social skills and lack of knowledge of the breadth of potential needs

Autism is generally described largely (or even entirely) as a social disability. The diagnostic criteria for autistic spectrum disorder (American Psychiatric Association 2013; World Health Organization 2018) and common diagnostic tools such as the Autism Diagnostic Observation Schedule 2 (ADOS-2) (Lord *et al.* 2012) and the Diagnostic Interview for Social and Communication Disorders (DISCO) (Leekam *et al.* 2002) focus heavily on social behaviours and social communication. These are the aspects of autism which are most noticeable to others and can be readily observed by diagnosticians. However, issues with social interaction are far from the only difficulties which autistic people experience. There is often limited understanding within health and social care services of the breadth of difficulties which autistic people may struggle with. This may lead to assumptions that autistic people will only have difficulties in one or two domains of need. This chapter will outline the impact which autism can have on a broad range of activities of daily living, as well as health outcomes.

3.1.4 Independence and recovery
A good deal of thinking and service provision in health and social care is built on reducing dependence and promoting independence from services. Services in the mental health field are particularly prone to focus on recovery, but wider service provision (such as reablement) is often geared to seeking to reduce needs. Unchallenged assumptions along these lines can be problematic and even damaging for autistic people. Autism is a lifelong disability. Autistic people may learn and develop, acquiring coping skills and strategies in some areas. However, autism does not go away. When needs are well met, that does not mean that those – or other – needs have disappeared.

EXAMPLE
Naomi (41), an autistic single parent with three children, underwent a review of her social care package. She had previously received 15 hours per week via direct payments which had enabled her to function effectively enough in her daily life to parent her children competently. For example, support workers would prompt her to respond to letters from school, help her keep the house from becoming too cluttered, prompt her to shop for food and support her with getting clean school uniforms and other necessary items ready for her children each day.

When Naomi's package of care was reviewed, she was suddenly found ineligible and her direct payments were withdrawn. The review paperwork stated that Naomi's house was relatively uncluttered, that she had a filing system in place for paperwork and that there was food in the house. This assessment failed to identify that these things were the *result* of Naomi's needs being met by her care package at the time of the review.

During the six months that Naomi was without support (before the local authority's decision was successfully challenged), her self-care deteriorated substantially (failing to wash, brush her teeth, take medication and, often, eat) as did her mental health (she was referred for further assessment for depression) as she tried her best to maintain adequate care for her children. Her house became increasingly cluttered and at least one referral was made to children's services, expressing concern about the state of Naomi's home.

> Can you think of ways in which increasing a person's independence would support them to have more control of their own life?

> Can you think of ways in which increasing a person's independence from support might actually conflict with them having control of their own life?

> Is your practice similar with clients with permanent, lifelong conditions or disabilities compared to those with conditions from which they may recover or is it different?

No one would ever expect a physically disabled person to 'learn strategies' to overcome their need for adaptations and/or support with certain tasks. For example, no one would suggest to a deaf person that they should learn strategies in order to cease needing a British Sign Language (BSL) interpreter. It is a common experience, however, for autistic people to be told or expected to learn strategies to overcome their need for support in some areas.

Independence is widely seen as a reasonable and positive goal. However, this is not always the case. Just as for people with physical disabilities and/or learning disabilities, taking away support from an autistic person to 'make them more independent' may actually merely serve to reduce their quality of life and cause or exacerbate other difficulties (such as mental or physical health issues).

EXAMPLE

Lionel is 54, autistic and works full-time in a university environment (where he also has support through Access to Work). His social care reassessment carefully analyses his needs in each domain, recognizing that difficulties are not currently arising due to the provision of long-term, high-quality, stable support through a team of Personal Assistants (PAs) (employed through direct payments) and clearly acknowledging long-term needs, despite these being well met. Amongst many other detailed analyses of aspects of Lionel's social care needs, his assessment identifies that:

> Risk of self-neglect would occur if Lionel was not supported around his needs relating to autism. He would become stuck without support and his property would become very untidy and cluttered. This disorganization would significantly impact upon his functioning in the home, which would then adversely impact his ability to carry out activities outside of the home.

The review of Lionel's support concludes:

> The support Lionel is receiving and the positive benefits to his life and wellbeing have a protective impact on his mental health and demonstrate how a person with autism can lead a full life and make use of their talents and abilities when correctly supported.

> How does Lionel's experience of social care differ from Naomi's?

> How do you assess and record met needs?

3.2 Thresholds or barriers?

The most substantial barrier to social care for many autistic people is getting an assessment at all. In theory at least, local authorities have a duty to make efforts to identify and provide information to disabled children (and their families) and disabled adults in their areas. The statutory thresholds for assessment are very low. All disabled children are Children in Need (CIN) (s.17(10)(c) Children Act 1989) and adults are entitled to an assessment if it appears they may have needs for care and support (s.9 Care Act 2014). However, severe pressures on local authority budgets, competing priorities and the impact of waiting lists means that experience of access to social care assessment often differs from theory.

3.2.1 Problem 1: Not knowing what social care is, what it is called and where to find it

From a social work perspective, this is hard to imagine. But try to imagine a world in which your only awareness of social workers is vaguely of child protection. You know there is a local council in your area – they are the people who organize the bin collection and council housing. You also know about the NHS and education. But social care?

EXAMPLE

Alistair knew that he struggled with many tasks in day-to-day life and found lots of things very difficult. He had heard of people having support workers or PAs and thought that one of those could be a big help, but he had no idea how to go about getting one. He had tried googling terms like 'help' or 'support' but could not find anything useful.

It was only after he attempted suicide that his need for support was identified.

> Do you think anything could be done to help people like Alistair at an earlier stage?

Generally, there is no advertising to encourage people to come forward for a social care assessment. Many people know very little about social care, autistic or not. However, autistic people are much less likely to 'pick up' information through casual interactions with a range of other people, such as:

- chatting to the hairdresser whose mum has just gone into a care home

- joining a support group and sharing personal experiences

- getting into conversation with the person next to them in the waiting room at the doctor's surgery or on the bus.

Gathering this type of information through social interactions requires asking about someone else's life and experiences and having the skills and inclination to initiate and sustain such interactions.

This is why autistics are even more unlikely than the general public to find out about social care and ascertain that they might be in need of an assessment in the first place.

Parents of autistic children may generally be more successful in acquiring this type of information, but only if we assume that they are not autistic themselves. Moreover, parents in general may be reluctant to approach social services, fearing that it may prompt concerns about their competence as parents.

Ways to help

There are statutory duties which may help some groups. The Autism Act statutory guidance requires local areas to develop an automatic referral to adult social care following adult diagnosis of ASD (Department of Health 2015, p.17). However, adults who already have a diagnosis are not included. Transition assessments are a requirement under the Care Act for young people who may require social care as they become adults (s.58 Care Act 2014). However, these are often only offered to children already receiving social care input and/or to those attending special schools. Nearly three-quarters of autistic children attend mainstream schools (Department for Education 2018), many of whom do not receive support from children's social care (Disabled Children's Partnership 2018). Consequently, for many autistic children and adults, a more universal and inclusive referral process is needed to ensure access to assessments for social care.

Information about social care is not always provided in ways which are accessible for autistic people. All local authorities provide information and advice about social care for parents of disabled children (under the 'local offer') and for adults who may have needs for care and support. Autistic people may find it difficult to follow this information if it contains: jargon, acronyms, non-literal statements, missing information and/or ambiguous statements. So, it can help to seek advice from autistic people to ensure information is communicated in ways which are actually effective.

It also makes sense to target information and advice at key transition points, such as:

- starting or moving schools

- beginning or ceasing to access alternative educational environments, including home education
- transition services, colleges, sixth forms, universities
- registry offices and funeral services.

3.2.2 Problem 2: Rationing by obstacle

There is a type of rationing in the public sector which, in my experience, although widespread is actually rarely discussed. Hard-pressed services with limited resources seem to have a tendency to create procedural obstacles to access in order to try to keep demand at manageable levels. One of those obstacles is not publicizing the service to those who may need it (see above). Beyond that, there are frequently policies which create barriers to accessing services, such as:

- only accepting referrals in a certain format
- some or all initial contact (before allocation) taking place by telephone (a form of communication many autistics find difficult)
- only accepting referrals from particular professionals
- automatic discharge from services for missing appointments
- social care and closely related services (such as occupational therapy, enablement, some mental health services, etc.) working only in 'episodes of care' (i.e. for fixed, time-limited periods regardless of need), even for those with complex, long-term needs.

These can be further compounded by administrative difficulties, such as:

- staff shortages or high turnover, leading to mistakes or inconsistencies
- failure to follow up, requiring the service user to repeatedly make contact to sustain communication

- frequent cancellation(s) and rearrangement(s) of appointments
- scheduling problems, making it impractical or impossible to attend appointments
- paperwork being poorly drafted or going astray.

These issues create additional barriers for autistic people. A significant proportion of autistics struggle with initiative in a variety of ways (Buckle 2019). Individuals who can readily engage in discussions about the latest theories in astrophysics or philosophical perspectives on disability may have extreme difficulty with mundane tasks such as: posting letters, washing up, or making a phone call to their bank. In particular, many autistic people struggle immensely to start things, and managing to get something done can be a huge undertaking. Consequently, making that initial phone call or writing that letter to ask for a social care assessment may have taken weeks or even months of trying.

There will also be key words/language which public-facing staff are looking out for in an initial approach which suggests that an assessment is required. Autistic people may well fail to use typical trigger-words and may fail to explain their needs in terms which staff at the first contact stage recognize.

And then nothing happens.

A proportion of autistic people will never recover from this. They will never ask again. They will go away, lick their wounds, give up and never be heard from again. The autism-specific difficulty here is that this can happen regardless of how badly an autistic person needs help or how motivated they are to obtain it.

For autistic people, it is not about 'being bothered'. The initiative required to try again may be a mountain so high that they cannot hope to climb it without support, but being without support is exactly why a social care assessment is needed. Some may have a family member or friend who can request an assessment, but many do not. Family estrangement and social isolation are common amongst autistic people. For others, family members and friends may also be autistic.

Other autistic people may respond by making formal complaints when services do not appear to respond in the way they expect.

Unfortunately, autistic rigidity and attention to detail can easily mean that such complaints are frequent, extremely lengthy and cover every single deviation from good practice. This response can easily result in the person being seen as vexatious and the genuine needs which underlie the complaints being overlooked.

WAYS TO HELP

Low-level universal support with requesting and pursuing a social care assessment (as well as other services) is very helpful where it is widely available. Providing up-to-date information online is also helpful, as is providing online forms and enabling communication by email (whilst being aware that many secure email systems work in ways which also pose barriers for some autistic people and additional adaptations may be necessary). Ideally, advice and information available should include realistic instructions and guidelines about what to do if there is no response or something goes wrong.

Effective autism-specific training for frontline staff taking initial referrals is essential. This training needs to include the importance of proactive follow-up(s), which does not rely on the autistic person to take the initiative. Staff need to recognize that an autistic person's failure to act may well be because they are unable rather than unwilling. This requires staff to identify and put aside common assumptions such as, for example, that someone with a high level of education 'ought' to be able to follow up their referral, or that the frequency with which a person asks for help reliably indicates how urgently they need that help.

EXAMPLE

Based in Inverness, the Highland One Stop Shop (HOSS) provides services to more than 500 autistic adults (aged 16+) across the Highland region. This service supports autistic people with a broad range of issues, including, crucially, accessing other essential services. Their work has helped people to avoid homelessness and mental health crises. An evaluation report produced by Autism Rights Group Highland (ARGH) (2018) included comments such as:

'It could actually put my life at risk [if]...I cannot get to the help I need.'

'I was homeless and very unwell. Staff at HOSS accompanied me through the process of housing, education, financial stability and health improvement.'

'If it hadn't been for the HOSS, I think I would have had a complete breakdown by now and would probably have been hospitalized.'

Can you identify any practices you are familiar with which might pose a barrier to autistic people accessing services?

How do you think support could be made more accessible for autistic people?

Similarly, it is vital that both frontline and complaints-handling staff have sufficient understanding of autism to recognize when complaints may disguise underlying need.

3.2.3 Problem 3: Falling between two stools

Traditional divisions within social care often excluded some autistic people who did not fit neatly into either 'Learning Disabilities' or 'Mental Health' categories. Many local authorities now have all-age or working-age adult teams to provide holistic coverage for adults with needs for care and support and Children with Disabilities teams to cover all disabled children. However, even where team structures have changed to be more generic and all encompassing, practices, policies and ways of working can be slower to change. Autistic people continue to commonly experience exclusion at the point of requesting an assessment.

EXAMPLE

Patrick has just been diagnosed as having 'high-functioning' autism by the multi-disciplinary team in his area. He has been given two leaflets: one about a social group for autistic adults run by a local parents' organization, and one about Community Care. He rings the Customer Service number given on the Community Care leaflet and asks for an assessment. The customer service worker asks him some questions. She then explains that people with autism are normally referred to the Learning Disabilities service (run jointly with health), but he does not meet the criteria for the Learning Disabilities team because they only take people whose IQ is below 70. She says she cannot refer him to the Mental Health service (also run jointly with health) because they only take people with severe mental health problems such as psychosis. She says there is a waiting list for assessment by the generic local authority adult social care assessment team and she can put him on it, but he is unlikely to meet the eligibility criteria anyway. She signposts him to the website of the National Autistic Society (NAS) and gives him the phone number of a Wellbeing Service (run by a local charity) which runs a 'drop-in' once a fortnight to help people stay healthy.

> Do you think that Patrick's local authority have fulfilled their statutory duties under the Care Act?
>
> Do you think the response Patrick experienced is an appropriate and effective one?
>
> How might Patrick have felt about his post-diagnosis experience of services?

WAYS TO HELP

A number of statutory requirements around social care assessment for adults were intended to help. The Autism Act statutory guidance points out that:

> Assessment of eligibility for care services cannot be denied on the grounds of the person's IQ. This is particularly important for some people with autism, including those with Asperger syndrome, who may face very significant challenges in their everyday lives, despite having average or above average IQ. (Department of Health 2015, p.19)[10]

The National Institute for Health and Care Excellence (NICE) guidance recommends multi-disciplinary autism teams which are autism-specific and not restricted to those who may also have a learning disability (National Institute for Health and Care Excellence 2012, Para. 1.1.13). This recommendation should apply not only to diagnostic teams in the NHS, but also to social care for both adults and children.

This shift towards working with autistic people right across the spectrum is evidence-based. Both of the main diagnostic criteria for autism have now integrated all forms of autism under a single diagnosis of autistic spectrum disorder (American Psychiatric Association 2013; World Health Organization 2018). Many individuals still choose to identify as having Asperger's syndrome, but the formal diagnosis of autism no longer makes a distinction between Asperger's syndrome and autism.

For autistic children, determining eligibility for social care support on the basis of the presence or absence of a learning disability or other additional conditions is even more common than for adults, despite concerns about the lawfulness of such criteria (Council for Disabled Children 2009; Disability Law Service 2019). A number of local authorities even use criteria which explicitly exclude 'high-functioning' autism or Asperger's syndrome.

Excluding the majority of autistic children[11] from social care support is short-sighted. The cost-effectiveness of early and preventive support for autistics is well established, as are the increased risks autistic adults face of unemployment, mental health issues, early mortality, victimization and involvement in the criminal justice system (Iemmi, Knapp and Ragan 2017).

3.2.4 Problem 4: Inappropriate services and lack of autism knowledge

In the current context of severe budget cuts in social care, signposting has become a common response to low-level needs and/or initial requests for support. The services which people are signposted to are most often voluntary sector or community groups or services, such as support groups, advice and information services, charities and so on. Whilst these may provide valuable sources of support for some people (including some autistic people), they are often inappropriate or inaccessible for many autistics, and such signposting may leave significant needs unmet.

Support groups generally focus on providing opportunities for social interaction with other people with an experience, difficulty, health concern or other issue in common. For some autistic people, social interaction is difficult and overwhelming and they may experience a support group as an additional demand rather than a form of support. Additionally, support groups for parents of autistic/disabled children are generally full of parents who are not themselves autistic or disabled. This may make them inappropriate, uncomfortable or unsuitable as a source of support for autistic parents.

Groups for autistic adults or children which are established and run by non-autistic people are common, and include the vast majority of groups organized by major autism charities. Groups for (rather than by) autistic people tend to focus on what non-autistic people believe autistic people need and so are often focused as 'social' or 'social skills' groups. While this may be experienced as supportive by some, such groups rarely promote social interaction in a way which is actually autistic friendly (such as around a common interest) and often assume that autistic individuals will naturally become friends with other autistic people, purely because they have the diagnosis in common. Such groups also rarely offer other types of support and are, therefore, unlikely to meet broader support needs (for example for advocacy, help with communicating with services and managing paperwork, support with daily living or household tasks).

A wide range of aspects of 'universal' services may make them inaccessible to some, or even many, autistic people. Adverse sensory environments, administrative demands (having to fill out forms, reliably return paperwork, etc.), communication difficulties (such as requirements to communicate by phone) and a lack of autism knowledge are all common difficulties autistic people face in/when accessing services.

Some autistic people, due to social difficulties, may express themselves in ways which (often inadvertently) offend or alienate other people. On occasion, some autistics may be perceived by others as abusive or threatening (again often inadvertently), provoking responses which frequently include denial of access to a service entirely or additional restrictions or requirements around accessing a service. This is not to say that it is ever acceptable for staff or other service users to feel threatened or be abused. However, lack of understanding of autism often results in autistic people being treated as having deliberately acted in such a manner when, in fact, the autistic person may have had little or no understanding of how others might perceive or experience their behaviour.

WAYS TO HELP

One of the most important ways to help is to carefully consider the accessibility and suitability of services for the individual autistic person when signposting to potential sources of support. For social and/or peer support, whenever possible, signpost to groups run by autistic people themselves.

It is also vital to consider whether the services to which autistic people are signposted are actually appropriate to meet their needs. One aspect of this requires considering whether an autistic person can actually realistically and reliably access and make use of the service without additional support. When doing so, it is important to be honest, realistic and forthright when communicating with an autistic person about the support they can expect. It is rare for 'customer-facing' staff to be trained or even allowed to make clear, direct statements such as:

> 'I am signposting you to that service but they actually have a nine-month waiting list.'

Or:

> 'The council hasn't got any money and is struggling to pay for really basic support, so you can ask for an assessment but you may not get offered much or any help.'

Such clear, honest and unambiguous statements are likely to be very helpful to autistic people in navigating health and social care. While it is acknowledged that most customer-facing staff are not qualified social workers, it is relevant to consider that the British Association of Social Workers code of ethics states that social workers should 'assist people to understand and exercise their rights' (British Association of Social Workers 2012, Principle 3.4).

Where appropriate, practitioners may need to consider providing or signposting to effective support in challenging decisions around denial of access or restrictions on accessing services and encourage mainstream services to access effective autism training (Health Education England 2019). It is also likely to be helpful to promote an Equality Act culture around autism, which recognizes needs for reasonable adjustments and encourages tolerance/understanding of social errors, recognizing that an autistic person may well lack ill-intent.

3.3 Autistic needs in daily living

Exact eligibility criteria will, of course, vary depending on the type of assessment being undertaken. I have used a generic framework here to set out an overview of the types of needs autistic people of all ages, from all across the spectrum and in any country, may have in daily life.

3.3.1 Personal care and physical health

As I discussed in Chapter 1, physical health conditions are common amongst autistic people, who are at increased risk of an array of conditions including epilepsy, other neurological conditions (including migraine), hypermobility syndrome (double-jointedness – which can cause mobility problems in later life), sleep disorders, gut problems, allergies and auto-immune conditions.

Some autistic people have needs around eating which may include eating disorders (Shea 2015). It is also common for some autistic people, due to rigidity and/or sensory issues, to significantly restrict what they eat. This may be defined by colour, texture or other criteria, but can result in a highly restricted diet which may or may not be nutritionally adequate.

Sensory needs can also affect needs around personal hygiene. Some autistic people have very specific and inflexible sensory intolerance of particular hygiene products, materials, fragrances and/or textures. Others may find some tasks (such as brushing teeth) or requirements (such as having to wear particular clothing) so aversive to their senses as to be unable to tolerate them at all. Autistic priorities and social perspectives may make it difficult for some autistic people to learn and internalize the social reasons why personal hygiene is important, and we can find it difficult to identify and choose suitable clothing for social situations. Difficulties with flexible thinking and different sensory perceptions may result in some autistic people failing to choose suitable clothing for the season or current weather conditions.

Autistic people who also have dyspraxia, a common co-occurring condition (Cassidy *et al*. 2016), and/or weak proprioception (poor awareness and control over body position) may struggle with any or all of the following: using cutlery; manual tasks involved in cooking; the fine motor control needed to brush teeth; washing the entire body effectively; or hair washing. Others may be highly distractible and unable to reliably turn off appliances. Many autistic people have difficulties with planning, organization and flexibility. Any or all of these problems may cause difficulty with shopping, planning and preparing meals and/or with reliably maintaining supplies of hygiene products and/or establishing and maintaining a personal hygiene routine.

Sensory perception can affect an autistic person's ability to recognize bodily signals of hunger, thirst, pain, discomfort or need for the toilet (due to weak proprioception). Difficulties starting, stopping or switching tasks are also common amongst autistic people. Some autistic people have particularly significant difficulties with initiative and features of catatonia. These types of issue may cause some to be unable to reliably meet their own basic needs without assistance.

Some individuals, mostly those who tend towards a 'passive' type of autism presentation, are particularly at risk of catatonia-like symptoms. Any marked deterioration in movements, pattern of activities and in self-care and practical skills in an autistic person should be identified as potentially a catatonia-like deterioration and expert advice sought as a matter of urgency (Shah 2019).

Issues with continence are quite common amongst autistic children and adults, including in the 'high-functioning' group (Niemczyk, Wagner and von Gontard 2018). Factors which may impact continence include sensory differences impacting on awareness of sensation of needing the toilet, inertia impacting on ability to initiate action to go to the toilet when needed and medication side effects which can improve or worsen continence issues. Consequently, some autistic people may need short- or long-term support around toileting.

Sensory issues may affect the ability of an autistic person to identify, describe and locate pain and may cause over- or under-experiencing of pain. Rigidity and difficulty coping with change can make it difficult for an autistic person to cope with medical procedures without good support and preparation (which is often not provided). These issues, combined with autistic communication and initiative problems and a lack of reasonable adjustments, can have a seriously negative impact for autistic people in terms of access to physical healthcare.

EXAMPLE

Summary from a Safeguarding Adult Review (Rees 2017)

As an adult, Mr C had lived semi-independently in supported housing in the same village for many years and was well known to both the community he lived in and the care team that supported him. He had well-known character traits that at times would see him barred from local shops and pubs, but then this would soon settle and he would again be welcomed. He attended church regularly and enjoyed football and cricket. He maintained longstanding relationships with workers and had a particularly strong bond with a manager at Mencap who supported him. Mr C found any change particularly difficult and found it hard to build new relationships when workers changed. These difficulties often manifested themselves in a deterioration in behaviour. A particular trait of Mr C was a refusal to eat and drink when he was distressed.

Mr C appeared to become unsettled after another resident with whom he enjoyed a good relationship moved away and he was briefly admitted to a mental health hospital. Between February 2015 and June 2016, Mr C was then moved between placements a further four times. These were planned transitions; however, they often actually happened in an unplanned way. During this period, Mr C's behaviour deteriorated, and he stopped eating and drinking, resulting in a deterioration in his physical health. Capacity assessments found that he did not have capacity to understand that he needed to eat and drink to maintain his wellbeing and that his health could be seriously impaired if he did not have an adequate nutritional intake.

Concerns were expressed by his care team that there might be an underlying physical cause for him not eating and drinking and consequently losing weight. He was admitted to the local acute hospital trust on 20 April 2016 for observations and diagnostic tests.

Mr C displayed signs of aggression aimed at staff on the ward and refused various interventions and threw his food on occasions if he did not want it. An initial plan to undertake an oesophageal gastro duodenoscopy (OGD) to rule out an obvious physical cause was not progressed due to the management problems that Mr C was causing for the ward staff, and it was felt by the hospital that his condition was due to behavioural and not physical causes. So it was concluded that he no longer required an acute hospital bed.

He was discharged to a nursing home on 13 June 2016. At the nursing home he received end-of-life care, before he passed away four days later on 17 June 2016 at the age of 66. The coroner recorded the medical cause of death as sepsis, pneumonia and urinary tract infection and severe malnutrition. The conclusion of the coroner at the inquest was that death was due to natural causes exacerbated by self-neglect.

A safeguarding enquiry was commenced due to concerns raised that during his admission to the acute hospital he had not received the necessary tests to rule out a physical health condition as the root cause of his physical presentation. There were also concerns that he was transferred to a nursing home, apparently for palliative care, despite potentially reversible causes of his deterioration not having been addressed and without his situation being raised with the community learning disability team.

> Do you think health and social care staff are widely aware of the health risks associated with autism?

> What role (if any) do you think social workers should have around a client's health issues, where those health issues may be related to and/or impacted by their autism?

Effective social care support can be essential for maintaining good physical health and wellbeing. Health services should make reasonable adjustments for autistic people under the Equality Act 2010, but practice is highly variable and it is often only possible to achieve sufficient adjustments to effectively access healthcare with support to advocate for those adjustments. Additionally, some autistic people will need someone who knows them well to provide communication support in healthcare interactions, prepare them for medical appointments and procedures and provide support with understanding and implementing health advice, including support with obtaining and prompting to reliably take medication. These types of support needs go well beyond any adjustments that health professionals are required by the Equality Act to make and health services routinely argue that these are social care and not health needs. It is not uncommon, at the same time, for local authorities to contend that any need which is in any way health-related is a health need. Unfortunately, autistic people can readily find themselves stuck in the middle without these needs being met by either health or social care.[12]

3.3.2 Activities of daily living (shopping, cooking, cleaning, tidying, laundry, etc.)

Autism can, and does, affect any, all or none of these areas in different individuals. As discussed in the previous chapter, it is important to avoid assumptions that the type and degree of difficulty any individual experiences will necessarily be related to factors such as:

- any particular diagnostic label within autistic spectrum conditions

- IQ

- level of education

- type and level of communication (such as having a wide vocabulary and verbal speech or being entirely non-verbal)

- presence or absence of a learning disability or difficulty.

There are a wide range of autistic difficulties and challenges which can impact on our practical ability to achieve these tasks, including:

- inertia and/or difficulties with initiative (these can cause an autistic person to be 'stuck' and unable to initiate a task, even when strongly motivated to do so, requiring large amounts of prompting to overcome on each occasion)

- organizational and sequencing difficulties (such as becoming stuck as soon as something interferes with completing the task, or having difficulty assembling all the necessary items to cook a meal)

- rigidity and lack of flexibility (such as being unable to conceive of, let alone cope with, a change in familiar routines, products or ways of doing tasks)

- sensory issues (such as being unable to tolerate the smell of a particular cleaning product, cope with the noise of a vacuum cleaner, or touch rubber gloves, etc.)

- attention or focus issues (such as being unable to shift attention from an obsessive interest to a practical task, or needing to start a task at the beginning and complete it thoroughly all the way to the end before doing any other task)

- communication difficulties (such as misunderstandings or causing offence)

- learning difficulties (such as struggling to generalize an ability to carry out a task from one location to another, or lack of types of knowledge 'picked up' from experience or other people)

- limitations on overall resources (many aspects of life are difficult and demanding for autistic people and autistics may simply 'run out' of resources and be unable to function as efficiently as a non-disabled person).

The presence of each of these difficulties and the impact on practical tasks will vary widely between individuals and may or may not change or fluctuate over time. However, it is relatively common for autistic people considered very 'able' or 'high-functioning' in some ways to experience significant difficulties with basic daily living tasks. The possibility of support needs around these types of tasks requires assessment and consideration with autistic people right across the spectrum. In some cases, short-term 'enablement' support may be all that is needed to achieve independence. However, autism is a lifelong condition which does not 'get better'.

Consequently, it is important to recognize that, for many autistic people, all types of support needs (including with activities of daily living) will be permanent and that 'independence' in the sense of not requiring assistance or support may be an inappropriate and unrealistic goal. The limitations on overall resources, mentioned above, mean that for many autistic people there may be trade-offs between independence in activities of daily living, overall quality of life and ability to contribute to society. Just as for those with other permanent disabilities, achieving control over one's own life, combined with as much independence as sustainably possible and consistent with quality of life, are more meaningful goals.

3.3.3 Mobility

Autistic people can have a wide variety of needs around mobility. For some, using public transport may be extremely challenging or even unmanageable due to adverse sensory environments, communication challenges and the risk of unpredictable difficulties and changes. Most autistic children, young people and even adults may need support in learning how to use public transport safely to make particular journeys. Some will need to repeat this learning for each different journey and may have difficulty generalizing the learning. Others will need ongoing support to make at least some journeys safely.

Public transport environments such as train and bus stations are generally busy, noisy and chaotic, potentially posing significant risks to autistic people. An autistic person who becomes overwhelmed or panics may behave in ways which attract negative responses from other passengers, staff and police, all of whom are likely to lack basic knowledge about autism.

Autistic people also vary in their spatial abilities. These are relevant to a person's ability to find their way, navigate an environment, remember a route, use maps or follow directions. As with many issues, autistic people tend to the extremes. Some are spectacularly good at navigation, whilst others are spectacularly bad. The latter group may have difficulties which affect their mobility throughout their life.

As will be discussed in Chapter 8, autistic people of all ages are particularly vulnerable to exploitation and abuse. Simply being in a public place can put an autistic person at risk of bullying, harassment and even assault, triggered by their 'strange' behaviour or social naivety. Some autistic people (even adults) will fail to pick up social information and clues or to connect up information. This can result in an autistic person unknowingly putting themselves in highly vulnerable situations, such as walking alone in a 'dangerous' neighbourhood or boarding a deserted bus or train carriage late at night. Explicit teaching, practice and being allowed to make (small) mistakes are all important protective support that autistic children and young people need to develop, maximize and generalize their skills in safely accessing transport.

EXAMPLE

Extract reproduced from Autism Injustice (2019) with kind permission from Kat

On 6 March 2018, Kat boarded the last Virgin train (the 11:30pm) out of Euston and went to the toilet. The next thing she knew there was a banging on the toilet door and a British Transport Police (BTP) officer was ordering her, 'You need to hop off the train.' Confused by what was happening – why should she hop off the train? – Kat's first thought was that if she did get off the train, she would be stranded in London, late at night and with nowhere to stay.

She tried to explain that she was using the toilet and was a legitimate passenger but the police continued to harass her and demand she get off the train. When they asked Kat if she had a valid ticket, she told them that she did have a return ticket (this was subsequently provided to the police by Kat's solicitor) but if it was the wrong one she would be more than happy to buy another. She even offered to put her credit card under the door and explained that she was trying to use the toilet. She asked for more time, after which she would be happy to discuss the problem. She explained that she was very anxious and needed to get home.

The police continued to insist that Kat get off the train, refusing to listen to her pleas that she needed to get home and could not be stranded in London. They also ignored the fact that she was confused and upset by what was happening, making things worse by telling her that the train would not move until she got off and that other passengers were getting upset because they wanted the train to depart. When Kat asked why they were insisting she get off the train, a woman police officer said it was because she did not have a valid ticket, even though she did. BTP officers then switched their justification for treating Kat in the manner they did, from suspecting her of fare-dodging to behaving in a 'strange' manner (see below).

At this point Kat started to panic, but the police made matters worse by allowing a message to go out over the train's loudspeaker that there was 'a difficult passenger on the train'. Kat explained that she suffered from anxiety and asked to speak to a train manager.

Eventually, Kat agreed to come out of the toilet because a woman police officer started speaking to her like 'a human being'. But on leaving the toilet she was immediately arrested, handcuffed, and removed from the train, even though she was not resisting in any way. Later statements by BTP officers claimed Kat was being obstructive.

She was told by the custody sergeant at Brewery Road Police Station that she was acting in a strange way. At this point it seems clear that the officers involved had no idea about autism, making the assumption instead that Kat was on drugs and ordering that she be strip-searched in spite of the custody nurse making it clear to BTP officers that Kat showed no signs of being intoxicated by either drugs or alcohol – but that for this reason she was fit to be interviewed. Neither was anything incriminating found in Kat's bag. And yet the officer considered her behaviour so strange that he insisted on a strip-search even though Kat refused to give consent.

> Can you think of any steps that could be taken by public services and/or transport providers to improve the experience of autistic people?
>
> What role (if any) do you think social workers should have where a client experiences discrimination or inappropriate treatment in their daily life?

However, mobility is not solely about using public transport. Some of the same issues also affect walking, cycling and other modes of transport. Some autistic people drive, but driving can be a particularly challenging skill for autistic people to acquire and sustain and will not be accessible to all. Issues include difficulties with co-ordination and multi-tasking, 'reading' others' intentions and the need to make decisions at speed. Finally, all forms of mobility may be adversely affected by dyspraxia.

3.3.4 Social needs

Social difficulties are the most well-known aspect of autistic needs and the most likely to be considered when deciding eligibility. However, there are some aspects of social needs which may be overlooked.

Access to appropriate and accessible social environments may be particularly important for autistic people. On the whole, autistic interaction is most likely to be based around mutual interests or activities. Therefore generic 'social groups', schools, employment environments and random social interaction (e.g. in shops, on buses, etc.) are generally less likely to provide sources of meaningful social interaction or developing friendships for autistic people. Social interaction focused on mutual interests or activities is more likely to be helpful. However, autistic interests can be unusual and highly specific, so it is often challenging to find and access suitable social environments and some autistic people may need support doing so.

Social skills courses or groups are often provided for autistic children through schools and, sometimes, for autistic adults by charities, community groups, health or social care services. These vary in quality and appropriateness. Those which focus on teaching autistic people 'correct' social behaviour may have an adverse impact on self-esteem by teaching an unspoken message that autistic behaviour is 'wrong'. It is more constructive to provide information about non-autistic social interaction and options for emulating it if desired, alongside a clear distinction between behaviour which infringes someone else's human rights (which is always unacceptable) and merely unconventional, weird or odd behaviour (which is perfectly acceptable, although the autistic person may choose to modify it at times to achieve a particular goal).

However, these groups and courses may not provide social education in key skills such as:

- recognizing healthy and unhealthy relationships

- unwritten social rules which can lead to risk (such as 'snitching', telling other people what to do or how to avoid inadvertently provoking someone by seeming rude)

- detecting deception

- identifying exploitation.

Even where such topics are covered on courses for children, follow-up education and support for learning such skills in adulthood is rarely provided. Because of the developmental delays and generalization difficulties experienced by autistic people, support for learning about these issues is just as important in adulthood as during childhood.

Often overlooked is the impact of autistic communication and social difficulties on essential communication and interaction in daily life. It is common for autistic adults to struggle to navigate and find themselves embroiled in chronic conflict and misunderstandings with public services and service providers of all kinds. These difficulties affect adults most acutely, but many of the same difficulties affect autistic children navigating educational, structured social and administrative environments, and these difficulties tend to worsen with age and increasing levels of responsibility.

This is also true of the crucial area of sex and relationships education (SRE). Autism affects social communication and understanding. Misunderstandings and social missteps are common and normal for autistic people. However, the area of sex and intimate relationships is one in which a single error or misunderstanding (around consent, for example) can have severe and long-term consequences. It is vital for all autistic people, including adults, to have access to specialist SRE, which includes explicit teaching on the complexities of public and private, consent, and online behaviour.

Unfortunately, in my experience public bodies frequently assume that 'someone else' is responsible for meeting this need. Special schools may or may not provide appropriate, sufficiently autism-specific, high-quality SRE. Mainstream schools (where around 72% of autistic people are educated (Department for Education 2018)) generally provide only 'mainstream' SRE, which is entirely inadequate to the specialized needs of autistic people (Hartman 2014).

Autism is a neurodevelopmental disorder. This means that autistic people may vary in the rates at which various skills and needs develop. Consequently, it is especially important for autistic people to be able to access appropriate SRE in adult life (Attwood, Henault and Dubin 2014). It is often the case that this is not available at all or, if it is, only for those with a learning disability (around 40%) and often not autism-specific.

The consequences of this unmet need can be severe, as will be discussed in Chapter 8.

3.3.5 Education

The difficulties autistic children and young people experience in education are extensive, with exclusions and/or school refusal common (Ambitious about Autism 2018). Even for those autistic children who continue to attend school throughout childhood, school is often not the happiest or most accessible of places. For children with sensory sensitivities, schools can be loud, chaotic and overwhelming. Peer groups vary in their tolerance and understanding, often subtly influenced by adult attitudes, but bullying and social exclusion are common experiences (National Autistic Society 2006). Compared to wider society, schools are a relatively small social 'pool' of individuals. This can, for some autistic children, leave them with limited options for friendship, as those with less mainstream interests may lack peers who they can relate to and who can relate to them. Making it through the school day can require navigating a constant barrage of confusing interaction and communication. Teachers and teaching assistants vary enormously in their autism knowledge, attitudes and understanding. It is common for autistic children to be viewed as having 'behaviours' and for the focus to be on 'normalizing' those behaviours rather than supporting their functioning and wellbeing (Milton 2018). This can be damaging to self-esteem and identity as autistic young people often emerge having internalized negative beliefs about autism and with a self-image of being somehow defective or lacking.

The language of special education has shifted in the direction of person-centred approaches, but there is a long way to go before every autistic child is effectively supported and educated to become a healthy and happy autistic adult, comfortable with themselves and having developed effective coping strategies for adult life.

Education, for autistic children, needs to extend beyond schooling. Support to access out-of-school activities, including 'mainstream' activities, is vital to developing skills for life beyond school. Autistic people often find it difficult to generalize learning and skills from one context to another. As a result, it is vital that learning and skills acquired at school are extended during childhood to a wide range of other contexts. Autistic children who are sheltered or excluded from mainstream society risk being limited to an *adult life* excluded from mainstream society.

Of particular importance are opportunities to take risks, make mistakes and practise decision making. Commonly, in my experience, the childhood of some autistic children (especially those with learning disabilities) can be limited to special schools, special out-of-school activities, the family home and little else. Disabled children are often excluded from the freedoms and unstructured learning opportunities commonly available to non-disabled children, particularly during teenage and early adult life, due to assumptions about ability, inaccessible facilities and attitudes and over-protectiveness from well-meaning adults (Hingsburger and Tough 2002). Lack of opportunity to experience taking risks and making mistakes is often then assumed to indicate a lack of decision-making capacity in adult life when, in reality, a young adult may never have been given the opportunity to develop skills in these areas.

There are also additional skills which autistic (and all disabled) children need to learn. Self-advocacy, explaining needs to professionals, navigating the benefits system, health and social care as a disabled adult, boundaries in relationships with professional carers and the employment responsibilities of employing support workers directly are all important areas of learning for disabled children and young people, and yet are rarely taught.

Investing in support for autistic children to access a wide range of out-of-school experiences, learn and generalize skills is likely to be a cost-effective investment with the potential to reduce support needs later in life and/or prevent other costs (such as in mental health or criminal justice) (Iemmi *et al.* 2017).

There is far more that could be said about education, but there are other books entirely devoted to the subject. For the purposes of this chapter, therefore, the above brief summary is simply intended as a guide to a small number of the potential issues of particular relevance from a social work perspective.

3.3.6 Employment and contributing to society

The challenges autistic people experience with obtaining, maintaining and succeeding in employment are well documented. Rates of employment amongst autistic people are believed to be particularly low and, where relevant needs are not effectively met, autistic people can be denied opportunities to contribute to society (National Autistic Society 2016).

Whilst for many autistic people (including those with learning disabilities) the obstacles to employment can and should be overcome, it is also important to recognize that paid employment may not be appropriate for every autistic person. For some individuals (all across the spectrum) paid employment can be unmanageable and/or may result in an overall negative impact on wellbeing and functioning. Therefore, it is important for autistic people to be empowered to consider whether paid employment is the most appropriate way for them to contribute to society and whether it has a place in their overall wellbeing. In some cases, alternative activities which are meaningful to the individual and contribute to society (perhaps in less conventional ways) may be more appropriate.

Either way, it is vital to identify, acknowledge and challenge assumptions (including unconscious bias (Kenyon 2015)). An autistic person who is working may well need more, not less, support as a result of the overall demands on their limited resources, and the prospects of an autistic person being able to undertake and sustain employment may well be most affected by whether or not they have sufficient and effective support in other domains of life, not just specifically with employment itself. On the other hand, many people with learning disabilities (with and without autism) are under-estimated and not provided with effective opportunities to progress, learn and contribute to society, both throughout education and in adult life (Shifrer 2013).

Support with obtaining and transitioning into work is often targeted primarily at young adults and may exclude older autistic people who have taken longer to become ready for that type of support. Whether or not support is available, recruitment processes, both formal and informal, often act as a barrier to employment for autistic people. Estimates vary, but it is received wisdom that many job opportunities arise via informal networking and social contacts, rather than through conventional recruitment processes. Many autistic people find 'networking' baffling and impossible to participate in, and attempts are often unsuccessful, probably because informal networking tends to depend heavily on social communication with little or no content explicitly relevant to the topic of obtaining employment. Formal recruitment processes can be just as challenging to navigate, often depending heavily on face-to-face interviews, in which autistic people are often at a significant disadvantage (Tostrud 2016). Even alternative recruitment processes which are intended to be more objective, such as aptitude tests, can unfairly disadvantage autistic people (The Government Legal Service v Brookes 2017). For some autistic people, where it is possible to arrange a job trial (spending a short period actually doing the job), this can be a more autistic-friendly approach to recruitment.

If an autistic person does manage to secure employment, the key difficulties they may face include:

- social interaction and communication differences

- difficulty with flexibility of thought

- sometimes difficulties with forward planning, thinking in abstract ways and/or making mistakes

- discrimination and intolerance

- overload, too much uncertainty and interaction, and stress.

The problems arising from autistic social interaction and communication differences, including for those with fluent speech, should not be under-estimated. In my experience, whilst most employers and people have the intention to be inclusive and tolerant (and generally believe they are), it is nevertheless common for autistic employees to run into serious difficulties as a direct result of our social interaction and communication differences. Typical difficulties include:

- when a miscommunication or difficulty arises, automatic assumptions that the fault lies with the autistic person and that the problem is their autism

- unconscious bias influencing decisions with a subjective element, such as recruitment, appraisal and promotion decisions

- under-estimation (both by the autistic person and their employer) of the importance of peer acceptance and being seen to be a 'team player' to how the autistic person is viewed within the organization

- the 'hidden' nature of autism causing some autistics, especially more 'high-functioning' individuals, to be seen as getting special treatment/making a fuss over nothing and/or as culpable for social errors (because someone that intelligent *ought* to know better)

- autistic honesty and bluntness worsening disciplinary situations leading to a worse outcome than might otherwise have been the case; for example, an autistic employee honestly listing all their faults or expressing themselves extremely precisely and being unable to promise to never repeat an error or completely eliminate a risk (because neither is literally possible)

- managers and peers being unable to adapt to autistic needs for precision, specificity, honesty, a slower pace and/or less verbal ways of communicating, reducing or limiting interaction.

These issues cannot always be overcome by short-term, introductory support at the point of initial employment. These types of issue may lie dormant for long periods before reaching a crisis point. As a result, patchy employment histories are common amongst autistic people, including having lost jobs and/or been subject to disciplinary procedures and having had time out from working.

However, autistic people also have potential strengths as employees (Lorenz and Heinitz 2014), such as:

- attention to detail

- honesty and reliability

- willingness to do repetitive tasks

- loyalty

- knowledge and technical ability (obsessive interests can be useful for this!).

Often, informal support such as the presence of a person who happens to communicate in a way an autistic person finds compatible or a particularly supportive and proactive colleague can make a huge difference to the success of an employment opportunity. These forms of support can be important, but cannot and do not replace formal support, which may also be needed, in many cases over the long term.

Before ending this section on employment, it is also important to mention the relevance of volunteering and of adult education. For autistic people who cannot manage or are not yet ready for paid employment, volunteering and/or adult education can provide valuable opportunities, both to contribute to society through these activities and to learn and develop new knowledge and skills. It is notable that the Care Act explicitly includes training and volunteering alongside education and work as valid and important ways of participating in society and in relation to which eligible support needs may arise.

3.3.7 Accessing and making use of services in the community

There are a wide range of community services which autistic children and adults may need or want to use. Nearly all are obliged, at least in theory, to provide reasonable adjustments for autistic people. However, even where adjustments are available, this does not necessarily mean that autistic people will be able to use these services without support.

For example, if an autistic person finds leaving the house overwhelming, it is unlikely to matter that their local sports centre runs an autistic-friendly trampolining session. Similarly, owning a laptop and being able to order shopping online does not overcome support needs around putting the shopping away and finding a solution when expected items are not available.

Many mainstream services can be inaccessible for relatively simple reasons: crowds; noise; smells or other sensory issues; requirements to communicate by telephone; communication and language difficulties; difficulties meeting paperwork requirements (understanding letters, filling and returning forms, providing documents, etc.); and the expectation that an individual will initiate and sustain actions. It is common for autistic people to have low-level support needs which, if met, can revolutionize their lives but which, if they remain unmet, can paralyse and seriously impair quality of life. Typical needs include: someone to make a phone call on the person's behalf; practical assistance with completing benefits forms; support with problem-solving; support with finding and maintaining employment, education and suitable housing; and facilitation to meet and socialize with other autistic people and/or people with similar interests in an accessible environment.

EXAMPLE

The Highland One Stop Shop (HOSS) offers free social groups and activities, scheduled drop-in times and 1:1 appointments for advice and support on a range of issues.

Staff working at the HOSS are available for 1:1 appointments to discuss a range of topics and support individuals to develop strategies for specific situations and areas of difficulty.

Typical topics that arise in 1:1 appointments are:

- Employment – including finding and maintaining employment. Support may be given for the application and interview process, as well as discussing difficulties that arise in the workplace.

- Benefits – assistance with ascertaining what benefits you may be entitled to and how to apply, or issues with current benefits you are receiving.

- Housing – including support with housing applications and

advice on financial or other issues that may help to maintain a tenancy.

- Problem-solving support can also be provided in the following areas: education, befriending and relationships.

In addition, HOSS is open four days per week for 'drop-in', which is a safe place where people can relax and stay for all or part of the time and take a break from the stresses of everyday life. This includes access to internet-accessible computers, which also have Microsoft Office software, games consoles, art materials, musical instruments and a library of autism-specific books and magazines.

> Do you think there is a role for autism-specific preventive/low-level support or do you think mainstream advice or other services (with adaptations if needed) are best to meet those needs an autistic person has which may not be eligible or may lie outside the remit of social care?

3.3.8 Parenting

Autistic people can and do become parents. Autistic parents, like all parents, vary in their parenting capacities. Autistic parents with or without learning disabilities must be given every opportunity to show that they can parent safely and be good enough parents, with appropriate support. It is essential that assessments, training and support are both timely and appropriately tailored both to any learning disability-related needs (Working Together with Parents Network 2014) and to autism-related needs (Brook 2017). Failure to build in, from the outset, reasonable adjustments and assessments which recognize the validity of different parenting styles puts autistic parents at a significant disadvantage compared to parents who are not autistic. Appropriate and effective communication is vital to enabling autistic parents to participate fully in assessment or other processes.

Joint working across all agencies is also crucial in effectively supporting autistic parents, especially between adult's and children's services. The Care Act eligibility criteria are explicit that support for disabled adults to carry out caring responsibilities for a child is a service to the adult, falling on adult social care (Reg. 2(2)(j) Care and Support (Eligibility Regulations) 2015). Appropriate support to enable disabled parents to parent effectively must be provided at a sufficiently early stage to minimize or avoid the development of child protection concerns, provided this support does not extend to a level which would be tantamount to substituted parenting (A Local Authority v G (Parent with Learning Disability) 2017). If difficulties arise in finding adult social care providers who are willing to work with children, alternatives need to be found either via direct payments or by the local authority using its dominant position in the social care market to influence the development of appropriate services.

Recognizing and identifying learning disabilities and/or neurodivergent conditions such as autism are often not a core feature of parenting capacity assessments and referrals to adult services are often made too late or not at all (Dugdale and Symonds 2017). When referrals are made to adult services, in my experience, they are often not followed up or pursued as vigorously as is necessary.

Support for disabled parents is often not a core part of the culture and approach of adult social care and is frequently seen as a low priority in the competition for scarce resources, coming up against the care needs of a growing population of older adults and working age adults with profound disabilities who are unlikely to parent. While adult social care assessments, under the Care Act, do generally ask about parenting, this is typically a separate section included almost as an afterthought rather than integrated within assessment approaches. Similarly, most Resource Allocation Systems (RAS) used by local authorities to guide decision making on personal budgets under the Care Act include parenting responsibilities only as an entirely separate area of need and do not take account of parenting responsibilities as a multiplier to the level of support needed. This can easily result in unmet needs. For example, an autistic parent who struggles with tasks of everyday living, such as laundry, would score the same points and be awarded the same budget as a single autistic person with the same difficulty, whilst 'parenting' would simply add a few extra points and perhaps a small amount to the overall care package. Good quality assessment and personal budget setting should, instead, recognize that an autistic parent is likely to need a higher level of support than a non-parent across all domains of need as a result of their increased responsibilities and, where appropriate, social workers may need to demonstrate that those needs cannot be met within the indicative budget generated by a RAS and must be readjusted to meet these needs.

It is also important that autistic young people, just like all young people, are provided with education and preparation to become parents in the future. Services for young people, particularly those with a learning disability, rarely consider or offer high-quality support and preparation for parenthood.

3.3.9 Mental and emotional health

It is well established that autistic people are at increased risk of a range of mental health difficulties, including anxiety, depression, obsessive-compulsive disorder, eating disorders and suicidality, but often struggle to access effective and appropriate mental health services (Camm-Crosbie *et al.* 2018).

Many autistic people experience alexithymia, a difficulty with identifying and verbalizing emotions, which may include lack of emotional awareness and/or confusion between emotional feelings and physical sensation (Poquérusse *et al.* 2018). These issues, along with chronic stress, genetic vulnerability and adverse life experiences, are likely to be contributing factors to the increased risk of experiencing mental health difficulties. However, the combination of alexithymia and autistic communication differences also means that therapies and interventions for mental health difficulties in autistic people need to be appropriate and, often, adapted specifically for autistic people (Muggleton 2018).

There is a high risk of death by suicide in the autistic community. It is important to be aware that rates of suicidality amongst the autistic population are significantly higher than in the non-autistic population, and that the risk factors for suicide in autistic people can differ radically from those in the general population (Cassidy and Rodgers 2017). Camouflaging and unmet support needs appear to be risk markers for suicidality specific to autistic people. Non-suicidal self-injury, unemployment/difficulties with employment, and mental health problems appear to be risk markers shared with the general population that are significantly more prevalent in the autistic community (Cassidy *et al.* 2018).

Effective, preventive mental health support is just as, if not more, vital than accessible and appropriate mental health services for those who already struggle with poor mental health. One relevant factor may be the development of positive autistic identity in childhood and early adult life, something which will be discussed further in Chapter 5.

3.4 Chapter summary and key points

- Challenge assumptions, recognizing:
  - uneven functioning
  - developmental delay(s) and the importance of well-planned and supported transitions
  - breadth of needs; not limited to social interaction
  - independence and/or recovery are not always an appropriate goal.
- Recognize the barriers, including:
  - not knowing what to ask for
  - rationing by obstacle
  - falling between two stools
  - inappropriate or inaccessible services.
- Identify autistic needs in daily life, including the fact that autism can impact:
  - personal care and physical health
  - activities of daily living
  - mobility
  - social needs
  - education

- employment and contributing to society

- accessing and making use of services in the community

- parenting

- mental and emotional health.

Recommended resources

St Clement's Practical Autism Video Guides (available on YouTube):

- *Gender Identity*

- *Mental Health*

- *Social Skills*

- *Sexuality*

- *School Refusal*

- *Food and Dietary Issues*

National Autistic Taskforce (2019) *An Independent Guide to Quality Care for Autistic People.* London: National Autistic Taskforce.

Westminster Commission on Autism (2016) *A Spectrum of Obstacles – An Inquiry into Access to Healthcare for Autistic People.* London: Westminster Commission on Autism.

CHAPTER 4

Person-Centred Care Planning and Autism

4.1 Person-centred approaches, needs-led planning and the wider context

Person-centred approaches have been at the heart of social work practice for many years. Following changes brought in by the Children and Families Act 2014 and the Care Act 2014, the legal framework underpinning social care fully supports a person-centred ethos. Even so, in a system under pressure from constrained finances and under-staffing, it is not uncommon for person-centred language to be used whilst the actual practice may be paternalistic, procedural and/or heavily resource led. The degree to which the service user's 'voice' is genuinely heard or even listened for in social care varies enormously.

Person-centred approaches can benefit all service users when implemented well. However, many current approaches to care planning (such as conversational approaches), specifically designed to be person-centred, risk narrowing care planning to focus exclusively on largely arbitrary 'outcomes' identified by the person, to the exclusion of a comprehensive, professional consideration of how the full range of their needs can be met appropriately. Where the person is autistic and may find it particularly challenging to imagine hypothetical futures, leaving all the responsibility for identifying potential options entirely to the adult themselves may not be an adequate mechanism for care planning.

The degree of social work involvement in care planning is also variable. In adult services, case-holding is now much less common than it once was. Both adults' and children's services suffer from high staff turnover and extensive use of agency social workers (Perraudin 2019). Typically, social work involvement is limited to assessment and care planning at the strategic level, largely consisting of commissioning a service provider and subsequent reviews (often undertaken by a different individual or team). It is now common for much of the care planning function to be effectively delegated to a service provider, where it is typically undertaken by care staff. These approaches inevitably constrain the options considered during care planning and often require decisions to be made about where the person should live and by whom their care should be provided before significant thought is given to the detail of precisely *what* care and support the person actually needs. The resulting care planning tends to be service-led and focus on use of the services available from the particular provider and the ways in which that provider organizes their services, rather than being genuinely person-centred.

Truly person-centred working can be particularly important and beneficial for autistic people. It is in the very nature of autism that autistic individuals tend to have needs, interests and preferences which differ more widely than average from those of others (including other autistic individuals). In my experience, universal or 'standard' services often do not meet the individual needs of autistic adults and children well or even adequately. For example, many domiciliary care agencies are unable to guarantee the timing of care visits and even staff continuity. The resulting degree of unpredictability can, for many autistic people, result in this type of 'care' having an overall negative rather than positive effect. Similarly, the activities available in many generic care services (such as residential care, supported living or day centres) cater to average or majority interests. These are much less likely to be desirable or appropriate for many autistic people, who are far more likely to have niche or unusual interests (such as role-play games or collecting lightbulbs) and to dislike or find stressful many common, mainstream activities (such as coffee mornings or shopping trips).

Research has repeatedly demonstrated that autistic individuals tend to have a 'spiky profile' of abilities and difficulties (Happé 1994). In Chapter 2 I discussed the importance of recognizing this when undertaking assessments and being aware that an autistic person may have strong abilities in some areas whilst having significant difficulties in others. When care planning with an autistic person, it is important to consider a range of possibilities such as, for example, whether they may need much more support and adaptations in some areas than others, or whether a universal service might suit them for some needs whilst for other needs their support might need to be arranged in a way tailored specifically for them.

For these reasons, person-centred approaches are in many ways ideally suited to autistic individuals. The advantages can include:

- assessment and planning processes that enable taking into account the 'spiky profile' of autistic individuals

- arranging support in ways which permit greater certainty and predictability than is possible in traditional social care services

- focus on atypical priorities and needs, rather than those 'expected'

- increased autonomy and control.

However, the way in which person-centred approaches to care planning are commonly implemented in practice can actually create significant barriers for many autistic individuals. These include:

- where person-centred language is used but the practice is actually service-led, professional-dominated and severely restricted by arbitrary (and often undisclosed) policies and rules

- assessment and care-planning processes which require considerable initiative on the part of the service user

- assessment and care-planning processes which are vague and do not follow a predictable format

- uncertainty and unpredictability

- communication challenges – particularly the use of open questions such as 'What outcomes would you like?'

Adaptations suggested in Chapter 2 for assessment are also likely to help in mitigating some of these difficulties in care planning.

Effective person-centred care planning with autistic people needs to start long before decisions are made about service providers or provision. In line with the statutory frameworks, it should be needs-led. Difficulties abound with achieving this in practice, not least the severe under-funding of social care and a widespread lack of suitable community-based service providers (National Autistic Society 2018). Nevertheless, it is worth considering carefully the benefits of starting from an autistic person's needs, identifying what suitable care might look like and then comparing to actual services available, rather than the other way round. When this is done, it can lead to the identification of options not previously considered and even to innovative and creative approaches from service providers willing to rise to the challenge.

4.2 What does good care look like? Goals

What, then, might a good care plan look like? The first question we need to ask is what the goal is. Current care planning approaches (underpinned by the statutory frameworks) focus on the person's 'outcomes'. This is great…in theory. In practice, however, at least two difficulties arise. First, the autistic person themselves may not know, may not be able to identify or may not be able to communicate the outcomes they desire. Second, there are often hidden, unconscious over-arching goals which underpin the thinking of family members, professionals, care providers and even the autistic person themselves and impact on the selection of these 'outcomes'. The report of the National Autism Project, which reviewed the research evidence on 'interventions' of all types, highlights the issues and is worth quoting at length:

> Proxy decision-makers who are not usually autistic themselves tend to make decisions in terms of what autistic people lack. They are seldom told by autistic people what a good autistic life is like. An autistic person may not place a high value on a trait that non-autistic people consider essential, and may have, and value, abilities or affinities that have never occurred to non-autistic people. Intervention may amount to trading one unconventional set of traits with a more conventional, but not objectively superior, set. Assumptions that everyone wants, needs and values the same things must be confronted and reframed to determine their applicability

to any individual. Infliction of conventional values may infringe individuals' rights to self-determination.

Of particular concern are interventions that may train autistic people to be unquestioningly compliant, increasing their vulnerability. There is also the potential loss of connection to people who are 'like them' and the risk of ending up rejecting all that is autistic while not being able to pass well enough to succeed in non-autistic terms. And then, there are the adjusted expectations that the autistic person is now doing 'so well' that they can manage without support and have no excuse for continuing to have difficulty.

Particularly for intensive childhood interventions, there is also considerable risk of turning every activity into therapy with 'learning goals' and 'observations', jeopardising the right of children to have free time for play and recreation (UN Convention on the Rights of the Child). Disabled children are not an exception, and turning every activity into therapy does not constitute giving them 'free *time*'. (Iemmi *et al.* 2017, p.19)

It is therefore well worth reflecting at an early stage and opening up discussion about what a 'good quality of life' for this autistic person might look like and what the over-arching goal of any care or support might be. This enables constructive challenges to assumptions that a 'normal' life, 'normal' behaviour or becoming less autistic are necessarily appropriate goals and openness to accepting non-neurotypical perspectives (where these do not infringe on the rights of others). Adopting an explicit focus on the autistic person's wellbeing and quality of life (from their own perspective) can help to open up these wider issues. There are any number of models, guidelines and frameworks which can inform this stage of planning (for example, Justice for LB 2018; Think Local Act Personal 2019), although very few that are autism-specific.

The definition of 'wellbeing' set out in s.1 Care Act 2014 is one such potential starting point for considering quality of life. Whilst the Care Act applies only to adults, the definition of 'wellbeing' is nevertheless also helpful when care planning with autistic children – particularly with an eye to their future and considering whether they are being supported in ways which lead towards wellbeing in adult life. I will make connections to the Care Act definition of wellbeing throughout this chapter.

4.3 What does good care look like? A framework

The model I have set out here as a basis for care planning is drawn from an autism-specific, independent guide to quality care published in April 2019 by the NAT, an autistic-run organization focused particularly on the needs and interests of autistic people who may be less able to advocate for themselves (National Autistic Taskforce 2019). I am part of the National Autistic Taskforce and led the development of the guide. So I am hardly unbiased; however, I believe that this guide has three main advantages which warrant it being used as a framework for care planning (and reviews). First, the NAT is not a care provider and, unlike many autism organizations, is entirely independent of care providers. Second, the NAT guide is autism-specific. Throughout this book I will, I hope, illustrate why autism-specific thinking is so important. Finally, the guide was written entirely by autistic people. The NAT does not and cannot directly represent autistic people who are unable to advocate for themselves, but, as fellow autistic people, we do have a unique and useful perspective which can contribute to improving care and support for all autistic people.

The NAT guide sets out ten recommendations which describe key elements of quality care and support:

1. Respect and promote autonomy.

2. Support communication effectively throughout the lifespan.

3. Provide care which is autistic person-centred.

4. Tackle environmental and other stressors.

5. Remove barriers to access.

6. Fight stigma and discrimination.

7. Recognize behaviour as distress.

8. Ensure better transitions.

9. Ensure ongoing, practical, autism-specific staff training.

10. Accept difference and support positive autistic identity.

I will briefly discuss each of these in turn, relating them to aspects of wellbeing and consider how each can be applied in practice to care planning.

1. Respect and promote autonomy

Autonomy is an abstract concept and it can be difficult to see how it relates to the day-to-day practices of care delivery, but, in my experience, nothing could be more fundamental. It is remarkably easy for any adult or child with needs for care and support to become disempowered and not actually to have control of their own lives. Disabled children may grow up in home or school environments where they are (often unconsciously) treated as younger than they are or just assumed to be incapable. Adult social care environments exist in a wider world in which negative and discriminatory attitudes towards disabled people persist and have a pernicious effect. Despite best intentions, these attitudes can quite readily creep into health and care environments. Research also demonstrates the risk of care workers becoming emotionally 'detached' in response to challenging work environments and the importance of empowering staff to take a proactive rather than a reactive approach to providing compassionate care (Harbottle, Jones and Thompson 2014).

Even where staff attitudes are positive and caring, anxieties amongst staff about risk and safeguarding can readily lead to caring empathy becoming paternalistic, over-protective and disempowering. Focusing on respecting and promoting the autistic person's autonomy encourages staff to discover and empathize with their perspective and promotes a collaborative approach to care and support between the autistic person and those who care for and support them. It is also relevant to maintaining the person's dignity, an integral aspect of wellbeing (s.1 Care Act 2014), and rooted in fundamental rights under the Mental Capacity Act (s.1 Mental Capacity Act 2005) and Articles 3 and 12 of the UN Convention on the Rights of Persons with Disabilities (UNCRPD).

This principle can be applied to all aspects of care in any environment. The key questions to ask are:

- To what extent is this autistic child or adult in control of their own life?

- To what extent is their control sustained?

- What factors affect their ability to maintain control of their own life?

- What can be done to increase their autonomy?

Putting autonomy at the heart of care planning requires challenging the answer that the autistic person is (as an inherent result of their autism and/or any other condition or learning disability) too profoundly disabled to be capable of controlling their own life and, instead, considering what practical and active steps can be taken to increase their degree of control over their life. Autistic children and young people may well have spent their entire childhoods in protective environments and may lack the experience of decision making and risk taking which are typically a part of teenage years for non-disabled young people. As a result, it is important to ensure that, at any age, autistic people have opportunities to learn, both theoretically and from experience, how to make their own decisions. Autistic people may experience difficulties generalizing information and experiences from one instance to another, and so we may need more and a broader range of experiences, coupled with high-quality, accessible and explicit teaching (particularly of unwritten social rules) in order to develop our ability to make more of our own decisions. I will discuss capacity and supporting decision making with autistic people further in Chapter 6 and Chapter 7.

EXAMPLE 1

Julia (41), an autistic woman with a learning disability, is offered a choice of activities every morning at the day service she attends. Staff offer these choices verbally, because Julia speaks. Each day she replies, 'I don't know' and, since they assume she is incapable of making choices, the staff make suggestions (effectively decisions) based on their observation of Julia's apparent likes and dislikes.

EXAMPLE 2

Julia (41), an autistic woman with a learning disability, is offered a choice of activities every morning at the day service she attends. Staff initially offered these choices verbally because Julia speaks. Each day she replied, 'I don't know.' Julia's keyworker noticed that, at lunch, she was able to choose her food from the physical options in front of her. So, over time, her keyworker took photos of Julia doing each of the activities on offer and made a simple decision board to offer a choice of two activities each morning. She also made sure Julia had sufficient time and quiet to look at and consider the choices. After a few days, Julia began to pick up one of the photos and hold it to indicate her choice. Once this system had been in place for some weeks, the keyworker increased the choice of activities to three options. Over time, using similar methods, Julia learned to express her choices and make decisions about a wide range of aspects of life.

How do you think Julia might feel about each approach?

What differences do you think there might be in the recruitment, training and culture of the two day services? Would those differences be apparent to someone commissioning each service?

It is particularly important to include not only control over everyday choices (such as clothing, food or activities), but also control over the major life choices which are a substantial part of adult life for non-disabled people, such as:

- where to live
- who to live with
- relationships (including intimate relationships, family and friends)
- exercising citizenship rights (such as voting)
- how to contribute to society
- how to use money and assets.

Other key questions to ask which are relevant to autonomy are:

- Are staff always honest and open with service users about their own lives even when that information might be upsetting?

- What restrictions are imposed on the autistic person? Are these actually necessary? What less restrictive approaches could be used?

- Do staff empathize with and respect the autistic person's perspective? Have they thought about questions like what it might feel like for an adult to:

  - have to depend on others for support

  - have other people make life choices for them

  - have care/support people in their homes and lives for substantial periods of time?

- And do they show respect for autistic ways of looking at the world, such as:

  - seeing all non-literal statements as lies

  - finding uncertainty and unpredictability stressful

  - disliking touch and/or small talk?

It is vital to avoid the assumption that an autistic person's autism (learning disability, or any other condition) makes any particular restriction necessary or inevitable. This is often used as a justification when, in fact, those in formal or informal 'carer' roles may be fearful of 'something bad' happening and believe (wrongly) that they have an absolute duty to eliminate all risks and keep an autistic person completely safe.[13] Positive risk taking must include constructive critique of the reasoning behind any restrictions to identify ways in which those restrictions can be reduced and the autistic person's autonomy increased. It is just as important, however, that positive risk taking is used to genuinely increase the person's autonomy and control, not to act as a 'justification' for failures to meet needs.

Good care is when autistic people have power and responsibility and are supported to be able to control our own lives. A good service for autistic people respects our perspectives and does not assume that 'normal' is always best. Personal preferences are respected, including for:

- how to contribute to society

- communication and interaction

- downtime

- variety and change versus repetition and routine

- sensory needs

- special interests.

Good care planning with autistic people will identify to what extent they are in control of their own life and what steps are being taken to increase this. Effective person-centred care planning with autistic people is not merely tokenistic about personalization, but demonstrates a profound respect for the autistic person's perspective and preferences on major aspects of their lives. This includes control by the individual over day-to-day life (including over care and support, or support provided to the individual and the way in which it is provided) (s.1 Care Act 2014).

Autistic people need greater certainty and predictability than neurotypical people. Autistics are, therefore, particularly likely to value control over their day-to-day lives, including how care and support are provided.

There is a very important distinction to be made here between autonomy and independence. Independence can be a good thing. Conversely, being dependent on other people can be hard and frustrating. However, no one is truly independent of others; everyone is dependent on others to some extent. For those with any disability (ASD or otherwise), it may be a practical necessity to be more dependent on others than non-disabled people need to be. Increasing independence is a worthwhile goal *as far as it is actually reasonably possible and compatible with the choices, safety and wellbeing of the adult concerned.* All too often, in my experience, 'promoting independence' is a euphemism for cutting services regardless of actual need.

Some disabled individuals actually need (and may always need) to be dependent on some types of support indefinitely. It is vital to recognize that what actually really matters in terms of quality of life is *autonomy*. That is what is encapsulated by this aspect of the Care Act definition of wellbeing. Autonomy is the ability to control one's own life. This is not the same as independence.

For example, an adult might be made more independent of support by having their care package cut from 16 hours a week to eight hours a week. The consequences for that individual might be that they are now only able to carry out basic shopping and health tasks and are no longer able to access the leisure activities that they want to do. So, by making the individual more 'independent', they have actually *lost* a degree of autonomy because they can no longer choose whether or not to access leisure activities – that choice has been taken away from them.

This distinction is critically important when thinking about care planning with autistic people. There might be little apparent difference in the amount of support provided by a large care provider versus employing a PA directly. But which would provide the client with greater control over when and how the care is provided?

A further issue is the model of support itself and how it is delivered. Many autistic individuals have a limited supply of the resources needed to cope with social interaction, decision making, initiative and sensory demands (all of which may cause significant stress to autistic individuals). These resources may well be depleted by the support itself, particularly when this is delivered in the traditional 'alongside the client' model. The strain of trying to navigate the communication demands of interacting with a (most commonly) non-autistic support worker combined with the sensory demands of being in busy, noisy environments (most places other than home) accompanied by the need to make choices and decisions (what would you like to eat, where do you want to sit, do you want to go to this place or that place first, etc.) can be exhausting and overwhelming. Many autistic people have a limited ability (although how limited will vary greatly from individual to individual) to tolerate this type of support and will need substantial 'downtime' in a quiet, familiar environment, interacting only with familiar people or not interacting at all to recover from the experience of being supported!

This does not mean that this type of support is not helpful or necessary. For the vast majority of autistic people who require support, this type of support is necessary and appropriate for at least some of their needs. However, it is not the only possible form of support and, for some autistic people, some of the time, alternative approaches to support which maximize autonomy may need to be considered – even if these sometimes involve support being provided on behalf of and away from the individual in order to make it possible for them to use their limited resources in ways which maximize their autonomy (and other aspects of their wellbeing).

2. Support communication effectively throughout the lifespan

Communication is so high up the list of the NAT's recommendations because communication differences are central to the nature of autism and because effective communication is critical for being able to exercise autonomy. In fact, autonomy and communication have been described as the only goals which are 'almost always good' in terms of care and support for autistic people (Buckle 2017).

In this area, it is especially vital that assumptions about fixed capabilities are challenged and rejected. An extremely small number of autistic people are truly incapable of developing some form of functional communication[14] (see example below). Autism is a lifelong developmental disability but autistic people can and do develop skills throughout our lives. Far too many autistic adults languish in services which (largely through lack of autism knowledge) simply assume that they are incapable of developing functional communication and cease trying. Many more are supported by services that consider supporting the development of functional communication to be someone else's responsibility (such as speech and language therapy), but do not address the absence of such services actually providing active support.

EXAMPLE

Surrey and Borders Partnership NHS Foundation Trust run an Augmentative and Assistive Communication Project whose aim is to engage and interact with service users who are autistic and have moderate to severe learning difficulties using low- and high-tech assistive technology, Augmentative and Assistive Communication (AAC), sensory and/or intensive interaction. The aim is to build and embed the use of individualized communication systems throughout the daily lives of the people participating and routine practice of the staff working with them. Led by a dedicated AAC project lead, the project initially started working with just one service user, but now involves 25 people living in four houses.

The project has at its core the wish to ascertain people's choices, dreams, desires and preferences through meaningful interactions. Most of the participants have lived in large hospital institutions for many years and have missed opportunities to converse and make choices. Interventions are regularly reviewed and adjusted as necessary to suit each individual.

The technology used in the project includes iPads, touch screen PCs and interactive whiteboards. Tactile, keyring-sized objects are being designed and 3D printed to assist people who process information that way. Paper-based communication books have been built and are being developed for individuals to support a visual schedule and communication.

The project lead is working to make information accessible to all, including people with complex needs. The onus is on the project lead and staff to find what works for the person – not for the person to fit some unreachable criteria.

> What differences do you think the people who are supported by this project experience in terms of control over their lives, compared to people with similar needs who do not have access to such specialist support?
>
> Where do you think communication support of this nature fits between health and social care services?

A good service for autistic people is one where:

- People are effectively supported with communication throughout their lives.

- Staff routinely use, offer, respect and are receptive to a range of alternative forms of communication (such as pictures, photographs, diagrams or symbols; objects; apps on smart phones, tablets, interactive whiteboards and touch screen PCs; switches/buttons; sensory items such as olfactory or tactile; writing, text messages, email or other text-based communication).

- There is a designated member of staff (preferably a specialist Communication Support Worker) responsible for exploration based on observations and trials to find the most appropriate communication systems for individuals. This must include continuous assessment and review of each service user's preferred form(s) of communication, including the development of functional communication (the ability to communicate needs) and the introduction of assistive technology.

- There is a designated member of staff (preferably a specialist Communication Support Worker) responsible for helping each person initiate and maintain contacts with family and friends and people in positions of authority (such as professionals).

- Service users (as well as staff) routinely have good internet access on an equal basis with others in society – this should be treated as a basic utility (like electricity or water) in care services, as it has begun to be treated in wider society. These days, it would be considered unacceptable not to provide fast, reliable internet access in a university or railway station. It should be just as unacceptable in a day service, residential care or supported living service.

- Assistive technology equipment is kept up to date, well maintained, and readily accessible by individuals at all times.

- Staff are supported and empowered to share, learn and develop communication knowledge and skills.

- The service communicates and provides information in ways which meet the Accessible Information Standard. (National Autistic Taskforce 2019)

Reproduced with kind permission from the
National Autistic Taskforce

If this is to be achieved, care plans for autistic people must ensure that each individual has their communication needs assessed and met, including where these are not in practice being met effectively via input from speech and language therapy (SALT) services. Where speech therapists with expertise in autism are able to assess and meet needs, their expertise can be invaluable. However, even where there is SALT involvement, there will still need to be provision for staff working directly with the autistic person to implement SALT advice. These basic needs, day-to-day communication, should be met within the scope of a normal care plan in both children and adult services. Where health services are failing to meet health needs, such as the provision of SALT, these decisions should be challenged. However, absence of SALT provision should not be used to excuse autistic people being left with unmet day-to-day communication needs. Whether or not the NHS is providing access to any or sufficient SALT provision, care providers and special schools can and should be encouraged or challenged to empower their staff to develop their own communication knowledge and skills, including specialist roles, so that services providing care and support for autistic people can reliably support and develop basic functional communication (National Autistic Taskforce 2019).

Technology can play a vital role in enabling functional communication, in addition to a wide range of other benefits. Staff training and support is crucial to ensure that all those working with an autistic person are comfortable and competent in using the relevant technology. Care planning should include consideration of whether adults (and, at appropriate ages, children) own their own tablets/smart devices on an equal basis with others in society, including any assistive technology they reasonably require. Where an adult (or young person) does not, this needs to be challenged and questioned during care planning.

In practice, unnecessary and spurious barriers are often raised. Funding should not be a barrier since the cost of purchasing a smart device is negligible compared to the cost of meeting ongoing care needs, and could be considered from a variety of sources including personal finances, disability benefits or personal budgets. Risks, health and safety issues should also not be used as a basis for denying access to such devices. Extremely robust protective cases are widely available, as are apps and settings which are capable (if restrictions are lawful and absolutely essential) of limiting or restricting access to certain activities or types of material.

3. Provide care which is autistic person-centred

It is, unfortunately, remarkably common for care to be provided which is labelled as 'person-centred' when, in reality, the care is dictated largely by family members (often parents) and/or the service provider, with the autistic person, at best, having some day-to-day choices between pre-set options. A particular challenge occurs where family members are responsible for managing a direct payment and/ or where a PA is a family member. This can drive decision making that may not be in the service user's best interests or properly reflect their wishes and feelings, especially where there is a large package of care and the service user becomes a major source of income for members of the family. However, social workers are not entirely powerless in such situations. Where there is concern about paying a family member as a PA or around the administration of direct payments, under the Care Act (Direct Payments) regulations, a person receiving direct payments can only employ a family member as a PA with the permission of the local authority (Reg. 3 Care Act (Direct Payments) Regulations 2014). Such permission can lawfully be withdrawn. Local authorities also have significant powers to place other conditions on the use and administration of direct payments and to judge whether a person is 'suitable' to receive a direct payment on behalf of an adult who lacks capacity (s.32 Care Act 2014).

Truly person-centred care recognizes the rights of adults (and the emerging rights of children to an age-appropriate extent) to self-determination and autonomy (Justice for LB 2018). This does not mean entirely disregarding the knowledge and role of (often dedicated) family members. But it does mean carefully considering the autistic person's perspective and, if necessary, providing appropriate challenges to any person (family, friend or professional) putting forward their views and perceptions of what the autistic person wants or needs. As a result, care planning should seek to ensure that person-centred care genuinely promotes an autistic person's control over their own life (as distinct from family and professionals).

Genuine person-centred care also needs to recognize and accept autistic differences (National Autistic Taskforce 2019). Whilst every individual is different, there are some issues where autistic people are more likely to have particular needs which require a different approach than for non-autistic people and good person-centred care planning will respect these autistic perspectives.

DO:

- ensure a minimum of staff variation and match staff to autistic people on the basis of shared interests and mutual compatibility whenever possible

- question the intended outcome of programmes and approaches, including those designed to manage behaviour, not just their effectiveness (Are they trying to help the autistic person's wellbeing and functioning and reduce distress? Or are they trying to make the autistic person more 'normal' and/ or stop displaying distress?)

- plan changes in advance whenever possible; provide preparation and information about upcoming events using written and/or visual information as well as words

- support and facilitate the development of autistic identity, access to autistic culture and autistic space.

DON'T:

- try to make autistic people 'normal'

- restrict an autistic person's life totally to within their current comfort zone – encourage new experiences that they might like based on their preferences

- make us join in if we don't actually want to

- tell us that non-autistic ways of doing things are 'right' and autistic ways of doing things are 'wrong'

- impose excessive or unnecessary changes when we may prefer repetition and sameness

- insist that we conform to social norms when we may prefer not to do so

- lie to us (including 'lying by omission'), even for 'good' reasons such as to avoid upsetting us

- tell us what to do without explaining why

- overwhelm us with excessive choices and/or insufficient time to make decisions

- use touch, forced eye contact and/or small talk to 'reassure' or establish rapport if we may not welcome this

- put words into our mouths that we did not say (e.g. by using 'I' statements when not quoting).

In care planning, consider whether the proposed service(s) for an autistic person:

- responds promptly and effectively to individual needs and preferences, as defined by the autistic person, including staffing decisions

- empowers service users and staff with the knowledge to understand different perspectives

- aims to maximize autonomy but without unreasonable risk of harm or excessive stress

- supports in ways which ensure dignity and works with existing family or community (including autistic community) strengths

- promotes social inclusion (defined as *voluntary* participation by autistic people)

- supports autistic people to meaningfully contribute to society in a way that makes sense to the individual

- values difference, ensures equality and does not discriminate (National Autistic Taskforce 2019).

It is worth discussing further the issue of contributing to society (s.1 Care Act 2014) as an important facet of care planning. Individuals can contribute to society in a variety of ways. All lives have value and enrich society, including those of disabled people. However, this does not mean that the contribution of those who have needs for care and support needs to be tokenistic. Nor do autistic people necessarily have to contribute in conventional ways such as through paid employment, voluntary work, charity fundraising or attending community events. Consideration should be given to each individual's skills, abilities and special interests and the role these could potentially play. Autistic individuals may choose to contribute in other ways such as:

- to knowledge
- to public discourse (through writing articles, books or pamphlets or by using social media)
- by challenging convention/expectations
- through activism
- through creative or artistic endeavour

or in their own unique ways.

EDUCATION

In the UK education system, children are divided between mainstream and special schools. The education system is strongly geared to a set level of attainment at fixed ages and to consistent rather than spiky profiles. This can pose particular difficulties for autistic children and young people. Many autistic children and young people struggle to access schools which can meet both their support needs and academic needs (Goodall 2018). So-called 'high-functioning' children (i.e. those with higher levels of academic attainment) who also have significant support needs are likely to struggle to get their needs on both fronts met in the same place. Autistic children with significant impairments in verbal language may find themselves placed in a special school which has an inappropriately low expectation of their academic capabilities. Broad level-based measuring of attainment can result in autistic young people being denied (sometimes for years) the opportunity to progress in areas of strength until or unless they achieve an equal level of attainment in areas of weakness (All Party Parliamentary Group on Autism 2017; Waddington and Reed 2017).

Similar issues arise around the timing of educational progress. Autism is a developmental disorder and it is common for autistic teenagers and young adults to be ready to do things at ages (sometimes early and often late) which do not 'fit' with the system. In England, there is no 'right' to repeat years or delay progression at school – only a rarely used discretion for headteachers to permit such delays. Following substantial funding cuts in further education, access to a more academically orientated qualifications route is often closed or considerably more difficult for those who are not ready to achieve GCSEs at 16 and A-levels at 18 (or by 19 at the latest), the assumption being that failure to achieve qualifications at the requisite age indicates that the young person would be better suited to less academic qualifications, rather than simply lacking the social and emotional maturity to achieve them at the specified age (which can easily be the case for an autistic young person).

These challenges mean that good educational planning for autistic children and young people needs to take account of all their needs (academic and non-academic) and may need to consider bespoke solutions. The importance of social care support to meet needs and develop skills outside of the school environment should not be under-estimated. For those in special schools, this can be crucial to accessing more 'mainstream' out-of-school activities which can develop social and communication skills, decision making, risk taking and resilience along with a wide range of other life skills. For those in mainstream schools, support outside of school can be vital in enabling autistic children and young people to develop 'soft' skills vital to employment and to access support to learn practical, relationship, communication, decision making and other life skills at a pace they can manage, with explicit teaching and additional help where needed.

EMPLOYMENT

For many adults paid employment can be a primary means of contributing to society and a very positive experience (see s.1

Care Act 2014). Evidence from the general population indicates that employment is broadly positive for mental health (Waddell and Burton 2006). This is also likely to be true of a substantial proportion of autistic people, but it is not universal. In care planning with autistic people it is important that paid employment is not automatically adopted as a goal without careful consideration as to whether it is an appropriate and helpful goal for that individual at that time. Paid employment can be an unhelpful goal where, for example:

- the person currently has difficulties/challenges which make paid employment completely unfeasible (such as severe inertia)

- the person does not currently have the skills or qualifications needed to attain the employment they wish to aim for

- the support the person needs to attain and/or maintain employment is not available

- the person has struggled in the past to sustain employment and the issues involved have not been adequately addressed

- the person has experienced bullying and/or trauma associated with employment and has not sufficiently recovered from these experiences

- the person faces significant discrimination in attaining and/or maintaining employment and this has not been adequately addressed

- the demands (sensory, interaction, communication, uncertainty, social and/or other) of employment cause excessive stress which has an overall detrimental impact on their wellbeing or ability to function and the issues cannot be addressed through additional support or reasonable adjustments (such as working reduced hours or adjusting the job role).

For these individuals, alternative goals and activities should be considered such as voluntary work, education, training and/or the wide range of other available ways to contribute discussed earlier in this chapter. It should be borne in mind that many of the same challenges may be encountered in activities other than paid employment. Nevertheless, for many people, alternatives can be constructive and worthwhile activities in themselves and/or may provide a stepping stone towards paid employment.

Where paid employment is a goal the autistic person wants to pursue, consideration of the support needed should be integral to care planning with them. It is important to be aware that the autistic population fares far worse in both attaining and sustaining employment than the general population, worse even than other disabled people (Taylor, Henninger and Mailick 2015). The reasons for this are complex, but one of the key issues is likely to be that autism is, broadly, seen by non-autistic people (and defined by the diagnostic criteria) as a deficit in social functioning in the autistic person. Put bluntly (as autistics generally prefer), this means that many autistics behave socially in ways which are not only atypical and different but which other people generally view as 'defective' in some way.

It is widely accepted that social networks play an important role both in finding a job and in career advancement (Halpern 2005). The disadvantage autistic people experience is readily apparent when common expectations in person specifications are considered. These frequently include requirements such as: team player; good communication skills; or excellent interpersonal skills. It is unsurprising, therefore, if autistic people often fail to measure up to such criteria. Less explicitly, promotion and job progression may be influenced more heavily by social acceptability than by competence in the job role itself and workplaces can be social environments in which individuals who do not 'fit' are vulnerable to exclusion and bullying.

A range of other difficulties can create barriers for autistic people when it comes to finding and sustaining employment. A common difficulty is lacking experience and/or the conventional background that employers typically look for to demonstrate relevant skills and competence. Some of these difficulties can be overcome through good support to access voluntary or internship opportunities. Autistic communication and social challenges can mean that interviews pose a significant barrier. Basic adaptations such as providing questions in advance can help, as can encouraging employers to offer alternatives such as job trials.

Employment support services can be invaluable for autistic people. Generic services for disabled people vary in their usefulness for autistic people due to our typically 'spiky profile' (see Chapter 3), because some services focus only on 'low-level' jobs which may be inappropriate or unsuitable for autistic people with significant skills or qualifications.

There are some autism-specific employment support services, mostly run by the voluntary sector and dependent on grants and/or charitable funding. As a result, many have significant geographical and/or age restrictions which often make them unavailable to adults over 25 and those who live in parts of the UK not covered by an autism-specific service. The age issue is particularly important for autistic people. Autism is a developmental disability and it is common for autistic people to take a lot longer to navigate the challenges of the transition to adult life and reach a point of being able to cope with employment. As a result, it is not at all uncommon for autistic people over the age of 25 to have never had a paid job (National Autistic Society 2016; Taylor *et al.* 2015).

Most employment support services offer only time-limited assistance in obtaining and settling into employment. This often leaves unmet autistic needs for ongoing and periodic support in sustaining employment over time, a particular issue in autism (Taylor *et al.* 2015).

4. Tackle environmental and other stressors

A good care plan for an autistic person is one in which the cumulative effects of stress are recognized and the person is enabled to balance demands in a way which is healthy for them and maximizes their ability to function and exercise autonomy (National Autistic Taskforce 2019). In my experience, managing and reducing stress plays an important role in a good quality of life for autistic people. Our stress levels, capacities and needs can change, even during the course of a day. So good care planning will involve considering all sources of stress and all times of day and carrying out regular reviews. This includes controlling and managing the level of stress an autistic person may be experiencing from all aspects of their environment. I will briefly consider four major ones here:

SENSORY NEEDS

Care planning should consider the suitability of the sensory environments where autistic people live or spend significant amounts of time, both in terms of the built environment and the behaviour of staff and other service users. This analysis must draw on information from the autistic person themselves about their sensory needs, whether these are communicated verbally, through alternative forms of communication or through behaviour. Where it is not possible to gather any information from the autistic person themselves, or where that information is insufficient, the expertise of other autistic people should be used to help identify sensory issues.

Sensory issues may be directly relevant to the suitability of housing and/or other services for individual autistic people and sensory needs must be factored in to consideration of the appropriateness of any option to meet an individual's needs. There should be clear differentiation between needs and preferences and recognition that what may be a preference for some people generally, can be a need for some autistic people with severe sensory processing difficulties (Caldwell 2014). Consequently, there are some autistic people who cannot share housing with other people and there are some autistic people who cannot live in urban areas and whose sensory needs can only be met by housing in a quiet, suburban or even rural environment.

Care planning should consider how to meet sensory needs, both for sensory stimulation and to avoid sensory overload. These days, most special schools have sensory rooms and, often, soft play areas, trampolines and access to large, outdoor spaces. However, similar access to sensory stimulation opportunities is rarely provided in adult services, which can result in 'challenging behaviour' when sensory needs go unmet (Caldwell 2014). Environmental modifications (particularly to living environments and environments where autistic people spend significant amounts of time) may be necessary to reduce sensory distress from some inputs (through sound proofing, for example) and/or to provide opportunities for needed sensory stimulation. Some environmental modifications can be relatively inexpensive or even free, such as reducing clutter, avoiding patterns on carpets, curtains and furnishings, using or not using certain colours. Others may require accessing additional funding, such as Disabled Facilities Grants. Consideration should be given to staff policies around autistic sensory needs and preferences, such as banning the use of scented personal hygiene products and ensuring respect for sensory preferences, including for touch. Staff responses to sensory stimulation behaviours ('stimming') should also be considered and care plans should ensure that staff only intervene in such behaviours on the basis of an agreed plan led by the autistic person if they are suffering distress or harm (National Autistic Taskforce 2019). Care planning should also include considering how appropriate sensory adaptation equipment such as noise-cancelling headphones, coloured lenses/filters, sensory stimulation 'toys', etc. can be provided, considering the full range of options (including personal finances, disability benefits and through a personal budget) to ensure that sensory needs are met appropriately. Last, but not least, overall balance between the amount of time an autistic person spends in adverse sensory environments and the amount of time they spend in favourable sensory environments should be considered in the overall appropriateness of a care plan. All these issues and needs should be reconsidered and revisited during reviews as sensory needs can and do change over time (Bogdashina 2003).

CHANGES AND TRANSITIONS

Care planning must consider autistic needs for:

- accurate, honest and specific information
- routine, structure and predictability
- preparation for transitions/changes.

The care-planning process should be one of honesty or openness with the autistic person themselves. In my view, the plan itself must also treat lack of honesty or openness with an autistic person as a totally unacceptable form of discrimination. Most decisions to withhold information are taken with the best of intentions, usually to minimize distress, but this approach is misguided. Uncertainty and/or the prospect of change is likely to cause an autistic person distress – that is simply in the nature of autism. Honesty, accurate and specific information (in accessible formats) and good preparation are far more effective ways to support autistic people in minimizing the stress caused by changes.

It is also vital to consider the role of public services and care providers in keeping changes and transitions to a minimum, advocating for clear information and preparation for transitions well in advance and in challenging decisions to withhold information (National Autistic Taskforce 2019). This needs to include considering the quality of staff communication when providing information to or answering questions from autistic people. Do staff actually give clear, straight answers to questions? Are they willing to patiently repeat the same answer as many times as the person needs? Are calendars/diaries/planners used to locate events in time? Are photographs available and used for people and places relevant to information being provided?

Care planning should also involve consideration of an autistic person's needs for routine, structure and predictability and whether support is needed to create or develop these (National Autistic Taskforce 2019). Most autistic people find routine and structure helpful, but can often find it difficult to create the degree of order that we need to achieve a good quality of life. We may need such support as:

- help drawing up a weekly or daily timetable that meets our needs

- prompting to initiate the next activity in a routine

- support to organize the practical supplies and/or information needed to carry out an activity

- help to undertake some activities.

INTERACTION AND COMMUNICATION

It is often difficult for non-autistic people (and even some autistic people) to understand that many autistic people may find interacting and communicating with others demanding, tiring or even unpleasant. The overall quantity and quality of interaction and communication with others which the autistic person wants and with whom they want to interact and communicate should be considered during care planning. Some autistic people can have difficulty regulating interaction and meeting our own needs and may struggle to recognize when we need a break. Others may know when they need a break but find it difficult to communicate this to others and actually get a break. Needs for 'downtime' and 'recovery time' (after a demanding activity), including breaks/rest from interaction and communication, should be considered and included in any daily or weekly routine for both adults and children. This can be challenging for services and staff, who may find it difficult to accept or justify 'doing nothing', but periods (and often longer and more frequent periods) of rest and lack of interaction can be vital to autistic wellbeing (National Autistic Taskforce 2019).

Support needed to reduce stress from interaction and communication should also be considered in care planning. Many autistic people (including those who are most independent and functional) need some support to navigate communication with public and other services. Support to make sense of a confusing letter, someone to make a phone call on our behalf and help organizing and completing basic administrative tasks (such as paying bills or posting a letter) are very common autistic needs. Support may also be needed to translate communication into accessible formats and to cope with and make sense of communication and interaction socially and in less formal contexts.

DECISION MAKING

Research evidence, as well as the collective knowledge of the autistic community, strongly suggests that many autistic people find decision making stressful. Decisions that need to be made quickly, or involve a change of routine, or require talking to others, are experienced as particularly difficult, and the process of decision making is often reported by autistic people to be exhausting, overwhelming and anxiety-provoking (Luke *et al.* 2012). We may avoid decisions at times, feeling that they are 'too hard'. This can have serious implications for autonomy, as it can easily result in an autistic person being assumed to be incapable of making a decision and decisions being made for them. On the other hand, though, where an autistic person is required to constantly make and communicate decisions and choices, this can cause crippling stress.

A middle ground is possible by effectively supporting decision making (see Chapter 7), both in the care-planning process itself and, through the care plan, in daily life.

All four of these areas need to be considered at an early stage of care planning, along with any other environmental factors relevant for a particular individual. This requires recognizing that these factors will render some environments wholly unsuitable for some or even many autistic people. Particularly stressful environments are likely to include most hospitals (whether psychiatric or acute), prisons, many mainstream schools and some care services, because these environments typically involve constant uncertainty, change, interaction, communication and decision-making demands, combined with a highly unsuitable sensory environment (bright lights, noise, lack of space). As a result, environments like these can cause massive stress to some autistic people. Environments which cannot be adapted and which are highly unsuitable should be avoided whenever possible and accessed only for the shortest period absolutely required in order to protect the person's human rights.

In Chapter 9, I will discuss the likelihood that these issues may underpin much autistic behaviour which is described as 'challenging', and, therefore, the importance of focusing on the removal of environmental and other stressors as a priority over modification of the behaviour.

5. Remove barriers to access

Care planning needs to consider ongoing and future needs for advocacy for an autistic person. In a consultation workshop I ran with autistic people at Autscape[15] in 2009, the top need identified was for advocacy. Whilst it is important that statutory rights to advocacy[16] are upheld for autistic people, it may well also be necessary to supplement statutory advocacy through specific care provision where advocacy can be identified as an appropriate way to meet needs.

I highlighted in Chapter 3 the barriers autistic people face in accessing healthcare and the above average levels of co-occurring conditions in autistic people. It is vital, therefore, that care planning includes consideration of both reasonable adjustments required and support needs around health, including preventive health checks, support needed to access healthcare, communicate with healthcare professionals and implement treatment, including medication.

Care planning needs to recognize and challenge discriminatory treatment of autistic people in health, social care and community environments and facilitate access for autistic people to the full rights of citizenship (including voting, activism, making complaints, being involved in research and consultations) and to rewarding activities, including leisure activities. A good care plan will identify and support individual interests, skills and strengths and provide an environment in which each autistic person can thrive, develop, learn and contribute (National Autistic Taskforce 2019).

6. Fight stigma and discrimination

In my experience, one of the best ways to do this is to make care planning rights-based, recognizing and promoting the human and equality rights of autistic people. This requires considering potential placements or services from the perspective of whether that service or placement is best placed to protect and uphold the autistic person's rights. This is most effective where it includes active support for two key principles which are challenging to the health and social care status quo for autistic people. These are:

- the right of autistic people to choose where and with whom they live on an equal basis with others in society (UNCRPD[17] Article 19)

- that no autistic person requires long-term institutional care and that all autistic people can and should live in the community (UNCRPD Articles 12 and 14).

Putting these principles into practice is not easy, but it is possible. The first requires the provision of sufficient, suitable housing and identification of autistic needs as needs. It is relatively common for an autistic person to have to fail repeatedly in group housing environments, often acquiring a criminal record and/or labels like 'challenging behaviour', before services will accept a need for individual housing. Clearly this approach is not consistent with promoting basic human rights, but it is also wasteful and counter-productive because it compounds the problem before attempting to improve it. It would be far more cost effective (as well as more appropriate from a human rights perspective) to carefully assess the viability of different housing options for each individual and really try to select the most appropriate placement first time (which, of course, means that a full range of placements must be available). There will still be missteps and times when an option does not work out, but they would be the exception rather than the norm. Good service commissioning for autistic people recognizes unusual and specific housing needs and does not force people to live with others for efficiency or cost reasons when it is not the individual's choice to do so (National Autistic Taskforce 2019). Whilst it is lawful for a local authority to choose a cheaper option from amongst those ways in which the need could be met appropriately, the cost of cheaper options which would not be appropriate (a matter of professional social work judgement) is *not* a relevant consideration.[18]

The second principle mentioned above is substantially more challenging and many professionals genuinely believe that it is not possible and that detention in hospital is genuinely necessary for some people, usually on the grounds of risk to themselves or others. The difficulty with that position is that it assumes that behaviours which involve risk are a result of the person's autism (or learning disability) and that hospital 'treatment' is capable of making a person 'better'. As I will discuss in Chapter 9, both of these assumptions do not stand up to close scrutiny. Good service commissioning for autistic people is organized locally for one person at a time and recognizes the long-term cost-effectiveness of good quality community-based support, before situations deteriorate to the point of crisis. A good service for autistic people is located in the area in which they live and have connections (National Autistic Taskforce 2019). Care planning should, therefore, be based around suitable housing in the person's local community and, if this is not the case, the plan must contain clear, measurable, time-limited steps to bring such a situation about in the shortest possible time.

It is also sometimes argued that community-based care is not necessarily less restrictive than hospital care. Whilst this is true at present, it is a fallacy to assume that the level of restrictions often placed on individuals with high care needs in community settings are actually necessitated by their disability (see Chapter 9 for further discussion). Care planning does need to address risk. But it also needs to address fear-driven decision making. In my experience, throughout health, care and education services, at all levels, many staff are fearful of being blamed if 'something bad happens'. This fear-driven thinking leads to risk-averse decision making. Consequently, care planning needs to address these unspoken fears and support all those involved to become confident and comfortable, enabling and empowering positive risk taking. This requires social workers to take a confident, legally literate lead in creating a reassuring, solution-focused, blame-avoiding culture, including in safeguarding activities (see Chapter 8 for further discussion of safeguarding). Good care planning involves positive risk taking, recognizing autonomy and emotional and social factors as at least as important as the physical safety of a service user (Department of Health 2014). This may also require supporting (and when needed challenging) families and friends to understand and become comfortable with positive risk taking and a rights-based approach. As I set out in Chapter 8, positive risk taking and promoting autonomy to empower autistic people to better protect themselves is, in reality, a highly effective way to reduce the vulnerability of autistic children and adults to abuse and neglect.

Care planning should also consider the need for a preventive approach to risk. Right across the autistic spectrum and throughout the lifespan, needs for individualized education and support in areas such as healthy relationships, decision making in social situations and recognizing exploitation, should be identified and met (see Chapter 8 for a detailed rationale). It is important to question assumptions about an individual's ability to protect themselves, particularly where these are based on factors like IQ or educational level.

Care planning should also question and challenge beliefs and assumptions about the cognitive or learning capabilities of an autistic person in all areas of life and support lifelong learning and development (Courchesne *et al.* 2015). Care planning is also a key opportunity to consider the potential vulnerability of autistic children and adults to bullying (National Autistic Society 2006) and to consider whether effective strategies to prevent, identify and challenge bullying are in place and whether those policies respect autistic perspectives on banter, teasing and similar behaviours, recognizing when this may be experienced as bullying. In an effective service for autistic people, everyone feels able to challenge discriminatory or inappropriate attitudes and beliefs (National Autistic Taskforce 2019).

7. Recognize behaviour as distress

Good care planning considers whether those supporting an autistic person have the training, skills and empathy to try to put themselves in an autistic person's shoes, get to know them as individuals and maintain relationships with them based on trust and respect (National Autistic Taskforce 2019). This requires an approach to care planning which pays close attention to the pay, conditions, training and career structure of those working directly with an autistic person on a daily basis and the suitability and long-term viability of informal care arrangements. Only once these issues are addressed does it become realistic to produce a care plan which expects those providing care or support for autistic people to work with them to modify their environment to meet their needs and minimize distress.

I will discuss the causes of and solutions for 'challenging behaviour' in more depth in Chapter 9, but it is important to note here that a care plan should fully consider needs for 'downtime' (but not as a punishment) and opportunities to meet sensory stimulation needs. It is also relevant to add that careful thought may be required on the suitability of some care services for particular individuals and whether additional funding may be needed to provide an appropriate service. For example, if an autistic person needs to be supported by a consistent, small group of support workers and needs visits to occur at reliable, consistent times, this may require a more costly package of care than typical domiciliary care. It is vital for practitioners to recognize that these sorts of issues may well be *needs* for an autistic person, where they might be considered merely *preferences* in another client group.

8. Ensure better transitions

This is not just about the transition from children's to adult's services. Transitions occur throughout the entire lifespan: from primary to secondary school, changes of key professionals, bereavement, moving home and many more. Good care planning takes a 'whole life' approach: recognizing and planning well in advance for transitions throughout the lifespan (National Autistic Taskforce 2019). This is, of course, good practice with all client groups. But it is particularly vital for autistic people. Autistic rigidity means that many autistic people find even small changes or transitions (such as ending an activity or moving to another room) very difficult and unsettling. More major transitions can, if mishandled, cause severe distress and even trauma, leading to serious consequences in terms of functioning, mental health and behaviour. Transitions will be discussed in more depth in Chapter 5. However, I will briefly cover some of the implications for care planning in this section.

For autistic people it is vital to plan well in advance for transitions whenever possible and develop with the autistic person contingency plans for predictable emergency situations. This may require advocating with service commissioners and other agencies for co-operation with such planning at a sufficiently early stage. Good commissioning for autistic people is when agencies work together with the autistic person and their family/friends. It begins early, is detailed and specific, and continues consistently throughout the lifespan. Good service commissioning for autistic people works collaboratively with autistic people and (if they wish) their family and friends to create concrete, specific and funded plans for transitions, including crisis planning (National Autistic Taskforce 2019).

It is also important to consider the necessity of uncertainty, changes and transitions and the degree to which it may be possible to minimize these. Some changes and transitions are driven by the needs of services or staff and not by the interests of autistic people. In care planning, critical reflection is needed to consider the impact of this on a day-to-day basis in the autistic person's environment.

Is there a high level of uncertainty? Are there frequent changes of staff or schedule? Do services believe that they should provide a constant variety of activities and other choices (such as food) and does this lead to effectively enforced variety more for the sake of staff and inspectors than for autistic service users?

A good quality of life for autistic people can look more restricted, more repetitive, more boring than many non-autistic people might find tolerable. But this does not necessarily mean that the autistic person's quality of life would be better by being forced into constant change. It is important to support autistic people to, on occasion, step outside our comfort zone to try an activity that our interests suggest we might enjoy or to achieve a goal that we want to achieve. However, there is a balance to be struck between this and imposing a non-autistic view of what a 'normal' life should look like. Generally speaking, autistic people find repetition and routine comforting and have a much higher tolerance for sameness than non-autistic people. Much of life is more demanding, tiring and overwhelming for autistic people. Consequently, we also often have limits to the overall demands we may be able to deal with without suffering incapacitating levels of stress and/or fatigue. We therefore need to balance the internal resources needed to cope with new experiences or change with those required to meet other demands. As a result, care planning needs to take careful account of these delicate balances and recognize that a 'good life' for an autistic person may well contain less overall activity and a lower level of variety than would be the case for a non-autistic person (National Autistic Taskforce 2019).

It is also vital to be honest and open with autistic people about transitions. Sometimes professionals do not give an autistic person information until the last minute or even lie to them, such as telling them that they are going to visit a new placement for 'a cup of coffee' and then leaving them there (see, for example, Rees 2017, p.6). In my experience, staff do this because they want to avoid upsetting the autistic person and they often believe that telling the person earlier will cause 'anxiety'. This is a fundamental misunderstanding. Lies, omissions and only giving information at a late stage actually increase distress and undermine trust. A short delay in disclosing information to an autistic person may be justified if this is in order to gather information and/or reduce uncertainty, but these advantages need to be weighed carefully against the importance of early preparation, honesty and trust. Lies, evasions and half-truths are simply unacceptable when supporting adults and only acceptable for very good reasons in very specific circumstances (which would also be valid for a non-disabled child) when supporting children (National Autistic Taskforce 2019).

Autistic rigidity does mean that many of us experience stress around changes and transitions. We also find uncertainty stressful. These causes of stress are in the nature of being autistic and it is unlikely to be possible to entirely alleviate the resulting stress. What can help is for those supporting an autistic person to empathize with the stress we experience (Milton 2012). In care planning, this empathy requires considering the impact of changes or transitions (including the combined impact of multiple changes at the same time) and reflecting carefully on whether they are absolutely necessary. It also requires consideration of the overall demands and sources of stress for the autistic person and opportunities to recover from stress.

Autistic people may also experience anxiety around changes, particularly where there is uncertainty, as we may struggle to gather sufficient information to reduce the uncertainty and create predictability. The most effective way to support autistic people with change and transition is, therefore, to provide information as this increases predictability and reduces uncertainty. A good care plan for an autistic person will consider needs for information and ensure that the autistic person is provided with honest, clear, specific and detailed information well in advance. Planning must be in place to work collaboratively with the autistic person and (if they wish) their family and friends to effectively prepare for transitions (National Autistic Taskforce 2019).

9. Ensure ongoing, practical, autism-specific staff training

At first glance, this may appear to be beyond the scope of care and support planning. However, it is such a vital area of need that the implications for care planning must be considered. The recent Care Quality Commission (CQC) interim report on segregation (Care Quality Commission 2019, p.6) found that:

Many staff lacked the necessary training and skills to work with people with autism who also have complex needs and challenging behaviour. Many staff who worked directly with the people in segregation were unqualified.

This reflects a wider picture of autistic children and adults, including those with the most complex needs and in 'autism-specific' services, frequently being supported by staff who have not been equipped with sufficient training and skills to do so effectively. As will be discussed in Chapter 9, the result can be placement breakdown and a downward spiral into increasingly restrictive (and expensive) environments.

Funding community-based care at a level that enables and promotes high-quality training for staff and good retention of those skilled staff may seem unrealistic. But it is highly likely to be cost-effective overall in the longer term in preventing the breakdown of community-based support (Iemmi *et al.* 2017).

Even where staff are trained, however, much autism training is overly theoretical and does not focus on the practical knowledge of support needs in daily living which frontline care staff actually need. The recent publication of the Core Capabilities Framework for Supporting Autistic People (Health Education England 2019) has set out for the first time a comprehensive list of this practical knowledge and I recommend referring to that when planning training. At a bare minimum, it must include:

- practical communication strategies

- supporting decision making

- sensory needs and how to meet them

- preparing and supporting people with change

- understanding, preventing and responding to distress (including behaviour which may challenge).

Staff (including social workers) with strategic, assessment and planning responsibilities for autistic people should also have access to training providing autism-specific knowledge in (at least):

- assessing needs

- care and support planning

- planning and supporting transitions

- supporting decision making

- mental capacity assessment and best interests decision making

- safeguarding and risks

- commissioning good care for autistic people whose behaviour may challenge.

10. Accept difference and support positive autistic identity

Good care planning with autistic people promotes and supports positive autistic identity and does not assume that 'normal' is always good (National Autistic Taskforce 2019). A good care plan (including for children) must include activities which are not 'therapy'. Whilst specialist, autism and/or disability-specific environments have their benefits, care planning should include consideration of equality of access to mainstream community groups, services and activities and the importance of not limiting people to 'special' environments. This is particularly important for children and young people so as to equip them for adult life in their community.

Good care planning with autistic people does not allow 'choice' or 'self-determination' to be used to justify failing to provide effective support, access to services (including healthcare) and opportunities to explore new experiences. The type, quality and nature of social interaction that an autistic individual would like needs to be considered and may range from a substantial amount of social interaction to very, very little. The range is much wider than for non-autistic people and it is not safe to assume that very limited social interaction is bad nor that a large amount of social interaction is good (National Autistic Taskforce 2019).

Good care planning with autistic people facilitates access to autistic-controlled spaces (such as Autscape) and to the wider autistic community (including online), including for children and autistic people who may also have a learning disability

(National Autistic Taskforce 2019). More broadly, it is important to recognize the need for and create opportunities for autistic people to have ownership and genuine control of at least some spaces, activities or groups within their lives. It is common in care services for 'service user' groups to be set up, but for these to be, in reality, run and controlled by staff or volunteers. In the wider community, groups for autistic people are often set up and run by large charities or parents' groups, but it is much rarer for groups to be set up by or handed over to the genuine control of autistic people.

In my view, promoting a positive and accepting attitude to autistic identity and differences is vital because of the implications for self-esteem. This is especially important for children. We have moved from 'special needs' to Education, Health and Care Plans (EHCPs) and plans are now focused around outcomes. But culture and attitudes in special education can still amount to saying that a child has a defect and this is what the child needs to do to fix it. Rarely are EHCPs and Individual Education Plans (IEPs) written in a way which is underpinned by the social model of disability. Care must be taken to distinguish between skills and abilities an autistic child needs to develop and adaptations and adjustments which should be made to their environment to accommodate them. Both are appropriate for all children and most adults, but plans must reflect a strong disability equality ethos which accepts each autistic person for who they are, rather than trying to 'make me normal'.[19] This should include considering whether the autistic person's environment provides opportunities to challenge discriminatory or inappropriate attitudes or behaviour, whether amongst service users, staff, senior staff, family members or professionals (National Autistic Taskforce 2019).

Care and support for autistic people should promote our emotional, psychological and social wellbeing. A positive, accepting attitude towards autistic people helps to create and maintain good self-esteem. This must be balanced with education about the rights and needs of others and respect for others, who may also be different in various ways. For autistic children and young people, it is important to be able to self-advocate and ask for help, but it is also important to develop abilities to be autonomous, problem-solve, manage emotions, experience empathy, be resilient and develop and sustain relationships.

4.4 Chapter summary and key points

- Effective person-centred planning is needs-led.

- What does good care look like? Goals – what are we trying to achieve?

- What does good care look like? A framework.

    1. Respect and promote autonomy – work to increase an autistic person's control over their own life.

    2. Support communication effectively throughout the lifespan – developing functional communication and embedding in everyday support is everyone's responsibility.

    3. Provide care which is autistic person-centred – recognize and accept autistic differences and provide appropriate support to access meaningful activity and contribute to society.

    4. Tackle environmental and other stressors – recognize stress and ensure a sufficiently adapted environment considering:

        - sensory needs

        - changes/transitions

        - interaction and communication

        - decision making.

    5. Remove barriers to access – provide advocacy and remove barriers to accessing community services and healthcare.

    6. Fight stigma and discrimination – rights-based care planning which ensures access to suitable housing and support options.

7. Recognize behaviour as distress – give proper consideration in care planning to the suitability of the care environment and the need for well-trained and supported staff.

8. Ensure better transitions – a 'whole life' approach with clear, coherent planning early. Eliminate unnecessary change and ensure the autistic person is provided with honest, accurate information.

9. Ensure ongoing, practical, autism-specific staff training – including ensuring adequate funding for training and successful development of practical skills amongst staff providing care.

10. Accept difference and support positive autistic identity – do not allow 'self-determination' to be used as an excuse for failing to meet needs; focus on strengths and recognize disabling factors in the environment; provide access to the autistic community and autistic space.

Recommended resources

St Clement's Practical Autism Video Guides (available on YouTube):

- *Diagnosis and Identity*

- *Coping with Change*

- *Sensory Issues*

Justice for LB (2018) *Justice for LB Toolkit*. Accessed on 9/8/19 at www.advocacyfocus.org.uk/justiceforlb.

National Autistic Taskforce (2019) *An Independent Guide to Quality Care for Autistic People*. London: National Autistic Taskforce.

■ CHAPTER 5 ■

Life Stages, Aging, Transition Planning and Autism

5.1 Introduction

Throughout the earlier chapters, I have stressed that autism is a lifelong condition. In this chapter I will focus on autistic development throughout the lifespan and key moments of transition. We know from neurological studies that there are a number of differences in brain development across the lifespan between autistic people and non-autistic people, and that these result in some differences in how the brain is structured, functions and is organized (Ecker, Bookheimer and Murphy 2015). We also know from autistic people that the difficulties, challenges and strengths we experience can change and develop across the lifespan. As D'Astous *et al.* (2014, p.14) put it, 'Taking a life course perspective and developing knowledge and understanding of the shadows of parent blame[20] and challenging the sustained social exclusion of people with autism may be helpful to practitioners new to this area of practice.'

This chapter will discuss how these developmental changes intersect with social and care transitions both large and small for autistic people across the spectrum. Transitions affect and are affected by all aspects of life, but some particularly relevant factors are housing, family issues and parenting, all of which will also be discussed in this chapter.

In social work, transition typically refers to the transition from children to adult services. However, from the autistic person's point of view, a lifespan can be full of overlapping and often messy transitions. How these are handled and how services understand and adapt to the changes autistic people may experience at various life stages can have a significant impact (positive or negative) on a person's outcomes and trajectory.

5.2 Autism and attachment difficulties

The first and most obvious point which needs to be made about the impact of autism on a child's development is that autism is one possible cause which needs to be considered when developmental delay is detected. Distinguishing between the impact of inadequate parenting and neurodevelopmental disorders is notoriously difficult. In the case of autism, the distinction is further complicated by a number of factors.

It is well established that disabled children are at greater risk of experiencing abuse and/or neglect than non-disabled children (Jones *et al.* 2012) and, within this group, learning disability, communication and social difficulties are known to be factors particularly associated with increased risk. From this observation, it is not difficult to reasonably conclude that autistic children face an increased risk of abuse and/or neglect.

There is also evidence, both statistical and anecdotal, that autistic children are significantly over-represented amongst the 'looked after' population (Dowling, Kelly and Winter 2012; Ford *et al.* 2007) and that autistic children show weaker indications of attachment to their parents than non-autistic children (including children with learning disabilities) (Rutgers *et al.* 2007). Autism is also notably heritable. Where there is an autistic child, the chances of siblings, other relatives and the child's parents being autistic increase substantially (Xie *et al.* 2019). In short, where there is an autistic child, one or both parents may well also be autistic. Autism increases the risk of a wide range of other conditions, including other neurological and neurodevelopmental disorders, mental health issues and other conditions such as epilepsy. Finally, anecdotally, autistic adults seem to report higher levels of family estrangement than non-autistic adults, with some research studies suggesting higher levels of parental stress and divorce in families with autistic children.

This overlapping and complex web of potentially relevant factors suggests that, much as it can be important to distinguish between autism and the impact of inadequate parenting, it is also important to recognize the high probability of overlap. Autistic children are at greater risk of abuse and neglect and may well be at increased risk of being rejected by one or both parents and/or may struggle to form bonds with their parents or caregivers. In addition, autistic parents are more likely to have autistic children. The parenting style of autistic parents may well be distinctly different from, although not necessarily inferior to, more typical parenting styles (Brook 2019). And, of course, some autistic parents (as is true of some parents in all groups) will be unable to provide adequate parenting for their children.

Nevertheless, children with attachment difficulties who are not autistic can present with behaviours which are, superficially, very similar to autistic behaviours. So, to summarize, some children have autism, some have attachment difficulties and some have *both*. No single characteristic is sufficient to draw conclusions and distinguish between autism and attachment disorder. An individual's characteristics should be considered broadly against the specific characteristics listed in order to guide thinking about whether autism or attachment issues appear to be the most likely underlying cause. Great care needs to be taken not to put excessive emphasis on 'either/or' thinking. There appears to be a particular overlap with a group of autistic children (and adults) who may also be identified as having 'pathological demand avoidance' (see Milton 2013 for a deconstruction of PDA). The picture is also complicated by the possibility of ASD among parents. Distinguishing between autism and attachment difficulties can be very difficult and it is, of course, vital that care is taken to avoid excessive focus on making the distinction to the exclusion of responding to the child's needs.

The Coventry Grid (Moran 2010) was developed to assist clinicians in distinguishing between attachment difficulties and ASD for diagnosis and treatment decisions. It was designed for use with those of broadly average/mild learning disability but not for children with severe learning disability. Recognizing and distinguishing between attachment or ASD reasons underlying behaviours can help with piecing together a fuller picture of a child's needs and help identify how/whether to intervene. Table 5.1 provides a brief summary of some of the key differences in children, adapted from the Coventry Grid (Moran 2010).

Some of the differences set out in Table 5.1 are fairly specific to children. However, similar distinctions can be made with regard to adults when it comes to distinguishing between autism and personality disorders (emotionally unstable personality disorder in particular, since this can be related to experience of attachment difficulties in childhood) (Flood and sharp 2019).

Table 5.1 The key differences between autism and attachment difficulties in children (adapted from the Coventry Grid) (Moran 2010)

Autism	Attachment
Routine	
Problems with birthdays and Christmas – finds it hard to cope with social and sensory overload and changes in routine	Gets distressed, or avoids anniversaries of life events such as Christmas, possibly because of difficult memories
Everything tends to revolve around his or her special interests	
Waiting upsets them because it upsets their routine	Waiting has an emotional significance
Language and communication	
Repetitive	Says things to shock for a reaction
Made-up words	Seeks to get their needs met by making loud or unusual noises for attention
Overly formal or stilted	Understands jokes and sarcasm
Over-uses 'stock' words/phrases (e.g. from TV)	Overly sensitive to tone of voice
Speaks in a pedantic fashion and gives excessive detail	Worries his/her needs won't be met if you are running late for them
Poor awareness of others in a conversation	
Play	
Collects, orders or arranges items	Plays dramatic or traumatic games that may mirror experiences
Prefers to play alone	Struggles to end role-play games

cont.

Autism	Attachment
Play	
Play may be mechanical rather than telling stories	Tries to make others approve of, or envy, his/her possessions
Over-uses stories from TV/books rather than made up	Deliberately destroys treasured objects when angry
Plays with unusual items	
Limited range of activities	
When given a new toy, still favours old toys	
Social interaction	
Struggles to understand how interactions with teachers may be different from interactions with friends/peers	Seeks to provoke strong emotional reactions in others
Shows less of an awareness to share than you would expect for his/her age	Shows an awareness of his/her own role in interactions
	Aware of sharing but too anxious, and so hoards possessions
	Steals or takes things to hoard
Understanding others	
May think you know about situations when you have not been present	Refers to other people's views and feelings
Sometimes struggles to tell fact from fiction	Aware of the types of information you are interested to hear about
	Exaggerates and elaborates on stories
	Hypervigilant to others' feelings and actions, especially anger
	Often tells sophisticated lies
Sensory	
Their awareness of hot and cold or pain is unusual	Able to learn new motor skills easily (e.g. ride a bike, swim)
Tends to bump into things, spill drinks or trip over	Actively seeks out danger
Lacks awareness of danger	Hypervigilant to sounds associated with a previous trauma
Seeks or avoids touch	Scans the environment to seek and recall information essential for maintaining their safety
Seeks deep pressure (e.g. firm hugs)	Reacts to smells associated with memory

Overly sensitive to clothing texture (e.g. labels)	
Unable to filter out background noises	
Seeks or avoids visual stimulus	
Seeks or avoids smells	
Eating issues	
Is food restricted by texture or colour?	Does the child hoard food or binge eat?
Is restricted diet about maintaining sameness?	

5.3 Human development and developmental delay in autism

Developmental delay in children is a particularly difficult issue to unpick in terms of causation. Autism itself can and does cause some developmental delays. About 40% of autistic people have a learning disability and about 30% of people with a learning disability have autism. There are also concerns that there may be under-identification of autism amongst people with learning disabilities (Emerson and Baines 2010). Delays in language development are particularly common in autism, although precocious language development (hyperlexia) is also quite common in autistic children (Treffert 2011). Delays and atypical physical development can be related to sensory issues (particularly weak proprioception) and/or co-occurring conditions such as dyspraxia. Delays and/or atypical social development are virtually universal in autism. However, these can be present in such a variety of ways that they can, in some individuals, be difficult to detect and may go undetected for a significant length of time.

Whilst almost nothing is universally true of all autistic people, autistic people are most likely (at all ages) to have a 'spiky' developmental profile with particularly marked contrasts between areas of strength and areas of difficulty. It is common for 'high-functioning' autistic people to be described as 'book smart' but not 'street smart'. Typically, social and emotional development lag behind intellectual development (Green and Carter 2014). Communication difficulties are extremely likely in autism, but these may be disguised by advanced vocabulary (Vicker n.d.). Those who do have delayed or atypical speech may or may not also have cognitive delays. Some autistic people diagnosed with a learning disability may have average or above average reasoning ability and cognitive development when assessed through some non-verbal methods (Courchesne *et al.* 2015). This pattern of uneven and delayed development often extends well into adult life and may persist throughout an autistic person's lifespan.

5.4 Autistic identity development

As well as posing difficulties in distinguishing between the effects of autism and the possible effects of trauma or inadequate parenting, these autistic differences pose challenges for services, professionals and approaches which are age-based. It is common for autistic people to be ready for changes or transitions well outside the typical age-range in both directions. Such variance can also, frequently, happen within the same autistic individual. So, an autistic young person may be intellectually gifted and ready to take university courses at an unusually young age, whilst the very same autistic young person may by the age of 30 still not be ready to engage in an intimate relationship. It is common for even the most 'high-functioning' of autistic people to have experienced setbacks and false starts and to have needed to take some life stages more slowly, such as, for example, learning to drive at the age of 33 or starting a first paid job at 44.

One area of development which can be particularly challenging for autistic people is developing positive self-esteem and a sense of identity. Despite anti-discrimination and equality policies, it is still very much the case that most autistic children and young people experience being seen as and even being told that they are inadequate, deficient or defective in ways that are beyond their ability to control. Many of the characteristics of autism (see the first column in Table 5.2) are (at least superficially) things typically seen in society as character flaws (the second column in Table 5.2).

The attitudes of others to autism and autistic people can make a huge difference to the sense of self which an autistic child develops. When parents, family members, friends, schools and support staff take a positive view of autism, recognizing and accepting those traits which are not within the control of an autistic person and recognizing and celebrating the positive aspects of many of those same traits (see the third column in Table 5.2), it can make a huge contribution to an autistic child growing up with a positive autistic identity and strong self-esteem.

Table 5.2 Common autistic traits and corresponding character flaws and positive traits

Autistic traits	Character flaws	Positive traits
Rigidity	Stubbornness/ unreasonableness	Persistence/ determination
Direct communication	Insensitivity	Honesty
Obsessive focus	Selfishness	Concentration
Difficulty learning social rules	Not a 'team player'	Independent thinker
Not understanding social hierarchies	Lack of respect	Confident/self-assured
Executive function difficulties	Irresponsibility/ disorganization	Possibly creativity
Inertia	Laziness	
Detail focus	Nit picker	Conscientious, accurate
Difficulty 'reading' emotional expressions	Not caring/lack of empathy	

Another key element of developing positive autistic identity, as well as a potential source of support for autistic young people, is becoming aware of and having the opportunity to access other and older autistic people and experience autistic space (a definition of this can be found in Dekker 2017). Meeting other autistic people and, for children and young people, contact with autistic adults can help autistic individuals internalize autistic norms and experience a sense of connection with others who are fundamentally similar. Because autistic people are a small minority within a broadly neurotypical society, this sense of connection to one's 'tribe' can be a novel and valuable experience (Silberman 2015).

5.5 Managing transitions

In public services, 'transition' typically refers to the transition from children's to adult services. However, it is important to recognize that transitions of various kinds happen throughout the lifespan. Multiple transitions occurring simultaneously or single transitions which seem small or unnoticeable to others can trigger significant difficulties for autistic people.

Unfortunately, the ways in which public services are organized often result in multiple transitions occurring together. For children, the month of September can mean changes of building or room, changes of teacher(s), changes to peer group(s), changes in transport arrangements, changes of routine/schedule and even changes of residence, all at the same time. Transition from childhood to adulthood typically spans a period of time, but it is common for young people to experience: high-stakes exams, changes of educational establishment, changes of teacher, changes of peer group, radical (and often multiple) changes of residence, extensive new responsibilities for money and independent living, learning new skills such as driving, first experience of employment and numerous other new experiences and changes within just a few years (or even months). For autistic young people, these are often accompanied by changes in benefits, assessments and reassessments, changes of all or most of the professionals involved in their lives, changes of care and support arrangements and completely new groups of support people. The sheer number of – often recurring – changes in adult life can also be bewildering and daunting, and they include: transitions into and out of employment, changes of residence, and relationship and family changes including relationship breakdown and bereavement packaged together with changes in care and support arrangements and personnel, changes in income source and administrative requirements (tax, benefits, salary, etc.) and changes of professionals involved.

All of these transitions tend to have a greater impact and be more difficult to adjust to for autistic people than for non-autistic people. Autistic people find it more difficult to imagine hypothetical and unknown future situations, so recognizing and anticipating our needs, the difficulties we will encounter and finding ways to cope are more difficult. The stress caused by uncertainty, unfamiliarity and unpredictability can be overwhelming. This is compounded when people around us do not understand how much stress transitions can cause and do not take account of this in the way they provide or organize services.

Many negative experiences are entirely or largely preventable with a small amount of knowledge and consideration of autistic needs.

EXAMPLE

Rose (52) has autism and a learning disability. She has struggled to cope with living with other people in a residential care environment due to her sensory needs, finding communication and interaction overwhelming and the unpredictable impact of other people on her routine stressful. A flat has been identified in a supported living block where she will be able to have her own space. She has been taken on several visits to the flat whilst the change of placement was being considered, but she was not informed at that stage that she might be moving there because funding had yet to be agreed, and so there was uncertainty as to whether the move would go ahead. The funding and placement have now been agreed and she will be moving next month.

Rose has used a visual timetable (which shows her what she will be doing today) for many years. Over the past year, Rose's keyworker and other familiar staff have worked with Rose to put her daily timetable onto a week planner on a whiteboard. They have gradually introduced additional information about other days (as well as 'today'), and used a moveable cardboard label above the board to identify 'yesterday' and 'tomorrow'. Once Rose became used to the week planner and was using it to engage in conversations and ask questions about past events and future plans, they introduced a year planner. Over the past few months, they have worked with Rose to extend her understanding and communication about the past and future to events further away from the present.

Now that Rose's move to the flat is definitely going ahead, her keyworker has made Rose a short 'book' explaining what will happen when she moves. The book includes photos of important people in Rose's life (including support staff) and different areas of the care home and her new flat. The support staff who will be supporting Rose at her flat have been gradually introduced to her and have begun working with her at the care home. The date of the move has been put on Rose's year planner, along with details of visits to the flat and other steps towards moving in the weeks before the move. Support staff (old and new) regularly mention these events and patiently answer Rose's questions about them.

Rose's week planner and year planner have been duplicated and support staff have helped her put them up in her new flat. She has been supported to take some of her things to her new flat. Rose's new support staff have learned her routine at the care home and will closely duplicate the routine when she moves to maintain continuity whilst Rose is settling in, before considering with Rose whether to introduce any changes.

> In what ways is the approach of the support staff in this example similar to and in what ways does it differ from changes of placement experienced by autistic clients you have worked with?
>
> What role might a social worker play in Rose's transition?

Key to the above good practice example is transition planning which allows for the additional staff time required to undertake this level of preparation, including funding two sets of staff to work across an interim period and arranging for staff from one setting to work with a person in another setting. All these factors pose challenges to typical service, contractual and funding arrangements. However, the costs and administrative difficulties need to be weighed against the benefits of a successfully managed transition and the potential costs of placement breakdown resulting from poorly managed transitions (Lenehan 2017).

5.5.1 From children's to adults' services

In England, most local authorities have transition workers and/or teams. Typically, these are intended to span an age group of 14–25 and, theoretically at least, they are designed to support and manage the transition from children's to adult's services for children and young people with disabilities or special needs. The legislative frameworks governing education, health and social care provision for children and adults have been brought into line[21] and there are strong policy steers to encourage the integration of education and social care for children and social care and health for adults. As a result of these measures, seamless transition should be not only possible, but increasingly the norm.

Unfortunately, the reality is very different. At their most extreme, poor transitions can have disastrous consequences, leading to crises and preventable admissions to inappropriate hospital placements (which can then last for years and be very costly). As Lenehan (2017, p.21) notes:

> The adult population targeted through the Transforming Care programme is young, with the majority in NHS commissioned inpatient care being for people between the ages of 18 and 34. Analysis of age on admission/transfer to hospital shows that around 38% of all admissions and transfers are of young people aged between 18 and 25. 21% are young people between 18 and 21 years of age. Many of those transferring into the population will be coming from other residential settings, but nonetheless it is clear that a strong focus on well-planned transition to adult care and support will be required for the Transforming Care Programme to achieve a sustained reduction in the numbers in inpatient settings.

Similarly, a Care Quality Commission (2019, p.6) interim report about a particularly poorly served group of children and young people, those being held in long-term segregation in hospital wards (79% of whom were autistic), commented:

> Typically, the people we visited had had a very unsettled childhood and had been in and out of different residential settings. Moves were often triggered by a breakdown of the existing placement. The last such crisis had been the immediate cause of admission to hospital – which was seen as the only available option.

What, then, might be done to prevent such disastrous trajectories from transition and to improve the process across the board for autistic people?

Autistic children and young people frequently cross service

boundaries and fall into more than one group. Health services, particularly for children, are often organized in groupings such as 'learning disability', 'mental health' or 'physical health'. Service remits may be defined by reference to IQ or the presence or absence of a learning disability, despite NICE guidance (National Institute for Health and Care Excellence 2012). This readily results in no one taking responsibility and some autistic children falling through the gaps, particularly those with multiple, 'complex' or overlapping needs (Lenehan 2017, pp.17–18). Educational boundaries tend to segregate 'special' schools and 'mainstream' schools and to assume that all children with significant Special Educational Needs (SEN) are educated in special schools. About 72% of autistic children are in mainstream schools (Department for Education 2018), but their needs can include complex and severe needs. Autistic children may need to attend a special school but have abilities and areas of academic attainment where their needs cannot be appropriately met in that environment. Children's social care is generally focused largely on child protection, with services for disabled children being a small, secondary area from which autistic children without learning disabilities are frequently excluded altogether (see Chapter 3). Of course, autistic children will also be (disproportionately) present amongst those seen through the child protection lens (as discussed earlier in this chapter).

Services rarely start holistically from the needs of the child and, even where there is good communication and partnership, these gaps frequently leave some children unable to access an appropriate service at all and many more with unmet needs (All Party Parliamentary Group on Autism 2017). Very common, and even more harmful, are funding disputes between services. These should not be, but sometimes are, allowed to impact on the care and support provided to the person, delaying hospital discharge and transition planning and derailing vital planning. Social workers can play a crucial role in challenging these types of poor decision making and advocating for autistic children and young people. Support in doing so can be found in the clear evidence for the cost-effectiveness of public spending on preventive support (Iemmi *et al.* 2017) and the vital role well-managed transitions can play in preventing placement breakdown, unnecessary and very expensive hospital admissions (Lenehan 2017).

Transition plans should be in place for children with SEN from Year 9 onwards (around age 13) (Regs. 20(6) and 21(6) The Special Educational Needs and Disability Regulations 2014). They tend to only happen at all for those with EHCPs and are often tokenistic and inadequate – indeed, in my experience it is quite common for transition plans to be written by education services without any involvement of health or social care, let alone adult services.

Local authorities are required (s.58 Care Act 2014) to carry out transition assessments prior to transfer to adult social care services at age 18, a responsibility generally undertaken by transition teams. However, in my experience, referrals to transition teams are usually made for one or more of these groups:

- children receiving social care support

- children with an EHCP

- children attending special schools.

Given the highly restrictive eligibility criteria applied for access to children's social care (see Chapter 3), many autistic children are not receiving such support. Some autistic children have an EHCP, but many do not. The 72% of autistic children who attend mainstream schools (Department for Education 2018) may well not be referred. Consequently, there are significant numbers of autistic children who may require and be entitled to a transition assessment for adult social care, but who are unlikely to be referred to a transition team for one to be carried out.

Even where transition assessments are carried out, in my experience they are frequently completed under time pressure at a late stage. Some transition teams appear not to accept or act on referrals until a fixed age (varying from 16 to 17½), despite the Care Act requiring that the timing of transition assessment should be when it is likely to be 'of significant benefit' to the child (s.58 Care Act 2014).

Continuing Care (CC) for children and Continuing Health Care (CHC) for adults have their own policies and rules regarding transition, with initial referral at 14 and transition assessment taking place at 16–17, before transition at age 18 (Department of Health 2016).

Another factor which adversely impacts on transitions is instability and high turnover amongst the professionals working with a child or young person. This can be positively influenced by 'named person' schemes and processes, but these are far from universal. The negative influence is perpetuated by shortages in many of the key professions, including social work, and the use of agency staff to fill gaps (Perraudin 2019). Service organization approaches which eliminate 'case holding' may be more efficient for services but do not promote the stability and continuity that can make a positive difference for autistic people (National Institute for Health and Care Excellence 2012).

These systemic factors are likely to increase the risk of autistic children and young people falling through the gaps and not receiving vital support at all at what can be a difficult time. Even where support is provided, systemic factors such as these are likely to increase the risks faced by autistic young people during this transition. These include:

- excessive dependence on parents
- social isolation
- behaviour which may challenge (including offending)
- family breakdown, estrangement and loss of relationships
- difficulties coping with change
- difficulties learning new routines and skills, especially all at once.

The support needed by those autistic young people perceived as 'high-functioning' is frequently under-estimated. It is vital for practitioners to be aware that high IQ/educational attainment can mask inadequate adaptive and functional skills for adult life (as discussed in Chapter 3). As a result, autistic young people may be unable to cope with the rapidly increasing demands on their organizational and social skills and to take initiative in communicating and meeting their needs, which typically arise in late teenage and early adult life. Where young people are unable to access adequate support, these issues are more likely to result in transition failures: dropping out of education; returning to live with parents; retreating socially; deterioration in mental health; and problems in employment – ranging from inability to secure employment, through disciplinary procedures and dismissal. I would argue that all autistic young people need to be supported by practitioners who reflect on their practice, identifying and challenging unconscious bias and assumptions, and who are willing to challenge assumptions made by other professionals.

Good practice in child–adult transition is widely understood theoretically (Scottish Transitions Forum 2017) but challenging to realize in practice. The key elements are to:

- start sufficiently early

- maintain consistent staff involved

- have effective inter-agency working with clear communication, co-ordination and one plan

- ensure the person's voice is heard clearly

- provide clear information for the individual and carer(s) and avoid jargon.

In addition, an important adjustment for autistic people can be understanding and flexibility to allow them to undertake the various changes and transitions of moving from childhood to adult life at a slower pace, separately from each other and/or at atypical ages. Simple acceptance that autistic people may need a longer period to make this transition is likely to be helpful, but may require challenging service norms and policies.

5.5.2 Leaving the parental home or childhood placement[22]

I have chosen to discuss the issue of autistic young people/adults leaving their parental home or childhood placement separately from the transition from children's to adult's services. This is because it is common for this to happen much later than and separately from that transition. Of course, many non-disabled young adults who are not 'looked after' remain living with their parents until their mid-twenties or even later, largely for financial reasons but also for emotional and practical support. However, disabled young adults, including autistic young adults, face additional hurdles to making this transition, including:

- lack of information about options

- lack of suitable housing

- reluctance to fund care where free, informal care from parents is available

- poor co-ordination between multiple services

- funding disputes

- anxiety about the transition and/or the new situation

- parental resistance

- lacking the functional and adaptive skills needed.

These issues can lead to delays, difficulties and, in some cases, not making the transition at all (Anderson *et al.* 2014).

Many of these issues can be overcome with good support and advocacy on the autistic adult's behalf. Transition workers and/or social workers can play a pivotal role in helping navigate the complex web of information and identify the specific options available to a particular autistic adult. It may be necessary to challenge any reluctance to fund care and support to enable an autistic adult to move out of the parental home, pointing out statutory responsibilities and the benefits (including cost-effectiveness) of planned transitions over crises arising from breakdown of care arrangements. Poor co-ordination between services can potentially be overcome by a proactive professional who is willing to go a little beyond their formal remit to act as co-ordinator and advocate. Funding disputes can be more intractable, but services may need to be reminded that such disputes must not be allowed to delay the provision of care and support (Department of Health 2014, Para. 19.55). Where an autistic young person is, understandably, anxious about the prospect of change, the provision of good, clear information and working with them to plan the transition can be enormously effective support. Finally, it often falls to social workers to navigate complex family dynamics. In this situation, what can be needed is constructive challenge and working to support parents to see autistic adults (whatever their needs or disabilities) as adults, providing information and support to help them see and access realistic support options which can actually allay their concerns and help them to contribute effectively to plan for their young adult's future.

A small number of young adults and their parents may make a positive choice for the adult to remain living with their parents. However, it is important to determine whether this is genuinely an autistic adult's own free choice, particularly where he or she may have limited ability to communicate their views, or where parental influence may be so strong that an autistic adult may find it difficult to assert their wishes. Similarly, where an autistic adult lacks capacity to decide where to live, care needs to be undertaken in best interests decision making to ensure that the autistic adult's voice and own interests are given sufficient weight and the parent's potential conflict of interest with their own feelings is acknowledged.

Even where remaining in the parental home is an autistic adult's own choice, planning is required for the probability that, at some point, parents will become unable to care due to age. Even if the intention is for the disabled adult to remain living in the family home, consideration needs to be given to care and support arrangements and to any possible conflicts between a parent requiring care themselves in later life and the needs of the autistic adult.

Most autistic adults, however, will want to make a move out of the parental home at some point, and most of their parents will want them to.

5.5.3 Housing

The biggest obstacle to successful transitions at any stage of life can be finding and securing suitable housing. This is a challenge for many non-disabled young people due to a general housing shortage in the UK. However, autistic people face additional difficulties because aspects of autism can significantly limit the types of housing that are actually suitable for an individual and because this may not be recognized or understood by organizations involved in housing.

The major issues which can impact on the suitability of housing options for an autistic person are:

- sensory issues

- difficulties coping with change and uncertainty – often leading to a need for a high level of control over our environment

- communication and interaction difficulties

- vulnerability and safeguarding concerns.

I will discuss each of these in turn.

Sensory issues vary widely between individuals, but most autistic people have significant differences in sensory processing which result in over- and/or under-sensitivity of one or more senses, including sight, hearing, touch, taste, smell, proprioception (knowing where your body is in space) and vestibular (sense of balance and rotation). For many, these sensory issues can impact on the suitability of housing options. Autistic people should not be subjected to sensory distress in our own homes (National Autistic Taskforce 2019). Home needs to be a safe space in which our sensory needs can be accommodated. When this is taken into account, it means in practice that some autistic people are not able to:

- share a home with other people

- share facilities with other people

- live in a location overlooked by other people

- live in a noisy location

- live in a city or town.

Some autistic people will need:

- easy access to outdoor open spaces

- housing which provides space for support people to 'live in'

- sound-proofing and/or an isolated location.

Difficulties coping with change and uncertainty are common to all autistic people, but we vary widely in how severely these affect our lives. Most autistic people require a higher level of control over our 'home' environment than most non-autistic people, but for some autistic people these needs can result in:

- being unable to share a home with unfamiliar individuals

- being unable to share a home with others at all

- being unable to share facilities with others (such as bathrooms or kitchens but also in some cases including entrances and outdoor space)

- being unable to access homeless hostels and/or temporary housing (due to its temporary and unstable nature and/or other factors such as noise and vulnerability)

- needing an understanding landlord who is able and willing to tolerate careful planning of any and all maintenance or improvement work

- being unable to live in any location which is affected by unpredictable events (such as near businesses or communal facilities)

- needing protection from unexpected callers.

For some autistic people, communication and interaction difficulties impact on relationships with neighbours and landlords. Conflict can be the result and, where this is the case, can lead to intractable difficulties sustaining suitable housing, particularly in the private rented sector. For these individuals, social housing or other options outside the private rented sector may be necessary to mitigate these difficulties.

Vulnerability to victimization and safeguarding concerns more broadly (see Chapter 8) may also be highly relevant to the suitability of housing options for an autistic person. Autistic people are at increased risk of becoming targets of harassment, bullying, damage to property and assaults and of exploitation and 'mate' crime. These risks are higher in some locations and some types of housing than elsewhere. As a result of these issues, some autistic people may need housing away from those areas.

The lists of needs set out above are not at all exhaustive as individual needs can vary widely, but they provide some idea of the degree to which 'suitable' housing options may be constrained by autistic needs.

For some people, adaptations will be required to an existing or future home. Autistic people with needs for care and support are potentially eligible for Disabled Facilities Grants (DFGs). However, the criteria for mandatory DFGs are strongly geared to physical accessibility and worded in terms of issues like access to the property and garden, bathing facilities, food preparation, heating, power and making the dwelling safe. Although discretionary grants are potentially available to cover wider needs, in practice the competing pressures on local authority budgets mean that discretionary grants are rarely available. Practitioners (including particularly occupational therapists) need sufficient awareness and understanding of autistic needs to be able to recognize the impact of those needs on the individual's ability to access the property and facilities within it and for a property to be safe for that person. Support from at least one professional with such knowledge is likely to be required to explain autistic needs effectively in terms of the DFG mandatory criteria to obtain funding for modifications.

5.5.4 Aging and older autistic adults

Older autistic adults face further transitions, including: from working-age adults to older adult services; changing health needs and mobility; retirement from employment; and bereavement. Again, these changes are particularly difficult to imagine and anticipate from an autistic perspective. It is also extremely difficult to change established patterns and coping strategies (Lawson 2015).

Options and support designed for older non-autistic adults may not serve them well. Older autistic people are still more likely than non-autistic people to have niche interests, information-focused communication, aversions to noise, crowds and uncertainty, dislike communication by phone and have limited appetite for 'small talk'. Aging does not make someone not autistic and the unique needs of autistic (and other neurodivergent) older adults need to be considered by generic care and support services aimed at older people.

An autistic adult who has sustained employment and/or brought up children may depend on that employment or those children to create structure, identity and automatic access to social relationships without needing initiative. The loss of these structured routines and social interaction can have a seemingly disproportionate effect on an older autistic person who may struggle to make the transition to a less structured life and/or needing to take the initiative.

Past experiences of social workers and social care may also impact on how older autistic people react to contact with social work in later life. As D'Astous *et al.* (2014, p.13) note: 'For older people with autism and older parents of an adult with autism today, experiences or absences of social care and support may have lasting implications on their engagement with current and future social workers.'

5.6 Chapter summary and key points

- Autistic people are at increased risk of adverse experiences, including abuse and neglect. Autistic characteristics may look superficially quite similar to attachment difficulties and it is important to distinguish between these, recognizing that some individuals will have both.

- Autism is a lifelong neurodevelopmental condition and autistic people are likely to have uneven and atypical patterns and ages of development.

- Developing a positive autistic identity and strong self-esteem requires positive attitudes to autism in families, schools and the community. Access to the wider autistic community also supports positive identity development.

- Services are often organized in ways which require transitions to be made at fixed ages and all at once.

- Transition from children's to adults' services needs to be well planned and co-ordinated, with provision for extended support and delays to transitions where appropriate.

- Active support and planning is needed to enable autistic adults to (in most cases) move out of the parental home at a time which is right for them.

- Provision of sufficient suitable housing options in the autistic person's own community is essential to prevent crisis and placement breakdown.

- The distinctive needs of older autistic adults need to be considered, both within autism services and within older adult services.

Recommended resources

Bradley, E. and Caldwell, P. (2013) 'Mental health and autism: Promoting Autism FaVourable Environments (PAVE).' *Journal on Developmental Disabilities 19*, 1, 8–23.

Council for Disabled Children (2019) *Transition Information Network*. Accessed on 6/12/19 at https://councilfordisabledchildren.org.uk/transition-information-network.

National Autistic Society (2019) *Transition*. Accessed on 6/12/19 at www.autism.org.uk/about/transition.aspx.

Scottish Transitions Forum (2017) *Principles of Good Transitions 3*. Dalkeith: Scottish Transitions Forum. Accessed on 4/10/19 at https://scottishtransitions.org.uk/summary-download.

Stobart, A. (n.d.) *Transition Toolkit*. London: Autism Education Trust. Accessed on 10/8/19 at http://dspl7.org.uk/data/documents/Transition-Toolkit.pdf.

CHAPTER 6

Assessing Mental Capacity and Autism

6.1 Introduction

Although the terminology used is distasteful to many autistic people, in England and Wales autism is an 'impairment of the mind or brain' within the scope of the Mental Capacity Act 2005 (s.2 MCA 2005). Similar legislation exists in most jurisdictions: in Scotland, the Adults with Incapacity Act 2000,[23] and in Northern Ireland, the Mental Capacity Act (Northern Ireland) 2016. In this chapter, I will focus on the principles and test for capacity contained in the MCA specifically. However, similar issues arise under equivalent legislation elsewhere.

Some autistic adults will, at certain times and for some decisions, lack capacity in the terms of the MCA (and most similar legal frameworks). Autistic children, like all children, vary in their decision-making capacity and being autistic may (or may not) affect the age(s) at which a child is capable of making their own decisions and which decisions they are capable of making.

It is a continuing reality that there is highly variable day-to-day practice around issues of capacity in our over-stretched health and social care systems (Care Quality Commission 2016a). In mainstream society, non-disabled adults routinely make unwise decisions unchallenged (visit any town centre on a Saturday night!). Despite the principles set out in the MCA (and in most similar legislation), decisions by adult service users (including autistic people) which are viewed by professionals as unwise, especially where they impact on organizational risk, tend to automatically result in questions, discussions and assessments of capacity. At the other extreme, and particularly in health settings, capacity is rarely raised at all where a patient is not refusing treatment (Select Committee on the Mental Capacity Act 2005 (2014), Para. 75). Autistic people may be at particularly high risk of acquiescing whilst actually lacking capacity to consent.

Where capacity may be in question, assessment is required in order to determine whether someone lacks capacity to make a particular decision. Despite some examples of good practice, there are also serious concerns about the quality of capacity assessments. A repeated finding from inspections of care services has been that:

> Many providers made assumptions that individuals lacked capacity without having carried out or documented assessments, or they assessed individuals as lacking capacity without ensuring this was time and decision-specific… Some providers also made blanket assumptions that individuals with particular conditions lacked capacity, such as people living with dementia. (Care Quality Commission 2016a, p.142)

These concerns apply to all service user groups. However, where those service users are autistic, there are further, additional barriers to achieving good quality, reliable assessments of capacity. Those carrying out capacity assessments often do not have sufficient, in-depth knowledge of autism specifically and are rarely afforded the time to develop adequate knowledge of the individual. As a result, concerns have been expressed about the quality of capacity assessments on autistic people specifically (Select Committee on the Mental Capacity Act 2005 (2014), Para. 71).

6.2 Who does the assessment?

Capacity assessment is typically undertaken by different professionals for different types of decision, but this does not always produce the most reliable result. In capacity assessment, as with assessment more generally, allowing additional time (including potentially multiple sessions) is a reasonable adjustment for autistic people. An autistic person's ability to communicate will vary depending on who they are communicating with. Familiarity and, perhaps even more importantly, compatibility of communication style between the autistic person and an assessor are often needed to achieve a sufficient level of communication to enable a fair assessment to be undertaken.

In considering who should undertake a capacity assessment, it is important to be aware that professionals in all fields (including psychiatrists, GPs, hospital consultants, psychologists, nurses, occupational therapists, speech therapists and social workers) may have very limited knowledge and understanding of autism. Health services, even more than social care services, are typically divided into categories and specialisms such as mental health or learning disability, and autism rarely fits neatly into such boxes. Particular professional backgrounds may influence perceptions of autism and autistic people and can sometimes result in wholly inappropriate approaches. For example, those with a mental health background may be accustomed to working within a recovery model which may not transfer well to a permanent lifelong neurodevelopmental condition like autism. However, professionals with generic learning disability backgrounds may lack autism-specific knowledge and under-estimate or misinterpret an autistic person's level of understanding. All professionals involved with an autistic person should be prepared to take an independent view, bearing in mind the legal rather than medical nature of the statutory tests of capacity and, in appropriate cases, consider whether recourse to a court (in England and Wales, to the Court of Protection) for a determination as to capacity would be appropriate.

6.3 Assumptions

We tend to make assumptions at a deep level about capacity without realizing it. Even when we do not hold any prejudiced beliefs, we are still conditioned by unconscious associations and assumptions (Dovidio *et al.* 1997) which can influence decision making.

6.3.1 Like me

When assessing capacity, professionals can be tempted to make judgements about an individual on the basis of a comparison with themselves. For example, if I tell someone that blue is Henry's favourite colour and then ask them which jumper they think Henry would choose – the blue one or the red one – I know that, if I were told the same information, I would understand that the correct answer is the blue one. So, when the person I am assessing says 'the red one', it is tempting to conclude that the person is *unable* to reason at the level required to give the correct answer.

However, such assumptions are particularly unlikely to be reliable when a (most probably) neurotypical professional is assessing the capacity of an autistic person. An autistic person might, for example, be perfectly able to understand if the question was written down, but is unable to process the spoken word fast enough to follow all the relevant information. An autistic person might have elements of echolalia in speech and be unable to control what they say well enough to communicate the correct answer and may be 'echoing' 'the red one' because it was the last thing said, even though they may have intended to give the answer 'the blue one'. An autistic person might look at the problem in a novel and atypical way and reason that some people like variety and defying expectations and therefore the person might deliberately choose to wear a jumper in a colour they favour less.

6.3.2 IQ = functional ability

In my experience, one of the biggest and most problematic assumptions about capacity is the widespread assumption that intellectual or learning ability is roughly equivalent to functional decision-making ability. The capacity of autistic adults and children who are particularly intellectually able is rarely questioned, whereas autistic people with a learning disability are often, despite MCA principles, assumed to lack capacity or at the very least find themselves having to 'earn' their right to make decisions for themselves.

The trouble with these generic assumptions is that they do have some general validity – intellectual ability *is* relevant to the MCA functional test. However, as discussed in Chapter 3, most autistic people have a 'spiky profile' of needs, skills and abilities. In autism, intellectual ability does not necessarily equate to functional decision-making ability.

These assumptions adversely affect assessments of capacity in autistic people in both directions. Autistic people who do not use speech and/or who have a learning disability risk being assumed to lack capacity when they may be more able than others assume. Research suggests that autistic people who perform poorly on conventional cognitive tests (which depend heavily on language skills and on thinking and reasoning in conventional ways), perform far better than expected on perceptual tests of cognitive ability (Courchesne *et al.* 2015).

On the other hand, autistic people who are highly intellectually able and/or highly verbal risk being assumed to have capacity when in fact understanding or ability to use or weigh relevant information may be impaired. Autistic adults report more difficulties with decision making than neurotypical peers. Decisions that need to be made quickly, or involve a change of routine, or talking to others, are experienced as particularly difficult, and the process of decision making is often exhausting, overwhelming and anxiety-provoking (Luke *et al.* 2012). Autistic people can have good theoretical understanding of issues but struggle to apply knowledge in practice. Autistic people can also experience obsessive or compulsive behaviour which may interfere with our ability to use or weigh information and actually make an informed choice. We may find it difficult to envisage hypothetical situations or imagine a future situation not yet experienced. For any of these reasons, and others, autistic people perceived as 'high-functioning' may lack capacity in relation to some decisions, at least at certain times.

6.4 Autistic people and the development of decision-making skills

Unfortunately, many disabled children (including autistic children) experience attitudes and behaviour from adults which are paternalistic and over-protective. Special schools and/or over-protective parents can inadvertently create training grounds for dependence, compliance and being easy to look after. Disabled children are frequently 'protected' from making age-appropriate unwise decisions and taking age-appropriate risks.

EXAMPLE

Mr Glass, the teacher of a 14-year-old autistic boy called Joseph, asked Joseph's mother to send a jumper to school for him because the weather was getting colder. Joseph's mother explained that her son disliked wearing jumpers and refused to do so. Mr Glass followed up by asking the mother to send a jumper into school anyway so that staff could 'get him' to put it on when the weather was cold.

Joseph had autism and a moderate learning disability and used speech (although atypically) to communicate. He clearly understood (and could explain and communicate his understanding) that the consequence of not wearing a jumper when the weather was cold would be that he would feel cold. He was simply choosing, in the typical contrary manner of a teenager, to make the unwise decision not to wear a jumper. Mr Glass, with the best and most protective of intentions, was actually proposing to paternalistically over-ride Joseph's unwise decision.

> Do you think that a similar scenario would occur around a non-disabled teenager attending a mainstream school?
>
> What assumptions do you think Mr Glass was making?
>
> Can you think of an example from your own practice where any of the professionals involved may have been making similar assumptions?

Trivial as issues such as wearing a jumper may seem (and frustrating as typical teenage behaviour may be to parents and teachers), developmentally these unwise decisions and risk-taking behaviours are vitally important to the development of adult decision-making capacity. Given the difficulties and challenges many autistic adults experience in coping with decision making, it is even more important that autistic children are supported and enabled to experiment and gain experience with small decisions and small risks in relatively safe environments during childhood.

For autistic people, the process of development is also likely to continue throughout adult life. Autism is a developmental disorder and it is common for autistic people to continue social, emotional and cognitive development throughout the lifespan. Many autistic people find it difficult to generalize skills and learning from one experience to another. One consequence of this is that learning gains can continue to be made throughout our lives from each individual new experience.

Applying this understanding of the development of decision-making skills in autistic people, it becomes clear that capacity assessments and the steps taken to support a person's decision making should be regularly reviewed. The MCA requires us to recognize that capacity is time and decision specific. When assessing the capacity of an autistic person, it is *also* vital to recognize that decision-making capacity can improve and develop over time and throughout adult life to a degree which is much less common in non-autistic adults.

6.5 Providing all relevant information[24]

The MCA reminds us that, before an adult is assessed as lacking capacity to make a decision, the steps taken to support them must include providing them with all of the information relevant to the decision in a way accessible to them (s.3(2) MCA 2005).[25] There are several types of information which are often relevant to decisions, but may not be made explicit in the information provided to an adult. These are:

- information about the thoughts, emotions, expectations or reactions of other people

- information about what factors a person might typically think relevant to the decision

- information about what other people normally or typically do (social 'norms')

- information about the potential consequences of a decision and their likelihood.

These are types of information which are often unconsciously held by neurotypical people and, therefore, implicitly assumed to be available to the adult needing to make a decision. However, they are precisely the types of information which are often not 'obvious' to autistic people. An adult undergoing a capacity assessment may actually be being assessed on their ability to predict the consequences of a decision, rather than being given that information and then their understanding of it being assessed. For autistic people, being able to predict hypothetical consequences and being able to understand those consequences once they are explained are two very different things.

Care is therefore needed to ensure that an autistic person has actually been explicitly provided with these types of relevant information prior to any assessment of their capacity (particularly the capacity to use or weigh information).

6.6 Types of decision

Although the MCA is clear that capacity is time and decision specific, most practitioners will have experienced being asked to carry out 'capacity assessments' which are then used over a period of time (often years, sometimes an entire lifetime) to provide an overall determination of whether an adult can make key life decisions – particularly regarding their residence and care. Resources and practicality are of course relevant reasons for this. But there is also an unspoken assumption that an adult who lacks capacity to decide a matter such as residence, will also lack capacity to decide other matters which are seen as having a similar level of complexity or importance.

Autistic decision making is fundamentally quite different to neurotypical decision making and the factors which an autistic person considers relevant to making a decision can be quite different, as can the process of decision making itself (De Martino *et al.* 2008; Luke *et al.* 2012). Consequently, it is perfectly possible for an autistic adult to have capacity to take what a non-autistic person might see as a difficult or complex decision whilst lacking the capacity to take what a non-autistic person might see as a simple decision.

On the whole, autistic people are likely to find it easier to make decisions:

- which are based on facts (objective information)
- which can be taken on the basis of logical reasoning

- for which there is complete information available

- between choices which they have directly experienced

- which have clearly predictable consequences.

On the other hand, autistic people are likely to find it harder to make decisions:

- which are based on opinions (subjective information)

- which involve emotional or social considerations

- for which there is missing or unknown information

- which involve options which they have not directly experienced

- which have consequences which are more difficult to predict.

So, for example, an autistic person might find it easier to decide whether or not to have serious medical treatment than whether to go and visit a close relative who is likely to die soon.

6.7 Timing

The MCA Code of Practice (Office of the Public Guardian 2007, Para. 3.14) is clear that timing should be considered in assessing whether a person can make their own decisions. This is particularly important with autistic people, who often need more time than non-autistic people to process the information relevant to a decision. Many autistic people find it difficult or impossible to process information whilst also communicating. In addition, for many autistic people, our capacity to make any decision will fluctuate depending on our overall stress levels and how overloaded we feel.

So, for many autistic people, the common, everyday situation of being given information during a conversation and then being asked to make a decision on the basis of that information during the same conversation significantly impairs our ability to make a capacitous decision. Some may get stuck or fail to respond at all, others may use a 'script', still others may acquiesce without having made a capacitous decision and, finally, some will refuse, also without having made a capacitous decision. In Chapter 7, I will discuss simple adaptations which can help to overcome these issues. Where such adaptations have not been made, there is a significant risk of an autistic person being unfairly and wrongly judged to lack capacity in relation to that decision.

Similarly, it is vital to consider an autistic person's overall stress levels, including the environment in which they are being assessed. So, for example, for many autistic people, a hospital (of any kind) is likely to be a high-stress environment with adverse sensory experiences, constant unpredictability and endless communication demands and difficulties.

Situations will vary as to the extent to which a decision can wait for a more suitable time for an autistic person to make it. There will always be some decisions which may need to be taken urgently in an emergency situation. However, in many cases, advance planning and advance decisions could be used to enable an autistic person to make their own decisions in advance of, rather than during, a difficult situation. Any individual, specific emergency may not be predictable, but the possibility (in general) of some types of emergencies occurring is predictable. If advance planning was undertaken, these situations could be considered and advance decisions made in far more instances than is typically the case at present.

6.8 The functional test

Having dealt with those preliminary issues, I think it is useful to discuss each element of the MCA capacity test in turn.

6.8.1 Understanding

As I have repeatedly pointed out, many autistic people have a 'spiky profile'. This means that global measures of 'IQ' and/or generalized diagnoses such as 'learning disability' can only provide limited (and sometimes highly inaccurate) information about an individual's understanding or potential for understanding information. The picture is further complicated in autism by the huge range of language, verbal and communication abilities and differences and variability in social and interaction perceptions and behaviour. As a result, a good assessor will proceed with caution, taking care to avoid general assumptions about an individual's understanding and using a variety of methods and approaches before coming to conclusions.

An adult's capacity is generally assessed on the basis of what they can communicate to the assessor about their understanding of the decision. Communication differences are a core element of autism. It is not at all unusual for an autistic person to understand something, but struggle to communicate that understanding. So, it is important for care to be taken to assess an autistic person's understanding fairly and to consider whether the autistic person may understand, even if they are unable to communicate that understanding to the assessor. Any capacity assessment which is carried out without meaningful attempts to adapt to and adjust for autistic communication needs should be seen as an inadequate assessment.

A crucial area to consider is making adaptations to methods of communication (see Chapter 7 for further discussion). Consideration needs to be given to methods of communication *both* for information transmission to the autistic person *and* for gathering information from the autistic person. I would also stress the importance of making adaptations for autistic people who *do* use speech, as well as for those who do not. Many autistic people who speak still find alternative ways of communicating more useful and accessible, as alternatives or in addition to speech. Basic adjustments such as:

- providing information in writing (instead or as well as spoken information)
- using diagrams
- providing photographs

can make a huge difference to an autistic person's ability to understand the information relevant to a decision and to communicate that understanding. For those who do use alternative forms of communication, it is vital that these are used effectively during any capacity assessment.

In some cases, however, despite adjustments, an autistic person may understand but be unable to communicate their understanding to the person assessing capacity. Thoroughly considering this possibility can be more challenging. One way to begin to compensate for this difficulty may be to consider whether there may be alternative means of determining whether an autistic person understands which do not require communication at all, such as considering behavioural evidence. For instance, an autistic person might find that the oven glove is missing and respond by going and getting a tea towel and using that to take a plate out of the microwave. From this behaviour, it can reasonably be inferred that the person understands that the microwaved plate is hot and might burn them.

There are certain areas where autism can cause difficulties in understanding information which may be relevant to a decision. In general, autistic people find concrete information easier to understand than abstract concepts (Green *et al.* 2014). So, for example, choosing whether to eat an apple or a banana (when both fruits are physically offered) is concrete; choosing between college courses to start next week is much more abstract. Most decisions involve some level of abstract information. However, it is often possible to increase the amount of concrete information available. One approach is to use objects, models, photographs or symbols to represent an abstract concept to make it more concrete. Another option is to increase the amount of information available about the choices in a decision, for example by researching online, asking additional questions or undertaking a visit to a relevant location.

EXAMPLE

Based on: *LBX v K & Ors* [2013]

Lee (29, autism) has a diagnosis of mild mental retardation and some learning difficulties with an IQ that has been assessed at 59. Dr Hall (a psychiatrist) assessed Lee's capacity to decide who he should have contact with. He wrote:

> L is able to understand some basic information relevant to deciding who he should have contact with. However, I do not think he understands sufficient information in order to make a decision and also is not able to weigh up different factors important in making the decision. Again, he is clearly able to express a preference about who he sees.

...

Relevant information we discussed included who he might see (his father, brother, aunt and his friend C) and what factors were important in making decisions about whether to see people, such as the positive aspects of their relationship, the risks of seeing people, the emotional factors, the importance of family ties, how the other person might feel about his decision and the nature of friendship.

...

Turning to contact decisions, although L was able to say who he wanted to see and who he did not, he was not able to understand relevant information with regard to the positive aspects of his relationship with his father and brother, the risks of seeing people, the emotional factors, the importance of family ties, how the other person might feel about his decision and the nature of friendship. With regard to weighing in the balance, this is, of course, hampered by the fact that he did not understand all the relevant information and that he therefore put too much weight on the factors that he did understand. For example…with decisions about contact he put too much weight on his own feelings without sufficient consideration, for example, of the importance of family ties and how the other person might feel.

Dr Hall confirmed that he undertook his assessment at the J placement and did not use any tangible techniques such as drawings but said the location of the assessment where Lee currently lived was useful to aid his oral assessment and he imagined that Lee's social worker would have made attempts to explain these matters to him (although he did not check that assumption, which turned out to be incorrect). He concluded that Lee lacked capacity to decide who to have contact with.

Dawn Whitaker (an independent social worker) was also instructed to carry out an assessment with Lee (and, in doing so, assessed his capacity). She used drawings and some pre-prepared resources to facilitate a more concrete conversation with him. This involved taking time to ascertain his understanding of their meaning, such as the differences between living at and visiting somewhere and between wanting something and not wanting something. Lee was able to link emotions to their respective visual representation and he described his understanding of the difference between 'happy', 'OK' and 'sad', saying that to him happy means 'no pressure', OK means 'some pressure'/'not bad', and sad means 'pressure and worry'. The assessor's approach to questioning was guided by Lee's responses.

Pre-prepared cards that were two-thirds blank, stating, 'DAD', 'AUNTY', 'LEE' and 'STAFF' were used and Lee was supported to add details and drawings to represent each person. Lee described his understanding of 'contact', by explaining that it means 'to visit a person', 'to go/or see someone'. He was able to differentiate between different relevant locations where he might meet someone.

The assessment was carried out by inviting Lee to place cards (including 'I want' and 'Not want' cards) on drawings to express his wishes about contact. Options offered included living arrangements and frequency of contact – all by placing cards on options. The drawings and cards facilitated this more concrete conversation about options. By use of the drawings Lee was able to demonstrate his tangible understanding of the abstract concept of contact.

Ms Whitaker explained that:

> During this process I endeavoured to enable and encourage L to participate in the assessment as fully as possible by paying regard to the SALT advice regarding tips to aid L's communication and understanding: use of short simple sentences, ensuring to speak at a normal volume with slow speed and basic words, taking extra time to pause and check understanding, breaking down difficult information into smaller points, allowing L time to understand and consider each point before continuing, repeating information where appropriate and summarizing to check shared understanding.

The Court of Protection endorsed Ms Whitaker's approach.

> What were the advantages and disadvantages of the approaches taken by Dr Hall and Ms Whitaker to assessing Lee's capacity?
>
> How do you think Lee might have felt about his interactions with Dr Hall?
>
> How do you think Lee might have felt about his interactions with Ms Whitaker?

Another important area of understanding where autistic people can have difficulty and which is often relevant to decision making (especially around risk) is consequences. It may be helpful to consider an individual's understanding of the concepts of cause and effect and their relationship. Research suggests that autistic people often have more difficulties making inferences than non-autistic people (Bodner *et al.* 2015), although precisely how much more difficulty varies somewhat between different types of inference. The most difficult are emotion-related inferences. Autistic people can also have difficulties with other types of inference including physical causation. However, older autistic people and those with higher levels of verbal language ability tend to function better in making non-emotion related inferences, which suggests that many autistic people may have the potential to understand risks or consequences which involve making inferences with greater life experience and support to develop these skills.

6.8.2 Retaining

Difficulties with retaining information will not usually amount to grounds for concluding that an autistic person lacks capacity. Some autistic people will struggle to some extent to retain information, especially if the information is only provided orally. Therefore, providing written or visual information or otherwise recording information in an appropriate format which suits the person (audio recording, video, email, etc.) is likely to be sufficient to enable an autistic person to retain the relevant information for long enough to take a decision.

6.8.3 Using or weighing

Autism can pose significant difficulties with using or weighing information and it is worth examining each of these separately. Many autistic people have some elements of obsessive and/or compulsive behaviour. In some cases, these can interfere with the person's ability to use information relevant to a decision. So, for example, an autistic person may understand that if they do not go and have their dinner when it is ready, it will get cold, but still be unable to stop doing the task they are currently doing until they complete it. Similarly, many autistic people have difficulties with inertia and/or with executive function (Donnellan, Hill and Leary 2013). These can prevent an autistic person from taking actions that they understand the need to take and wish to do. As a result, for example, an autistic person may be in chronic pain and understand that they need to take prescribed medication, but persistently fail to actually do so. In most cases, these issues can be overcome by providing the right support, such as a skilled person providing prompting. However, in a few cases, these difficulties may result in an autistic person being unable to use the information relevant to a decision, even with adequate support to do so.

When it comes to weighing information relevant to a decision, difficulties imagining the unknown and rigidity are areas of potential difficulty and can affect capacity right across the autistic spectrum, including for 'high-functioning' individuals. Difficulties imagining the unknown may result in an autistic person failing to predict consequences. However, it is crucial when assessing capacity to ensure that the autistic person is given sufficient, explicit information about the likely consequences of a decision, rather than being expected to guess at what they might be. The MCA test concerns whether the person is unable to weigh the relevant information (once they have it), not whether they can work out the potential consequences. Similarly, autistic rigidity can make us more likely to focus on just one issue relevant to a decision or to hold firmly to a familiar option and struggle to consider alternatives. Providing additional time, information and direct experience of options may all help an autistic person to be able to weigh relevant information in making their decision.

As will be discussed in Chapter 7, there is a great deal which can be done to effectively support autistic people with these difficulties and, in many cases, autistic people will be able to weigh relevant information if we are given the right support to do so.

It is important that autistic people are not held to a higher standard of decision making than non-disabled people. For example, in a case which reached the Court of Protection, a psychiatrist took the position that a 20-year-old autistic person had failed to learn from negative experiences and use this to support her future decision making (as young adults are typically able to do). The judge disagreed, identifying that there was in fact some evidence that she had learned from experiences and modified her behaviour. Where her decisions were unwise, these were within the scope of adolescent risk-taking behaviour and did not by themselves indicate that she was 'unable' to weigh evidence of risk (*WBC (Local Authority) v Z (by her litigation friend the Official Solicitor & Ors [2016]*).

6.8.4 Communicating

This element of the capacity test is often assumed to be relevant to autistic people, since autism significantly affects communication. However, the MCA allows a conclusion that a person lacks capacity due to being unable to communicate only where they are completely incapable of indicating a decision by any means (MCA Code of Practice 4.23 and 4.24). Refusal to communicate, reluctance to communicate or communicating by non-verbal methods are not sufficient to conclude that someone lacks capacity (Brown, Barber and Martin 2015, p.27). Refusal to communicate may require some further exploration to consider whether it may be masking a lack of capacity in some other respect. However, unless suffering from an additional condition, no autistic person lacks capacity on this ground as even the most severely affected individuals are *capable* of indicating a choice (at least by their actions or behaviour), even if they may not always do so.

6.9 Chapter summary and key points

- Poor quality capacity assessments are a particular concern in autism.

- Consider the compatibility of communication and familiarity, not just type of decision and service boundaries, in deciding who should undertake a capacity assessment.

- Be wary of assumptions, especially:

    - that an autistic person's thinking or reasoning would be like the assessor's

- that IQ roughly equates to functional ability to make decisions.

- Consider the impact of lack of experience and developmental delay on the development of decision-making skills.

- Ensure that all relevant information is actually being provided to the autistic person.

- Recognize that different types of decision may be easier or more difficult for an autistic person and that which is which may be different for autistic people compared to non-autistic people.

- Consider the timing of an assessment and, particularly, stress levels and the need for quiet time to process information.

1. Understanding – allow for a 'spiky profile' and adapt to communication needs. Avoid assessing ability to communicate understanding. Consider behavioural or other evidence of understanding.

2. Retaining – adaptations (such as providing written/visual information) should be sufficient to enable retention of relevant information for long enough to make the decision.

3. Using or weighing relevant information – obsessive-compulsive difficulties and/or executive function difficulties or inertia can interfere with using relevant information. Ensure support needs are met before reaching opinion on capacity. Difficulty imagining the unknown and rigidity can interfere with weighing relevant information. Provide information about the consequences and experience of options before reaching an opinion on capacity.

4. Communicating – should not result in finding a lack of capacity, however limited an autistic person's communication may be (even behaviour only). Ability (not willingness) to indicate yes/no at all is sufficient to satisfy this criterion.

Recommended resources

See also Chapter 7 on 'Supporting Decision Making'.

Butler-Cole QC, V., Edwards, S., Allen, N., Scott, K. *et al.* (2019) *Mental Capacity Guidance Note: A Brief Guide to Carrying Out Capacity Assessments.* London: 39 Essex Chambers. Accessed on 4/10/19 at www.39essex.com/mental-capacity-guidance-note-brief-guide-carrying-capacity-assessments.

Butler-Cole QC, V., Edwards, S., Allen, N., Scott, K. *et al.* (ongoing) *Mental Capacity Report.* Accessed on 6/12/19 at www.39essex.com/tag/mental-capacity-newsletter.

Alex Ruck Keene's *Mental Capacity Law and Policy.* Accessed on 6/12/19 at https://www.mentalcapacitylawandpolicy.org.uk.

Internationally: *ASAN toolkit.* Accessed on 6/12/19 at https://autisticadvocacy.org/2016/02/the-right-to-make-choices-new-resource-on-supported-decision-making.

Validity (formerly Mental Disability Advocacy Centre) Accessed on 6/12/19 at https://validity.ngo.

CHAPTER 7

Supporting Decision Making and Autism

A person is not to be treated as unable to make a decision unless all practicable steps to help him [or her] to do so have been taken without success.

Mental Capacity Act 2005, Principle 2

7.1 Introduction

Practice, however, continues to lag well behind principles, particularly when it comes to major life decisions (rather than day-to-day decisions such as which clothing to wear). The Mental Capacity Act post-legislative review found that supported decision making is 'not well embedded'. There is 'institutional obstruction due to prevailing cultures of risk-aversion and paternalism', which prevents people with disabilities from being allowed to make the decisions they want, and 'the wishes, thoughts and feelings of [the person] are not routinely prioritized. Instead, clinical judgments or resource-led decision making predominate. The least restrictive option is not routinely or adequately considered' (Select Committee on the Mental Capacity Act 2005 (2014), p.8).

There is some research on decision making in autism which usefully identifies what some of the issues can be. This research suggests that autistic people tend to be more consistently logical in decision making and less influenced by the emotional and social context of a decision than non-autistic people (De Martino *et al.* 2008). We also know that autistic people are more likely to experience difficulties with the decision-making process and to avoid decision making than non-autistic people. In particular, as I mentioned in Chapter 6, decisions that need to be made quickly, involve a change of routine, or talking to others are experienced as particularly difficult, and many autistic people report that they find the process of decision making exhausting, overwhelming and anxiety-provoking (Luke *et al.* 2012).

Whether or not an autistic person currently has the capacity to make a particular decision (within the meaning of the MCA), there is a great deal that can be done to support us with decision making and to increase our capacity to take decisions, including major life choices.

7.2 Lack of experience

As I discussed in Chapter 6, all disabled children, young people and adults, including autistic people, may simply lack experience of making our own decisions. It is common for well-meaning carers (and parents) to act protectively towards disabled people, sometimes treating us as younger than our chronological age. Although this may be done unconsciously, the effect can be that disabled young people and adults may well have fewer opportunities to develop skills and experience in judging risk and making decisions than their non-disabled peers. For example, many disabled children in the UK attend special schools and travel to school by 'school transport' – usually an escorted taxi journey. This protective bubble can easily be extended to out-of-school activities, which are often 'special' as well. Whilst some special schools are excellent at providing a range of opportunities and challenges, the overall effect easily becomes one of training disabled children to be easy to care for and sheltering them from experience of the wider world (Hingsburger and Tough 2002). When this approach extends into teenage years and early adult life, disabled young people often do not have the same opportunities as non-disabled young people to make mistakes, make silly decisions and irresponsible choices and live with the consequences.

These limited experiences can adversely impact on the development of decision-making skills for many disabled people. The decision-making skills of autistic people, however, are likely to be particularly badly affected by any lack of experience. Autistic people often find it difficult to generalize knowledge and skills from one situation to another, so we tend to need more and a greater range of experiences to fully develop our skills.

Taking the above into account, a crucial first step in supporting decision making is to recognize that an autistic person of any age may well be capable of further developing their skills and capacity to take their own decisions and to consider how they can be supported to gain a broad range of experience, including experience of making mistakes and experiencing adverse consequences, to develop their skills. I am not suggesting that autistic people should be left unsupported or exposed to unreasonable levels of risk, but positive risk taking with autistic people must include opportunities at any appropriate level to push boundaries, get things wrong and experience meaningful challenges. Consideration of these issues in care planning could significantly improve care and support for autistic people (National Autistic Taskforce 2019).

7.3 Adapting communication

COMMUNICATING IN AN APPROPRIATE WAY

- Could information be explained or presented in a way that is easier for the person to understand (for example, by using simple language or visual aids)?

- Have different methods of communication been explored, if required, including non-verbal communication?

- Could anyone else help with communication (for example, a family member, support worker, interpreter, speech and language therapist or advocate)? (MCA Code of Practice, Chapter 3)

Much of the advice and adaptations I suggested in Chapter 2 for the process of social care assessment also applies more broadly to supporting decision making. Consideration needs to be given to communication adaptations in both directions: in the communication of information to the autistic person and in how communication from them is transmitted to others. A communication-friendly environment, providing information in a variety of formats suitable to the person and, crucially, providing time free from communication for an autistic person to process the information before expecting them to make a decision are all crucial ways to support decision making.

EXAMPLE

Hamid (22, autism, LD) currently lives with his parents and younger siblings in the family home. Lisa, a social worker with the transitions team, wanted to explore with Hamid the possibility of moving to a supported living flat in a nearby town. Lisa had discussed the idea with Hamid and his parents and arranged a visit for Hamid to view the supported living flats, accompanied by his parents. However, Hamid has limited verbal language and experiences repeated bouts of echolalia. When Lisa has talked to him about the possible move, he has replied with apparently unrelated phrases from his favourite TV show, *The Simpsons*. Lisa is not sure whether Hamid understands what she is proposing and suspects he may lack capacity to decide his residence. Nevertheless, she is keen to work with Hamid to try to ascertain his wishes and feelings and, either, support him to make the decision or (if he does lack capacity) ensure his wishes and feelings are fully considered in a best interests decision.

After getting some advice, Lisa obtains photos of Hamid, his parents, siblings, other family members and friends, as well as photos of both Hamid's family home and the supported living flats. She attaches each of the photos of a potential place to live to the outside of a cardboard box. Lisa then spends some time with Hamid (by himself) using the laminated photos of Hamid and people in his life and moving them between the cardboard boxes to explore Hamid's understanding of the choices (also using a clock and lights to demonstrate day and night). So, for example, Lisa moves the photos to physically demonstrate the differences between Hamid living in the family home (e.g. sleeping, eating) with his parents and siblings, and friends coming to visit and then Hamid living in the flat (e.g. sleeping, eating) and his parents, siblings and friends coming to visit and Hamid visiting his family. When she moves the photos, she clearly demonstrates to Hamid that his family members would not live with him in his flat.

She gradually encourages Hamid to move the photos around between the boxes. Over several sessions, Lisa is able to clarify, in this largely non-verbal way, that Hamid does understand the differences between living somewhere and visiting and that he is able to express a clear preference for moving to the flat.

Why do you think that Lisa spoke to Hamid by himself (without either of his parents)?

Do you think any particular adaptations are more important than others?

Can you think of any other ways of adapting communication which might help in a similar situation?

In Chapter 6, I clarified that autistic people are not, generally, 'unable' to communicate according to the terms of the MCA, even where an individual has no spoken, written, sign or symbol-based form of communication. However, this does not mean that practitioners will not at times face significant challenges achieving sufficient functional communication to assess an autistic person's capacity in other domains and to effectively support decision making. So, it is worth setting out here the most basic components of communication: what might an autistic person need to understand in order to be able to communicate sufficiently to ascertain their wishes and feelings (particularly on major life choices)?

In my view, there are three essential components:

- two-way exchange

- representation

- first–then

The concept of two-way exchange requires the autistic person to understand the point of communication. On the simplest level, this can be demonstrated by considering whether the autistic person is able, by any means, to make others aware of their needs in order to get those needs fulfilled. So, for example, a pre-verbal autistic person who uses the Picture Exchange Communication System (PECS) to hand over a card with a line drawing of a banana in exchange for an actual banana would be demonstrating understanding of two-way exchange.

The concept of representation is the idea that something can be represented by something else. For example, objects of reference is one simple method of communication which depends on this concept. It involves using an object, such as a cup, to represent a concept, such as needing a drink. At incrementally more advanced levels, photographs represent objects/places/people in the real world; generic photos (e.g. a stock photo of a house, rather than a photo of the person's own house), drawings or symbols are more abstract representations; written or spoken words or signs are even more abstract representations.

'First-then' is a system in widespread use with children, young people and adults with learning disabilities. I provided an example in Chapter 2. At its simplest level, using a first-then frame to order objects, photographs, symbols, drawings or words enables communication about sequence. As a result, it can be used to communicate to and understand communication from an autistic person about the order in which events occur. Once a person understands first-then at the level of sequence, it can then be developed to a slightly more sophisticated level to enable communication about cause and effect. This level of communication is probably the minimum required to effectively communicate with a person about decisions involving concepts of risk and/or major life choices.

So, for example, a practitioner might use a first-then frame, a photo of a person stepping into the road (in the 'first' section) and a choice of photos for the 'then' section to explore with an autistic person their understanding of the risks and potential consequences of running into the road.

As I discussed in Chapter 4 and will touch on further in Chapter 9, where an autistic person (of any age) does not yet understand all three of these concepts and/or does not have any method of functional communication (communicating to get basic needs met), it is vital to ensure that they are being supported to learn and develop these concepts.

Even where an autistic person lacks capacity to make the decision, they should still be fully involved in best interests decision-making processes (s.4(4) MCA 2005), including ensuring that they are provided with information in alternative formats and accessible forms of communication are used (Equality Act 2010).

7.4 Providing information

PROVIDING RELEVANT INFORMATION

- Does the person have all the relevant information they need to make a particular decision?

- If they have a choice, have they been given information on all the alternatives? (MCA Code of Practice, Chapter 3)

First and foremost, it is also important to ensure that all the relevant information has actually been provided to the autistic person (or, indeed, any adult needing to make a decision). This is easier said than done in social care. For example, any adult may need to make a decision about where to live, but for those with social care needs, their choices of where to live may be constrained by decisions by local authorities about how to meet their social care needs and in which accommodation options the local authority can and is willing to meet their needs.

Only once the adult knows which options are actually available to them and how their care needs would be met there, can they be supported to make a decision about where to live.[26] In such situations, it helps to be clear that there are typically two separate decisions involved: first, decisions by public bodies or other organizations about what they will or will not fund or offer; followed by a decision for the person themselves (or a best interests decision with their involvement) between the available options. In real life, the boundaries and order of these two distinct decisions can become blurred. In my experience, this often requires robust advocacy on the part of an involved social worker to ensure that there is clear and timely identification of the options open to the person (and what, if anything, they depend on) *before* the person can reasonably be expected to make a decision.[27]

It is also likely to be helpful to consider carefully the information an autistic person might need to make the decision from (as far as possible) their perspective. Consider whether it may be helpful to:

- *Make contextual information explicit.* Is there information which is implied, 'common sense' or seems 'obvious'? Is there socially derived information about general knowledge, social norms or typical choices which the autistic person might not know? Might the person need to be given explicit, additional information about the feelings of others who would be affected by the decision? Might the person need to be given explicit information about how realistic/likely options are? This is likely to require providing information in a more honest, direct and blunt manner than may be comfortable for non-autistic people.

- *Provide additional information* or information on aspects of the decision which may not be important to others but could be important to the autistic person, such as timing or the probability of an outcome or how the decision may affect things which are important to them. Often information provided is much too vague from an autistic point of view. Make sure that the information provided is as concrete and specific as possible and, if some information is unknown, explain why and what it depends on.

- *Minimize irrelevant information.* Is there information which might be important to others but is less important to this autistic person?

- *Provide all of the information relevant to the decision again at the time it needs to be made*, including information which has previously been given to the autistic person (but which they may have forgotten or not have immediately in mind).

7.5 Weighing information and making a decision

MAKING THE PERSON FEEL AT EASE

- Are there particular times of day when the person's understanding is better?

- Are there particular locations where they may feel more at ease?

- Could the decision be put off to see whether the person can make the decision at a later time when circumstances are right for them?

SUPPORTING THE PERSON

- Can anyone else help or support the person to make choices or express a view? (MCA Code of Practice, Chapter 3)

7.5.1 Time and space

The most crucial adaptation to support an autistic person's decision making is to give them quiet thinking time, free from communication, in which to process information and make the decision. This is usually possible, but rarely done. It is commonplace for an autistic person to both be given important new information and be asked to make a decision during the same conversation. Simply providing information in advance, or in one conversation, and then asking for a decision later is likely to make the difference between an autistic person being able to make an informed, considered decision and them expressing something which does not reliably reflect their true opinion or being unable to make a decision at all. Autistic people who *appear* to take decisions under time pressure are often either acquiescing without understanding or instinctively resisting, rather than actually making a capacitous decision.

Even in an emergency situation where a decision is required very quickly, it is often possible to, at least, provide a few minutes of quiet thinking time. If at all possible, communication about a decision and time to think should take place in an environment which is comfortable, familiar and not stress-inducing for the autistic person.

EXAMPLE

Tony (64) has peripheral arterial disease (PAD) and has previously suffered a blood clot in his lung and pain in his legs from blocked arteries. Tony is autistic and finds hospitals frightening and overwhelming. Tony's speech is apparently 'normal' and he does not have any diagnosed learning disability. However, his receptive language is much weaker than his expressive language and he struggles to fully understand a lot of what 'official' people say to him. During previous hospital admissions there has been some vague talk about possible surgery involving angioplasty or a stent, which Tony has understood as meaning doctors might want to put a balloon in the artery in his leg. Tony attends an appointment with the vascular team at the local acute hospital to review his treatment. He is accompanied by a relative and a support worker.

In the first part of the appointment, Tony has various tests. This involves sitting in waiting areas for unpredictable periods of time, going in and out of different rooms, meeting and communicating with a variety of health professionals, often without knowing what to expect next. Then Tony finds himself in a treatment room for a long period with his relative and support worker. He can hear snatches of conversation from the room next door where the doctors have gathered to review his scans. After a long wait for an uncertain period (by now Tony has been at the hospital for 3½ hours), the vascular consultant and three other 'team members' come into the room. The consultant explains that Tony's scans indicate that there are multiple blocked arteries in both of Tony's legs, but that the right leg is particularly bad. He goes on to say that the team has discussed the surgical options and concluded that the only viable option is a full amputation of his right leg at the hip.

The consultant asks Tony if he understands and agrees to the operation. The consultant says that he would prefer to admit Tony right away and operate the next day, though he states that the timing is not critical, so long as the surgery is done within the next couple of weeks. Tony is sitting in a wheelchair hugging his knees to his chest and shaking. He does not look at the consultant and does not reply. Tony's family member and support worker try to explain what the doctor has said to him, but his distress increases. Tony's support worker suggests to the consultant that Tony goes home to have time to think and that she could help him communicate his decision to the team in a few days.

The consultant responds that Tony obviously does not have the capacity to make the decision since he is not responding in the conversation, and adds that, as he is the decision maker, he will make a best interests decision that Tony should have the surgery. So, Tony will be admitted to a ward immediately and the surgery will go ahead the next day.

How do you think Tony felt during the interaction with the consultant?

What adaptations do you think could realistically have been made to support Tony to make his own decision about the surgery?

What role (if any) do you think a social worker could or should play in a largely health-focused decision-making situation such as this?

The only caveat to the above is the importance of proactively checking back with the autistic person, rather than relying on them to initiate communication of their decision once they have made it. Many autistic people struggle with initiative and may not be able to reliably initiate communication.

7.5.2 Open versus closed questions

The next most important adaptation to support decision making is to ask closed questions and/or offer a menu of specific choices. This, of course, directly conflicts with what is generally considered best practice in person-centred working! The difficulty for autistic people is that we find vagueness very confusing and can really struggle to work out what the range of potential responses might be.

EXAMPLE

A typical question from a person-centred planning toolkit: 'What's working/not working?' (Helen Sanderson Associates 2019).

From an autistic perspective, it is difficult to be sure exactly what this question is asking about. Could it mean whether I understand the idea of being employed? Could it mean whether any of my household appliances are broken?

Even if an autistic person manages to infer that this question relates to social care support of various kinds, the openness of the question then requires us to be able to imagine the unknown and consider hypothetical options of which we may or may not have any direct experience. It is common for an autistic person to get so stuck trying to work out what possible answers might look like that either: they do not answer at all or they simply give a familiar option as the answer, regardless of whether it is 'right' for them or not.

From an autistic point of view, the question also raises difficult issues about how 'right' should be judged. Does this mean:

- Geographically closest?

- Involving the least change?

- Support that someone has described using the word 'right'?

- Provided by someone I get on with?

- That helps me do the things I want to do?

- That helps me do the things I need to do?

- That enables me to have the most autonomy?

- Something else?

- Some complex combination of the above?

Seeing all these complexities, and needing precision, clarity and certainty, can easily derail autistic decision making and actually result in decisions being made which are a very long way from being genuinely 'person-centred'.

> Can you think of ways in which a person-centred question (such as 'What's working/not working?') could be adapted to be clearer for an autistic person?
>
> How can changes to make a question clearer be balanced with the need to avoid influencing the person's answer?
>
> Are there any disadvantages to making those changes?

It is possible to avoid unduly influencing or steering an autistic person's decision whilst also supporting them effectively. The key elements are:

- Provide information about why the question is being asked and what the answer will be used for – this helps an autistic person to identify what sorts of options might be relevant.

- Provide specific, concrete options to choose from, whilst also making it clear that the autistic person is welcome to come up with additional or alternative options of their own – very often, the options given may help an autistic person to work out what other options there could be.

EXAMPLE

Jenny is a support worker for Sarah, an autistic parent. Sarah wanted to arrange for her teenage son, Andrew (who is also autistic and has moderate LD), to go to an indoor skiing facility during the school holidays with his support worker, Carrie. Sarah had asked Jenny to look into this.

Jenny then sent Sarah the following email:

You wanted to arrange for Andrew to go to Anytown Snow Park with Carrie on Tuesday (28 May). You had asked me to book 'for skiing and playing'.

Carrie reminded me that last time Andrew went skiing there, the ski instructor had said that he had done well, but that it might be better in future to book via Disability Snowsports (website link) as they would be able to spend the extra time supporting Andrew in ways beneficial to him.

I phoned both the Snow Park and Disability Snowsports to get more info about the various options.

Here is what Disability Snowsports told me:

- They provide Snowsport lessons to people with any disability.

- Their instructors are 'adaptive qualified' – they are trained to work in a different way and adapt to people's disabilities.

- The vast majority of lessons they provide are 1:1.

- Their lessons are subsidized by Disability Snowsports UK, so are cheaper than usual 1:1 lessons.

- Ski lessons with them, at Anytown Snow Park, cost £52 for non-members (of Disability Snowsports UK) or £42 for members.

- Membership (of Disability Snowsports UK) costs £21 per year.

- A ski lesson with them would last one hour.

- They have good general availability for lessons next week; the only day they do not have availability is Tuesday (which is the day that you had planned for Andrew to go there).

Here is what Anytown Snow Park told me:

- If booking with them (and not arranging anything with Disability Snowsports), in order to get skiing and playing, we would need to book a 'ski taster and snow fun combo'.

- See here for details: www.anytownsnowpark.com.

- Cost: £25 per person.

- Includes: 50-minute (group) ski lesson + 60 minutes playing in the snow play area.

- This would be available at 10am or 12 noon on Tuesday 28 May.

- Support workers go free, so there would be no cost for Carrie to go with Andrew.

Do you want Andrew to:

1. have a 1:1 ski lesson with Disability Snowsports when he goes to Anytown Snow Park next week (this would involve changing the day of the trip, as Disability Snowsports don't have any availability for lessons on Tuesday 28)?

2. do the 'ski taster and snow fun combo' at Anytown Snow Park on Tuesday 28?

3. do something other than the above options?

Jenny

In what ways do you think Jenny has adapted her approach to support Sarah's decision making?

Could a similar approach be taken to supporting a client's decision making in contexts which occur in your practice? If so, how? If not, can you think of other adaptations which might help clients to make more decisions for themselves?

Obviously, all autistic people are individuals and will vary in the methods of support we find most helpful. However, in my experience, the technique used in the above example, of including 'something else' or 'none of the above' as an option in a list of concrete options, can be an effective technique for supporting an autistic person's decision making. What is really important is to guard against assumptions and ensure that people supporting an autistic person are working from the autistic person's perspective. This is much more likely to produce a genuinely person-centred outcome than slavish adherence to the principle of open questions, even where this is actually disabling to an autistic person.

That said, it is important that the options given are concrete, specific and actually available! It is important to try to avoid presenting an autistic person with options and having them choose one, only to then discover the option is not actually available to them. This cannot always be entirely prevented; sudden changes and emergencies can and do happen. But, often, it can be avoided simply by the person supporting doing a little basic information gathering and checking before presenting the options for a decision.

7.5.3 Support with foreseeing consequences

As discussed, autistic people may find it challenging to project potential and hypothetical consequences, particularly where these are outside our direct experience. Our social and communication issues can also be relevant here. Generally, we are more likely to be able to foresee physical and practical consequences and be less likely to foresee consequences which require us to predict the behaviour or emotions of other people (De Martino *et al.* 2008).

Autistic people also tend to focus on one thing at a time (Murray, Lesser and Lawson 2005). This has many advantages. However, a disadvantage can be difficulties connecting and spotting relationships between information from different sources or obtained at different times. This can be the case for autistic people at all levels of intellectual functioning.

EXAMPLE

Sarah, a highly intelligent autistic adult, is a member of a karate club. Her club started a new class on Friday evenings. The next Friday, Sarah was available and she decided to go to the new class and drove herself there.

Sarah is also a parent. Her son, Andrew, goes to Scouts on a Friday evening. On Wednesday afternoon, Andrew's support worker, Carrie, had checked with Sarah that the family's car would be available for Carrie to drive Andrew to Scouts, as they were doing a 'night hike' in a rural area.

As Sarah went out the door to the karate class, she told Andrew to have a good time on the night hike!

Sarah knew and remembered Andrew's schedule, but failed to connect Carrie's need for the car and her own during the same time period. Sarah's mind did eventually process the separate items of information more deeply and then made the connection, but unfortunately, she was driving home from the karate class by the time that happened.

> This sort of error, with similarly minor consequences, might be made by a non-autistic person from time to time. Can you think of any more serious consequences that an autistic person might fail to foresee?

> What role, if any, do you think support could play in a situation where an autistic person may fail to foresee the consequences of a decision?

7.5.4 Support to cope with potential change
Autistic people tend to find change difficult. This can impact on

decision making which involves change. For instance, an autistic person's instinctive and immediate response to a decision between something familiar and something new may well be to reject the new option. This may be because the autistic person freely chooses to weigh change negatively and more strongly in making their decision than a non-autistic person might. However, it may also be that the prospect of change is so frightening that they are struggling to weigh or use any other factors at all. This might, for example, be indicated by the person saying that the option involving change is impossible.

A good deal can be done to try to support an autistic person to cope with change sufficiently well to be able to properly consider all their options. Again, time is a significant factor. It might be an idea to simply provide information about the option involving change on one occasion and then, even if the first occasion appears to have prompted a negative decision, provide further opportunities to reconsider or remake the decision once the person has had time to process, research and consider what is actually involved in the change.

It is likely to be helpful to provide accurate, sufficiently detailed and specific information about the options in a format which the person can refer back to as many times as they need (see Chapter 4).

A further, but more demanding, adaptation would be to provide extensive and repeated access to the new situation prior to a final decision.

EXAMPLE

Edwin (ASD and mild LD) was in Year 10. His current school offered a 'Sixth Form' for Years 12 and 13. Alternatively, a nearby college also offered a potentially suitable programme for Years 12 and 13. Following Edwin's annual EHCP review in the autumn term of Year 10, Edwin, his parents, transition worker and school agreed to arrange a placement for Edwin to attend the college for one half-day per week in Year 10 and one full day per week in Year 11 to do an 'Introduction to Construction' course, alongside his education in Key Stage 4 at his current school.

The placement was duly arranged. By autumn of Year 11, Edwin had been attending the college each week in term time for around a year. Two weeks before Edwin's Year 11 annual review, his transition worker shared with him a booklet she had created explaining the choices open to him for Years 12 and 13 (between remaining at his current school and moving to the college). She left the booklet with Edwin and encouraged him to look at it several times and think about what he wanted to do.

At Edwin's Year 11 annual review, he was able to actively participate in the discussion about the choice and express clearly his view that he wanted to move to the college to study a more advanced construction course which was not available at his school.

> Do you think autistic people receive sufficient preparation and exposure to a potential new placement or other new situation in practice contexts you are familiar with, before they are expected to make or participate in any decision making?

> Can you think of any ways in which an autistic person's decision making could be supported in a situation involving potential change where a decision is needed in a short timeframe?

7.5.5 Avoiding the person becoming overwhelmed

Many autistic people find decision making demanding, tiring and overwhelming (Luke *et al.* 2012). The strategies outlined in this chapter can go some way towards helping. But, even with the best support and adaptations, some people may regularly and quickly become overwhelmed by being asked to make a large number of decisions. It is still possible to successfully support an autistic person to maximize their autonomy (see Chapter 4) where this is the case. This can be done by empowering the autistic person to make strategic level decisions which minimize the need for an excessive number of day-to-day decisions, such as, for example, deciding what to say in their care plan about how they want to be supported rather than being expected to tell each individual support worker what they want them to do on every occasion.

Another way of doing this is by supporting an autistic person to have a default choice. So, if I find it hard to decide what to have for lunch each day, I can decide to choose a particular lunch as my default choice. Then, on any given day, I can decide to have something else if I want to. But, crucially, if I am unable to manage to make the decision, then I am automatically having the default choice (because I have made an advance decision to do that). This helps to avoid becoming overwhelmed by excessive choices and allows the autistic person to concentrate their decision-making resources on a smaller number of the most important decisions.

7.6 Communicating and executing the decision

Once an autistic person has made a decision (with or without support), they may also need support to communicate and/or execute that decision. It is important that reasonable adjustments are in place to enable the autistic person to effectively communicate and execute their decisions and to ensure that any support needs in these areas have been considered during care planning. Some good questions to ask might be:

- Are all those who may need to know the autistic person's decision receptive to the ways in which the autistic person can best communicate?

- Might the autistic person need support and/or advocacy to communicate their decision effectively to others?

- Is the autistic person able to put their decision into effect without assistance? Do they need prompting, help with ensuring what they need is to hand, practical support or anything else?

- Is anyone or anything else impeding the autistic person's ability to execute their decisions?

7.7 Chapter summary and key points

- Provide experience and take steps to increase capacity (including planning these in care planning).

- Adapt communication.

- Provide information:

  - Make contextual information explicit.

  - Give additional information which may be important to the autistic person.

  - Minimize irrelevant information.

  - Ensure access to all relevant information at the time of asking the question.

- Give processing time, even in emergencies (as far as possible).

- Ensure a low-stress environment for thinking and decision making as far as possible.

- Offer a menu of choices including the option to add choices.

- Provide support with foreseeing potential consequences.

- Provide support to cope with change, including extended experience of and additional information about new or unfamiliar options.

- Avoid overwhelming an autistic person's ability to make decisions by supporting them to make strategic level decisions to avoid too many day-to-day decisions if they find this helpful.

- Provide support needed to communicate and/or execute decisions.

Recommended resources

Justice for LB toolkit: www.advocacyfocus.org.uk/justiceforlb.

CDC decision-making toolkit: https://councilfordisabledchildren.org.uk/sites/default/files/field/attachemnt/Final%20Decision%20Making%20Toolkit.pdf.

TLAP supported decision-making tool: www.thinklocalactpersonal.org.uk/_assets/Resources/Personalisation/london/Supported_Decision_Making.pdf.

SCIE directory of decision-making resources: www.scie.org.uk/mca-directory/making-decisions.

CHAPTER 8

Safeguarding and Autism

8.1 How big is the risk?

8.1.1 Victimization

Safeguarding of both children and vulnerable adults is the priority focus throughout social care and related services. Due to the inconsistent collection of data on autism in the UK, it is not possible to measure the proportions of autistic children and adults amongst those involved in safeguarding enquiries, but it will be clear to practitioners that the numbers are substantial.

People with disabilities are at greater risk of abuse than non-disabled people. At particular risk are those with speech and language difficulties (three times greater risk), intellectual disability (four times greater risk) and behavioural difficulties (five times greater risk) (Jones *et al.* 2012). Given that most autistic people have difficulties that may fall within one or more of these groups, it is clear that autistic children are at heightened risk of victimization. Similarly, autistic adults report high levels of victimization, particularly 'hate crime' (i.e. bullying, verbal abuse, name calling, assaults) and 'mate crime' (i.e. being exploited or taken advantage of by someone purporting to be a friend; examples include being coerced into illegal activity, financially or sexually exploited) (Wirral Autistic Society 2015).

Abuse or neglect of autistic people is never acceptable and these disproportionately high rates of victimization should not be considered inevitable. However, it is important to be aware of factors that may increase the vulnerability of autistic people to abuse and obstruct access to support and protection. Autistic people may:

- tend to take what people say literally and assume they are telling the truth

- not recognize and avoid 'high-risk' situations (such as walking alone late at night in a 'bad' part of town)

- not recognize subtle indicators of deception or risk in other people's speech, body language or facial expression

- have limited social networks leading to a lack of trusted people to turn to for help

- fear being labelled as the perpetrator rather than the victim (unfortunately this is a real risk due to public perceptions of autism)

- experience communication difficulties in trying to report abuse or seek help

- not have been taught the vocabulary to describe inappropriate touching or other abuse

- be wrongly assumed on the basis of intellectual ability to be able to effectively protect ourselves[28]

- have good 'book knowledge' but not be 'street wise'

- be wrongly assumed (on the basis of being autistic) to be unable to give evidence or be a reliable witness[29]

- need support (formal and/or informal), leading to relationships with unequal power balance

- lack awareness of social 'norms' and struggle to identify behaviour as abusive or neglectful

- have disclosures dismissed or overlooked because of a prior pattern of vexatious and/or trivial complaints and/or supplying far too much irrelevant detail.

8.1.2 Perpetrators

Autistic children and adults are far more likely to be victims than perpetrators. Generally, autistic people are particularly likely to follow rules and laws rigidly and most autistic people are law-abiding (Allely 2018; King and Murphy 2014). However, it is also true that autistic children and adults can behave in challenging or problematic ways and these can sometimes result in autistic people coming into contact with the criminal justice system. Some 16% of people placed in custody meet one or more of the assessment criteria for mental disorder (Maguire 2010), and 'a consensus figure of 50–60% of young people who are involved in offending having speech, language and communication needs is emerging' (Gregory and Bryan 2011).

It is possible to describe some loose categories (Gwillim 2009) of potentially offending behaviours of autistic individuals:

- innocent behaviour being misinterpreted (including 'social error' offences)

- distress and/or 'challenging behaviour'

- not knowing something was wrong/illegal

- being exploited/manipulated

- obsessions and rigidity (including in arguments)

- offending behaviour for non-ASD related reasons (just like anyone else).

8.2 Types of abuse

8.2.1 Physical abuse

Autistic people may be at risk of physical assault, both by family/carers and by strangers. The communication difficulties, conflicting needs and stress which can arise within families can be particularly acute in families which include an autistic person and this can increase the risks. Autistic people are at particular risk of being assaulted by strangers because our unusual behaviours or ways of moving may attract adverse attention or because social errors or miscommunication can trigger an aggressive response. Autistic people of all ages experience bullying to such an extent that we may consider it 'normal'. In care environments, particularly those where autistic needs are not well understood or which subject autistic people to high levels of environmental or other stress, autistic people may behave in ways which challenge care staff and other residents. This puts them at risk of abusive responses, including physical restraint, seclusion and the misuse of sedative medications.

Autistic adults and children may occasionally perpetrate violence and may be particularly vulnerable to inadvertently perpetrating threatening behaviour. Particularly when distressed, autistic people may speak at a volume, use language, gestures or otherwise behave in ways which are unacceptable to other people (such as encroaching on the personal space of others). These behaviours may be perceived by others in the social situation as threatening or aggressive. The autistic person may or may not (no matter how 'intelligent') be aware at the time of how their behaviour is being perceived by others and may fail to anticipate such reactions.

8.2.2 Domestic violence

As noted above, autistic people may experience abuse from parents and other family members. However, autistic people are also particularly vulnerable to domestic violence from partners. Contrary to popular myth, autistic people are capable of forming close emotional bonds with others and autistic teenagers and adults can and do form healthy intimate relationships. However, autistic teenagers and adults may also struggle to identify patterns of behaviour towards them from a partner as 'abnormal' or 'unhealthy' and may lack the social networks to have any basis for comparison. Most autistic people are accustomed to receiving negative reactions from other people in social relationships and to being told or believing that they are the person at fault. Most autistic people also have less knowledge and awareness of social 'norms' than their neurotypical peers. So, autistic teenagers and adults are particularly vulnerable to believing that they must be the one at fault and failing to recognize behaviour from a partner as exploitative, manipulative, unhealthy or abusive.

Autistic people can also (with varying degrees of awareness and culpability) perpetrate harassment, stalking or similar behaviours. Issues in this area can arise from a combination of obsessive tendencies and a potentially poor understanding of how social interactions may be perceived or experienced by others.

EXAMPLE

Jordan (19) is in his first year at university. He has spent some weeks plucking up the courage to ask a young woman on his course (Laura) out for coffee. When he finally manages to ask her, she politely declines, saying that she is too busy. Disappointed but determined to solve the problem, Jordan uses the web and social media to research Laura's timetable, find out what social and leisure activities she attends and which buses she takes to travel to university. In an effort to be helpful, he sends Laura a series of lengthy emails explaining several different ways in which she could make time in her schedule to have coffee with him.

What do you think Jordan's reasoning may have been?

How do you think Laura would have experienced Jordan's behaviour?

Can you think of anything that could have been done to prevent this situation occurring?

8.2.3 Sexual abuse

Sexuality, in the context of modern life in the UK, is an area of human interaction which involves complex and constantly evolving social rules and norms. Social communication about sex is rarely clear, literal and explicit. Much is implied or inferred and innuendo is commonplace. This communicative and social environment is very confusing from an autistic point of view.

Recent years have seen increasing awareness and public discussion of child sexual abuse and exploitation. However, the high levels of victimization amongst disabled children and adults are less visible and less discussed. Increasing awareness is to be welcomed and it has led to a flurry of new sexual offences, including some focused specifically on protection of people with 'mental disorders'[30] (a legal term which includes autism). Politically popular as introducing new offences may be, the evidence base is quite clear that good quality sex and relationship education for children and young people is far more effective in actually reducing rates of victimization (Finkelhor 2009).

Specialist sex and relationship education, specifically for autistic children, teenagers and adults, is essential to improve safeguarding in this area. This is because autistic people (including those who do not have an intellectual disability) often need more explicit and literal teaching than may be considered appropriate for a general audience and it is particularly important that sex and relationships education is embedded within wider teaching and support with social relationships (Hartman 2014). Unfortunately, provision is limited and patchy. The needs of autistic children in mainstream schools and autistic young adults beyond school age are often overlooked. Autism is a developmental disorder and it is common in the autistic community for young adults to mature over a longer period of time than neurotypical peers. So autistic young adults in their late teens and into their twenties and beyond may be continuing to develop and explore their sexuality. They may have further questions and need additional levels of knowledge at this point that they were not able or ready to take in at a younger age.

The massive impact of technology on social norms, including sexual relationships, has both positive and negative results for autistic people.

Table 8.1 Some positive and negative aspects of technology for autistic people

Positive	Negative
Increased accessibility of information	Highly variable quality of information
Easy access to a much wider social group, including niche and non-mainstream identities and interests	Social interaction can extend into private spaces 24 hours a day, including bullying, victimization and exploitation
Peer support for those who identify as LGBTQI+	Easy to inadvertently cross social or legal boundaries

On the positive side, information about every conceivable subject is now available through mediums which autistic people often find more accessible and without requiring human interaction. The growth of online dating and social media have provided new opportunities and ways of developing relationships which can have significant advantages for autistic people. Autistic people often have interests, traits and identities which are less 'mainstream'. Common interests in the autistic community include (amongst many, many others) trains and transport; role-playing and trading card games; Star Trek; maths, computing and physics. Although reliable statistical data is difficult to come by, it appears to be the case that autistic people are more likely to identify as questioning their gender, trans or non-binary (Van Der Miesen, Hurley and De Vries 2016). There may also be a somewhat higher proportion of autistic people who are (or at least who publicly identify as) gay or bisexual than the proportions found in a neurotypical population. The accessibility of a much larger range of individuals online compared to those in an autistic person's immediate physical community offers valuable opportunities to form social relationships with peers with similar unusual characteristics, identities, interests or traits.

On the negative side, the quality of information available online is highly variable. Autistic people are particularly vulnerable to scams and exploitation (including sexual exploitation) online. There are particular risks around being pressured or manipulated into transmitting explicit 'selfies' and then becoming vulnerable to blackmail and 'revenge' porn. Social (and sexual) interaction extends into what were formerly private spaces 24 hours a day and this can include bullying, victimization and exploitation.

Autistic people are highly unlikely to be sexual predators or pose any sort of risk to others. However, some autistic people may pose a risk of perpetrating particular kinds of sexual offending. Lack of knowledge and the complexity of the social rules in this area of human interaction can result in some autistic children and adults seeking to meet their sexual needs in ways which contravene the law and/or infringe on the rights of others, usually without deliberately intending to do so. Nick Dubin, an autistic self-advocate living in the US, has bravely written about his experience of being convicted of accessing child pornography following naive exploration of his emerging sexuality in his early twenties.

> Like many people with Asperger's who have little social contact, my computer was my major link to the outside world. I relied heavily on it to gather research for my studies, to obtain information about my special interests, and as a way to connect with others. For example, I would spend hours every day on the internet finding jazz music and then I would post all my recommendations on Facebook.

At the time it seemed like a natural progression for me to go from looking at pornographic magazines to viewing the same type of material on the computer. Using the computer was certainly a more comfortable and safer way to explore my sexuality than dating, travelling to Nevada, or going to adult bookstores. (Dubin 2014, p.98)

He explains that his psychological and sexual development was (as is typical of autistic people) substantially at odds with his intellectual development and his chronological age. Whilst in no way condoning or seeking to justify the viewing of child pornography, he painstakingly sets out how he felt internally like a young adolescent and sought images of those he saw as his 'peers', without, at the time, realizing that those children had been victimized in the making of the images or even that his actions were illegal. Following his conviction, he became aware that he was not the only autistic young adult to have made a similar, catastrophic mistake. He concludes that autistic people 'simply have a different psychosexual development from their neurotypical counterparts and this difference can sometimes affect interpersonal relationships and encounters with strangers, as well as sexual exploration that can take place on the computer' (Dubin 2014, p.125). A great deal can be achieved to mitigate the risk of autistic children and young adults becoming either victims or perpetrators of sexual abuse through providing good quality and autism-specific education from an early age and continuing access to such education throughout transitions and life stages (including in adult life).

8.2.4 Psychological abuse

Psychological abuse is a particularly problematic area for autistic people. Autistic people may experience as distressing interactions which others do not intend as abuse. So, it is particularly important in this area to recognize that unintentional abuse is still abuse and not dismiss an autistic person's experience merely because a neurotypical person might not experience the same behaviour as abusive.

A typical example is the concept of 'teasing', which is often experienced by autistic people as distressing because it can be very difficult to determine whether a comment is intended to be taken literally. Repeated 'teasing' of an autistic person who is distressed by it is a common form of bullying.

Autistic people may experience social exclusion, which can be a form of psychological abuse. Sometimes this is deliberate discrimination. However, it can also, readily, occur simply because others are unaware the person is autistic and are hurt or offended by what, from a neurotypical perspective, they may perceive as rudeness, when they would be more tolerant if they were aware of the person's autism.

Another example is the issue of honesty. Autistic perceptions of honesty tend to be much more black and white than neurotypical perceptions. Consequently, an autistic person may consider all statements which are not literally true to be lies. This lack of mutual understanding between autistic people and neurotypical professionals can result in behaviour which the neurotypical professional considers entirely normal being experienced as a violation of trust by the autistic person.

EXAMPLE

A neurotypical counsellor assures Issac that his conversations with her are confidential. After the counselling sessions have finished, Issac receives a copy of the report which his counsellor has sent to his GP summarizing the outcome of their sessions. She considers this an entirely normal action. To her it is just a summary and does not contain the types of details she would consider confidential. From Issac's point of view, however, the assurance of confidentiality was an absolute. The counsellor had not drawn his attention to her mention of feedback to his GP during their discussion about confidentiality. So Issac experiences this as a betrayal of trust and feels angry. On a future occasion, he refuses an offer of counselling, saying that he can't trust counsellors.

What (if anything) do you think the counsellor could have done differently?

Can you think of any other situations which an autistic person might experience as psychological abuse, where the other people might not perceive the behaviour as abusive?

Blaming and controlling behaviours towards autistic people are particularly common. Autistic people who speak and are not identified as having an intellectual disability are frequently treated as culpable for making social errors which are a result of being autistic – because others (often unthinkingly) assume that someone who is intellectually able should 'know better'. Controlling behaviours towards autistic people are often excused as being a necessary response to an autistic person's 'challenging' behaviour (i.e. victim blaming). These include inappropriate and unnecessary restraint (including inappropriate use of medication), unnecessarily rigid and inappropriate policies and procedures.

Controlling and paternalistic behaviours towards autistic people are also often excused as being 'in their best interests'. Disabled children and adults are frequently treated in ways which are inappropriate for their chronological age and paternalistic cultures remain deeply embedded and widespread within special schooling, care environments and in healthcare.

EXAMPLE

Ferenc Virag, an autistic artist, lives in specialist residential provision. He has a particular focus on light and shade and is interested in working with glass. Since at least 2004, Ferenc has been expressing his desire to have his own kiln. Ferenc is a meticulous and careful person with good fine motor control. Ferenc's friend, Dinah Murray, remarks that staff always promise to 'look into it' but nothing ever happens. On one occasion, Ferenc showed his drawing of a kiln to a member of the administrative staff. She responded by saying 'No, Ferenc! You know very well that it's too dangerous.'

Dinah arranged for Ferenc to visit a local jewellery school accompanied by his support worker and a manager. Ferenc rolled up his sleeves as soon as he realized he was being allowed to cut glass, and proceeded to cut a set of perfectly matched straight-edged rectangular small panes which stacked into a gleamingly varied transparent block. He did this with immaculate efficiency and speed. The jewellery school instructor explained the pros and cons of the two small kilns she uses. Ferenc again made it clear that he would very much like one of his own. By highlighting the importance of person-centred care and pointing to MCA principles, Dinah was finally able to persuade staff to support Ferenc in getting a kiln of his own.

Ferenc finally, in 2017, was enabled to obtain a kiln, tools and materials. Since then the limitations of this small kiln have sharpened his ambition to develop glass-blowing skills. Ferenc was happy for me to tell the story of his long wait for a kiln in this book, and his hopes for the future.

The background to Ferenc's story is told in Murray (2013). Real names are used at Ferenc's request.

> How do you think Ferenc felt when his requests for a kiln were not acted on?
>
> Can you think of examples of risk-averse practice from your own experience?

Another common experience for autistic people is that of being isolated and excluded from social groups. This can easily occur inadvertently as a result of misunderstandings (such as an assumption that an autistic person does not wish to interact) or uncertainty as to how to facilitate the inclusion of an autistic person. However, exclusion from social groups can readily become a persistent experience for autistic people and, when the exclusion is involuntary and unwelcome, can be abusive. Effective strategies for making social environments 'autistic friendly' include:

- clear, consistent and detailed information about times, locations and expectations

- time to adjust to new environments and to process information or questions

- absence of direct pressure to interact (e.g. being asked a direct question in front of an audience)

- facilitated opportunities for interaction (e.g. being part of a small group to whom questions are generally directed where it is clear that anyone is free to respond; being 'introduced' to people)

- if possible, a quiet, interaction-free space to retreat to

- tolerance and forgiveness of social 'errors'.

8.2.5 Financial or material abuse

Financial abuse occurs in a variety of situations and forms. So-called 'mate' crime, exploitation by those who claim to be friends, is a form of abuse which autistic people are particularly likely to experience. A full 80% of autistic people over the age of 16 report having been a victim of mate crime (Wirral Autistic Society 2015). It can be very difficult for autistic people to distinguish between stated intent and actual intent. In other words, autistic people are generally very trusting and tend to believe what people say. This can increase vulnerability to exploitation of all types.

Autistic adults and children also experience financial abuse from those in positions of trust with responsibility for supporting an individual with managing their money or financial affairs.

8.2.6 Modern slavery

There is no definitive evidence that autistic people are at increased risk of this form of abuse. However, recent forced labour and labour exploitation cases in which the victims have been British nationals do appear to involve the victimization of individuals with various vulnerabilities, such as homelessness, learning disability, mental health issues and autism.

8.2.7 Discriminatory abuse

Disability discrimination, unfortunately, remains remarkably widespread and difficult to eliminate. The Equality Act 2010 (and its forerunner the Disability Discrimination Act 1995) is a positive step, but its weakness in practice limits its practical benefits. Disability discrimination is extremely difficult to prove and day-to-day struggles to obtain the most basic adjustments and establish that they are 'reasonable' are the norm for disabled people.

Autism is an invisible disability. There is no obvious sign that someone is autistic. This has positive and negative implications in terms of discrimination. On the one hand, it is possible for some autistic people to avoid the risk of discrimination by not disclosing our disability. Many autistic people feel forced to do this at times (especially in order to access employment). However, trying to 'act the part' of a neurotypical person (often referred to as 'masking') is usually very demanding and stressful and is rarely an entirely positive experience.

On the other hand, the invisibility of autism leads many autistic people to constantly have the existence, reality and severity of autistic difficulties questioned, denied or trivialized. Autistic people who use speech and do not have an intellectual disability are often assumed (even by some autism professionals) to have a 'mild' form of autism. This is a dubious assumption and for many individuals it is highly unhelpful. As I discussed in Chapter 3, autistic people typically have 'spiky' profiles – we tend to have highly varying levels of ability and disability which are not particularly consistent across different skills. So autistic people also experience discrimination in the form of being treated as not disabled or as 'not really' disabled.

Discrimination and discriminatory abuse are widespread and most autistic people experience them frequently. But it is also fair to say that there are autistic people who tend to ascribe every negative experience to discrimination and struggle to recognize the difference between fair and reasonable differentiation on objective grounds (such as giving different grades to recognize different levels of academic attainment) and unreasonable discrimination on the grounds of a protected characteristic (such as disability). In combination with obsessiveness and focus on details, this common autistic difficulty can result in an autistic person failing to be heard when seeking to report actual abuse or discrimination.

EXAMPLE

Morgan (23) submitted a formal complaint to her council via their complaints process. She attached 25 documents, setting out a two-year long history of her complaints to Horizons Care Agency (who provided her support workers). All of her complaints alleged discrimination and psychological abuse. She described trivial events in great detail. These included an incident on a day trip to the seaside when, she alleged, a support worker discriminated against her because she asked if she would like an ice cream, but didn't ask what flavour she wanted and returned with a vanilla cone instead of the strawberry one she would have preferred. Another complaint concerned what she described as 'bullying' by another support worker who had pushed a note under her door one evening reminding her of an appointment the next day. She viewed this as bullying because he had not knocked on her door and spoken to her in person.

The council believed that it had conscientiously considered and responded to the complaint, although it concluded that it was unfounded. The council helped Morgan to move her support to another agency (Sunshine Support).

Morgan was not satisfied with the council's response and continued to write letters to the Ombudsman, the CQC and her MP about her previous allegations. Soon she made new allegations of verbal abuse and bullying about a member of staff from Sunshine Support and began to include these in her regular complaint letters.

How do you think council staff would have felt about Morgan's complaints?

What do you think would be likely to be the outcome of any investigations undertaken into Morgan's new allegations?

What might the consequences of those reactions be for Morgan, if (from an objective perspective) Morgan is actually now experiencing ongoing psychological abuse (such as bullying and verbal abuse) from a member of staff from Sunshine Support?

8.2.8 Organizational abuse

When considering organizational abuse, thoughts inevitably turn to the Winterbourne View case. It is undoubtedly the case that a significant proportion of those detained in assessment and treatment units and in other institutional care environments are autistic. Abusive cultures must be recognized and challenged and it is important to be aware of the potential for care environments to develop into abusive environments and develop strong approaches to prevention.

Total attachment theory suggests that abusive care environments may be more likely to develop where staff become overwhelmed by the pressures of the caring role and respond by dissociating and detaching emotionally from those who they are caring for (Harbottle *et al.* 2014).

EXAMPLE

Sisi (an autistic adult who does not speak) is rocking and staring at the floor. Ian – a care worker – comes towards Sisi, sits on the floor in front of her and says 'Hello'. Sisi jumps up, screams and pushes Ian away from her.

Ian describes the incident to his line manager: 'I tried to engage Sisi but she didn't like me saying "Hello" to her and pushed me away. Perhaps she would engage better with a female worker?'

How might Sisi see the encounter? Perhaps she was watching a fascinating pattern of sunlight on the floor and enjoying the sensory experience. Suddenly an object disrupted the pattern which made it 'wrong' and she needed to get her pattern back to make it 'right' again. She expressed her distress at the disruption by screaming and pushed the object out of the way of the rays of sunlight.

Can you think of any situations in which an autistic person's behaviour might put them at particular risk of organizational abuse, especially where staff working with them may not understand or relate to the causes of their behaviour?

Autistic people may be particularly likely to experience organizational abuse. Autistic people can present with behaviour which poses significant challenges for staff working with them. If staff struggle to understand and relate to the likely causes of an autistic person's behaviour, then they can easily become overwhelmed.

Key factors:

DIFFERENT WAYS OF SEEING THE WORLD

Autistic people see the world in a fundamentally different way to people who are not autistic. The majority of people in society (approximately 99%) are not autistic. Therefore, it is highly probable that the majority of care workers are not autistic. One understanding of some of the cognitive issues in autism suggests that autistic people tend to be strong at systemizing (the drive to analyse and construct systems) whilst not being as naturally inclined towards intuitive or empathetic thinking (Baron-Cohen 2009; De Martino *et al.* 2008). Within the care sector, on the other hand, empathetic thinking and behaviours are strongly encouraged and individuals with strong intuitive or empathetic thinking and behaviours may be more likely to be selected for care work during recruitment processes. This can result in a particularly wide gulf between an autistic person's perspective and the perspective of the care worker who is supporting them.

BEHAVIOURIST APPROACHES

Behaviourist approaches are ubiquitous within care services. Positive Behaviour Support (PBS) has been widely adopted and is widely trained as the 'gold standard' of support for those presenting with behaviour which challenges (many of whom will be autistic). As the National Autism Project report highlights, 'PBS is built upon theory and an evidence base that is not autism specific' (Iemmi *et al.* 2017, p.90). In theory, PBS is person-centred, includes the perspective of the autistic person, and has the goal to enhance quality of life. In practice, however, PBS is all too often simply used as a label for crude behaviourist approaches which 'train' individuals to stop displaying a behaviour which is deemed 'inappropriate' by others. The functional analysis (usually using the 'ABC' approach)[31] advocated by PBS focuses on 'triggers' of 'behaviour' and 'consequences'. This promotes a focus on containment and management of the 'behaviour' that is troubling or challenging to neurotypical staff members and their perceptions of what immediately 'set it off'.

Behaviourist approaches can form a useful part of a professional 'toolkit' and can be beneficial when used appropriately – for example to support an autistic person to manage an obsessive-compulsive behaviour which is troubling them. However, they do not address or deal with the actual underlying causes of behaviour. When they are used inappropriately, even by well-meaning staff, they can easily become a form of organizational abuse. An autistic person may well behave in a manner which does not conform to the needs or expectations of a care environment and which challenges those around them. Underlying causes are likely to include pain, sensory distress and acute stress. 'Training' an autistic person to stop displaying their distress, whilst failing to address the environmental causes of that distress, is abusive.

POOR UNDERSTANDING OF AUTISM EVEN WITHIN SUPPOSEDLY AUTISM SPECIALIST SERVICES

Issues (1) and (2) are worsened by the poor level of knowledge and understanding of autism amongst staff. In my experience, few staff have had access to more than basic 'awareness' training, which is wholly inadequate. Even where staff have had more advanced training, the content is often largely theoretical and lacking in practical strategies for actually working with autistic people day to day. Most autism training presents a rather dated model of autism in terms of differences from the neurotypical (predominantly social) 'norm' as the problem, rather than addressing causes of stress and distress for autistic people and how these can be reduced in the environment. This reinforces a perception that 'normalization' is an appropriate goal of support for autistic people.

Poor understanding of autism at the management level can (usually inadvertently) lead to policies and practices which are not at all autistic friendly. A common example is the prevalence of approaches to working with autistic people which impose constant activity and constant social interaction. Many autistic people need large amounts of 'downtime' with low levels of activity and an absence of social interaction. This can be vital to autistic wellbeing. Rarely is this respected by care services, where regulatory regimes, commissioning systems and management approaches all tend to operate on the unspoken assumption that imposing constant activity and social interaction on service users indicates 'good' care.

8.2.9 Neglect and acts of omission

One key issue for autistic people in this area is access to healthcare. The autistic population has increased health risks and reduced life expectancy at the same time as facing multiple obstacles to accessing healthcare (Doherty *et al.* 2020; Westminster Commission on Autism 2016). Current pressures on local authority budgets mean that it is ever harder for autistic people to access support to: eat nutritious meals, monitor health conditions, obtain and take medication and communicate with health professionals. NHS pressures mean that health services are more noisy, busy and chaotic and often require coping with long waits to access. Increasingly, healthcare resources are rationed by 'gatekeeping' procedures such as telephone triage systems using algorithms which depend for their accuracy on the patient communicating their sensory experiences in a way which is consistent with descriptions written by neurotypical people.

As a result, it is very easy for an autistic person to be inadvertently neglected and excluded from access to essential resources, particularly healthcare.

8.2.10 Self-neglect

In some instances, self-neglect can be a safeguarding concern. Where an adult is unable to protect themselves by controlling their own behaviour, they may need external support to protect them from self-neglect. Autistic people may self-neglect in a variety of ways, including:

- poor self-care due to lack of social awareness and/or sensory factors
- poor self-care due to inertia or catatonic symptoms
- poor self-care due to executive function deficits (poor sequencing, organizing)
- hoarding (autistic rigidity can lead to OCD)
- eating disorders.

8.2.11 Patterns of abuse

It is particularly important for autistic people that professionals record and appropriately share information in order to identify patterns of abuse. Autistic people may have difficulties with autobiographical memory (recall of personal experiences) and may not retain all their experiences over time.

8.3 Prevention

In their relationships with families, children and vulnerable adults, social workers are well positioned to undertake essential preventive work to reduce the risk of victimization. One of the most significant sources of risk is over-protective and paternalistic attitudes towards autistic children and adults (especially those with intellectual disability).

8.3.1 The 'prison of protection' (Hingsburger and Tough 2002)

As a society, we tend to treat children with disabilities and adults with intellectual disabilities (of whom about one-third are autistic (NHS Digital 2012)) in over-protective and paternalistic ways. Parents (understandably) are keen to protect their disabled children and professionals, families and friends alike can unconsciously tend to 'shelter' disabled children and adults from access to age-appropriate information (for example about sex); from relationships with people outside of their immediate family and carers – including with non-disabled peers (e.g. by attending special school); from making unwise or risky decisions (a normal part of growing up for most young people); and from wider society (e.g. by attending special after-school and holiday clubs, etc.). Disabled children, particularly those with the highest levels of need, are often effectively excluded from mainstream activities, although this exclusion is rarely acknowledged. The combined effect of these apparently protective measures has been criticized as forming a 'prison of protection' around disabled children and adults (see Figure 8.1) which actually results in increased vulnerability because they lose opportunities to learn knowledge and skills and to develop relationships essential to protecting themselves from exploitation and abuse.

Autistic children and adults are likely to be particularly adversely affected by these factors. This is because central autistic characteristics include difficulties with learning social rules, learning through experience (rather than rote or book learning), generalizing social knowledge from one situation to another and forming and maintaining social relationships. So, it is more difficult in the first place for autistic people to learn the knowledge and skills needed to protect ourselves and we are also likely to find it difficult to form a robust, broad social network. If autistic people also experience a 'prison of protection', we are likely to be left extremely vulnerable to exploitation, manipulation and abuse.

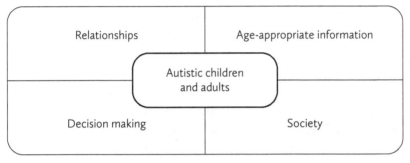

Figure 8.1 The 'Prison of Protection' (adapted from Hingsburger and Tough 2002)

8.3.2 Under-estimating vulnerability

Those autistic adults who do not have an intellectual disability, however, often encounter the converse problem of under-protective attitudes from professionals, family members and others who do not see them as vulnerable due to their intellectual ability. Autistic individuals tend to have a much more 'spiky profile' than non-autistic individuals. In other words, we may be very capable in some areas whilst struggling with other areas. The pattern of these abilities and disability may be confusing and appear contradictory to people unfamiliar with autism. For example, it is common for autistic people to be 'book smart' (such as having high academic qualifications) whilst struggling to pick up and understand 'street wise' knowledge. Common areas of difficulty include anticipating how others will perceive behaviour, knowing what other people typically do in common situations and generalizing knowledge from one situation to others.

All autistic people may also encounter some difficulties with people around them under-estimating their vulnerability in certain ways (even whilst they may also be over-estimating their vulnerability in other ways). For example, an autistic person who is very good at maths may be assumed not to be at risk of financial exploitation. But they may in fact be at high risk of being defrauded because they tend to believe what people tell them and lack the social experience to recognize a probable scam.

8.3.3 Effective preventive measures

Effective preventive work in safeguarding autistic people needs to include education: education of those working in social care about the autism-specific risks of both over- and under-estimating vulnerability; and education of all autistic children, young people and adults in important social, cultural, sexual and financial knowledge. This education should include: healthy and unhealthy relationships, unwritten social rules, recognizing exploitation and manipulation and explicit teaching of 'common sense' knowledge.

EXAMPLE

Joe (22) is autistic and has a learning disability. He had been working with his support workers on learning to cross the road independently. His support workers had used visual supports and repeated practice to teach Joe how to use different types of pedestrian crossing. Joe set out on his first independent journey, along a familiar route using a pedestrian crossing. While he was waiting for the lights to change (and the green man to be displayed), a member of the public stepped off the kerb a few metres away from the crossing and began to cross the road. Joe yelled at the man and told him that he needed to use the pedestrian crossing and wait for the green man (as Joe himself had been taught to do). The man reversed his steps and came back towards the pedestrian crossing. He walked straight up to Joe and punched him in the face.

Anyone can be a victim of crime, but it is notable that Joe's support workers (with the best of intentions) had taught him the explicit rules of crossing the road, but no one had thought to teach him the unwritten rule that most adults do not like strangers telling them what to do and may react badly in such a situation.

> Can you think of any other situations in which not understanding 'unwritten rules' could put an autistic person at risk of abuse?

Some good practice exists in certain services for autistic children – particularly in special schools. But it is common for autistic children attending mainstream schools not to be included in specialist provision. The nature of autism means that *all* autistic children need specialist and explicit teaching in these areas because they do not pick up this sort of learning from their peers, as typically developing children do.

Effective prevention more broadly can be promoted through increased autonomy and the reduction of inappropriate, paternalistic practices. Autistic people who are supported to make their own decisions and take appropriate risks are more likely to learn to manage risky situations effectively.

8.4 Safeguarding enquiries

8.4.1 Involvement, advocacy and questioning

Progress is being made on ensuring that the person being safeguarded is more involved and that their views are more central to safeguarding work. Making Safeguarding Personal, the Care Act advocacy provisions, the Children Act and Signs of Safety (amongst other developments) have aided this progress. However, paternalistic and risk-averse cultures persist in patches throughout the system. Safeguarding continues, all too often, to be something done to people rather than truly with them: person-centred in name only.

The communication difficulties inherent to autism can make it even more difficult to ensure that autistic people have a genuine voice within safeguarding processes and that their voice carries weight when set alongside professional views. There are small adaptations that professionals can make which can greatly improve communication for an autistic person. These are to:

- provide information in writing (with pictures where appropriate) – as simple an adaptation as writing a bullet

> point list or a quick email after a meeting, summarizing the
> key information covered, can really help

- allow and facilitate communication from the autistic person
  in alternative formats (such as drawings, writing, text
  messages, email, etc.)

- adapt your communication style towards being unusually
  blunt, direct and honest

- allow processing time (providing periods of silence, without
  staring at the person, to allow an autistic person to process
  what you have said)

- provide new information and questions in advance of asking
  for a response – again to allow sufficient processing time.

It is fairly easy for practitioners to recognize that these sorts of
adaptations are needed when communicating with an autistic person
who has an intellectual disability and/or who does not communicate
through speech. But these sorts of adaptations are often just
as important for autistic people who do not have an intellectual
disability and for those who do use speech to communicate. Being
perceived as 'high-functioning' disguises the extent of the huge
difference between how neurotypical people communicate and how
autistic people communicate. Adaptations such as those above can
make all the difference in helping to bridge that gulf and improve
communication between autistic people and professionals.

Many autistic adults and children, including those who use
speech, may need an advocate, supporter or intermediary to achieve
effective communication with professionals, especially under the
stress of a safeguarding enquiry. The potential conflict of interest of
involving family members or existing staff to support communication
can, in some situations, be appropriately outweighed by an autistic
person's need for familiar support. An autistic person may not be
able to quickly adapt to an unfamiliar person and family members,
friends or existing paid carers may be uniquely able to interpret an
autistic person's particular style of communication.

Nevertheless, there will, of course, be situations where
it is imperative to exclude some or all familiar people from

communication with the autistic person. This should not be done arbitrarily or unnecessarily, but, where the familiar person is potentially implicated in the safeguarding concern, it may be essential to ensure that the autistic person is provided with opportunities to communicate independently of possible influence. In many such circumstances, the autistic person may be entitled to statutory advocacy. However, care should be taken to ensure that an advocate actually has sufficient knowledge and expertise specifically in autism to communicate effectively with the autistic individual. An advocate without sufficient autism-specific knowledge and skills is unlikely to be effective at ensuring the autistic person is fully involved in the safeguarding process.

Where legal proceedings are likely and/or the police are involved, early steps should be taken (when appropriate) to secure the support of a registered intermediary with suitable autism-specific experience. Excellent good practice advice on preparation for questioning autistic people is available (see The Advocate's Gateway 2016) and should be carefully followed.

8.4.2 Risk assessment and decision making

Research suggests that autistic people are more likely to make decisions in logical and analytical ways, whereas neurotypical people are more likely to make decisions in emotional and intuitive ways which take account of social context (De Martino *et al.* 2008). Both decision-making styles have strengths and weaknesses.

Generally, autistic people are more likely to be risk averse than neurotypical individuals. However, an autistic person may be less likely to foresee, and so be able to avoid, social risks. Accurately foreseeing the potential emotions and behaviour of others is particularly difficult for most autistic people (as in the above example of Joe). Consequences that may be obvious to others are quite likely to be invisible from an autistic point of view.

It may, therefore, be a highly effective safeguarding intervention to provide an autistic person with information about and support to understand relevant social behaviours or reactions. It is not particularly helpful to just tell an autistic person to do or not do something, assuming that the reasons why are obvious. It is likely to be helpful to spell out and explain the likely thoughts, emotions and motivations of other people and how these are likely to be affected by various factors.

Many autistic people find making decisions difficult, demanding, tiring and overwhelming. We may struggle to make some decisions at all. Ways to support decision making are set out in Chapter 7.

8.5 Chapter summary and key points

- Autistic adults and children experience high rates of victimization across virtually all types of abuse and neglect. Like many disabled people, autistic people may be at increased risk due to perceptions of vulnerability, isolation and/or behaviours which do not conform to social norms.

- 'High-functioning' autistic people are often wrongly assumed not to be vulnerable due to their language and intellectual skills. However, they too experience high rates of victimization.

- Autistic people are generally law-abiding, but may (mostly inadvertently) encounter the criminal justice system.

- Over-protection and paternalism towards autistic children and adults increases vulnerability. Good quality autism-specific education around sexuality and social interaction and the promotion of autonomy increase safety.

Recommended resources

Triple A (All About Autism) project, Cumbria. Accessed on 6/12/19 at http://tripleaproject.org.uk.

Health Education England (2019) *Core Capabilities Framework for Supporting Autistic People.* Capabilities 9, 10 and 15. London: Department of Health and Social Care. Accessed on 6/12/19 at www.skillsforhealth.org.uk/learningdisabilityandautismframeworks.

■ CHAPTER 9 ■

Behaviour which May Challenge and Autism

Autistic adults and children may sometimes (or even quite often) behave in ways which others may find challenging. Sometimes this is simply a matter of perspective and all that is required is improved tolerance, acceptance and understanding from the non-autistic world around us. However, more commonly in social work practice, practitioners will encounter behaviour which infringes or seriously risks infringing the human rights of others and/or is seriously harmful to the person themselves. Examples would be:

- violent behaviour

- behaviour which causes others to believe they are at risk of violence from the person

- severe self-injurious behaviour[32]

- repeated, frequent 'running away'.

These types of 'challenging' behaviours are *not* an inevitable consequence of autism: *autism does not cause 'behaviours'*. It is the interaction between the autistic person's environment and the autistic person which results in the behaviour that others consider 'challenging' (MacDonald 2018). It is absolutely vital that those with responsibility for supporting autistic people day to day and those making strategic decisions about the placement or support needs of autistic people do not accept ongoing instances of 'challenging behaviour' as some inevitable result of labels like 'autism', 'severe', 'complex' and so on. Persistently or regularly behaving in such ways is likely to *indicate distress* and something about the situation (other than just the person's behaviour) needs to change (National Autistic Taskforce 2019).

9.1 Overload: fight, freeze or flight

When distressed, some autistic people shut down while others become aggressive or run away. These behaviours are a result of a normal, human, neurobiological response to perceived threat, but which appears to be much more frequently and readily triggered in autistic people than in typically developing people (Caldwell 2014) (see Chapter 6). An autistic person may become overloaded by the stimuli they are experiencing and this can trigger an overwhelming 'autonomic storm' (Ramachandran 2011). This massive over-reaction within an autistic person's brain triggers the body's self-defence system. The exact response may vary between individuals, but measurable physiological changes take place and the instinctive fight–freeze–flight response is triggered.

9.2 Managing behaviour: reaction

Once an autistic person is experiencing an overload at this level, they are unlikely to be able to process or respond to verbal communication and may well be largely oblivious to the presence and behaviours of others, except as a source of distress. Most 'de-escalation strategies' tend to rely on a non-autistic understanding of verbal communication and/or body language and are, therefore, likely to be of limited use. Similarly, responses which involve trying to reason with the person are unlikely to be at all helpful. To respond effectively, what is critical is an empathetic willingness to consider the autistic person's perspective and experience. From our perspective, we are experiencing what feels like a life-threatening emergency. What we need is to feel safe!

Responses which are likely to be helpful are to:

- Act for essential safety. If an autistic person is lashing out, then move other people away. In the very rare circumstance of a genuine emergency situation involving extreme danger (such as the autistic person running into a road with fast-moving traffic), the use of a minimum level and duration of restraint may be justified.[33]

- Set aside what you were trying to do. Recognize that it is no longer appropriate to focus on whatever was occurring just before the autistic person became this distressed and that they are no longer able to reason or engage.

- Crucially (and counter-intuitively for most non-autistic people), *stop* trying to communicate! Just shut up. Really!

- Reduce sensory and other demands. Whatever your view of what may have caused the autistic person to become this overloaded, this is likely to help:

  - move people away

  - stop people from staring at them

  - provide access to a safe space (and a clear route free of people to reach it); individuals may vary in what they find 'safe', but examples are likely to be a familiar retreat like a bed or a sensory room, corners of rooms, under tables, etc.

  - avoid physical contact (touch) with the person, unless you are certain that they find physical contact pleasurable or reassuring (likely to be strong, rhythmic touch – such as firm stroking or being tightly held)

  - turn off lights and reduce noise as much as possible

  - provide sensory protection options such as sunglasses and noise-cancelling headphones within reach.

- Provide comfort. The form this takes may vary between individuals. It may help for a familiar person to be with them, sharing their space and focus but not verbally interacting. It may help to provide a familiar, comforting object or experience such as an iPad, comfort toy or familiar video.

- Meet physical needs – provide access to food and drink, the opportunity to go to the toilet, and the opportunity to rest/

sleep. This is important because some autistic people may not receive or respond to internal body signals. The unmet need may cause or increase the distress and the distress may interfere with their ability to identify or meet the need.

- Slowly use autistic-friendly communication and feedback (described in far more detail in Caldwell (2014) and other writing on intensive interaction).

- Confront your own discomfort with silence and lack of distractions. Many non-autistic people find silence awkward and feel as if they always need to be doing something. Being quiet and not interacting may not come naturally.

The point of all the above is to support the person to feel safe and recover in their own time. However, achieving a good quality of life for autistic people requires an approach which seeks to enable a pattern of life in which we are able to avoid experiencing distress to a level so high that the fight–freeze–flight response is triggered.

9.3 Managing behaviour: prevention

Before setting out a strategic approach to preventing behaviour which may challenge in autistic people, I need to address some fundamental issues around the goals of any intervention. Consider first *whether* the autistic person's behaviour genuinely requires modification. As I mentioned at the beginning of this chapter, it is discriminatory and can be harmful to attempt to modify behaviour which is merely not 'normal'.

Having dealt with that issue, I acknowledge of course that everyone in society needs to be able to respect the human rights of others and avoid breaking the law. If an autistic person is behaving in a way which jeopardizes one or both of those, it is inevitably tempting to focus on the behaviour itself and set a goal of eliminating that behaviour. However, this is short-sighted, often ineffective and can be harmful because:

1. If the person's behaviour indicates they are distressed, focusing on eliminating the behaviour may result in an autistic person

who is just as distressed but has been 'trained' to hide their distress!

2. Some autistic people who are very distressed become passive, compliant, withdrawn and even catatonic. Because these individuals are not behaving in a way which others find challenging, they are easily overlooked and they remain trapped in a distressing environment/situation.

3. Generally, those carrying out a 'functional analysis' of an autistic person's behaviour are not autistic. This results in a significant risk of misperception and bias due to the radical difference in perspective between the autistic person and the person completing the analysis.

EXAMPLE

Over many years of running training sessions about autism, I have occasionally used an exercise which (unscientifically) often illustrates these different perspectives. Small groups are each given a card which describes a very simple behaviour, such as: walking back and forth across a room; taking all her clothes off; staring out of a window; saying the words 'fifteen, fifteen, fifteen'. Groups are asked to brainstorm as many different explanations for the behaviour as they can come up with. After five to ten minutes, groups are asked to list the explanations they came up with. I then categorize the explanations (roughly) into the following categories:

- functional explanations (e.g. to get something)

- cognitive explanations (e.g. because she's thinking it through)

- emotional explanations (e.g. because he's frustrated)

- communicative explanations (e.g. he's trying to tell us that he doesn't like an activity)

- sensory explanations (e.g. because she likes the feel of the carpet)

- social/behavioural explanations (e.g. because they don't like me).

224 ■ SOCIAL WORK WITH AUTISTIC PEOPLE

Most groups come up with at least one explanation in each category, but often many more in some categories than others. In my experience, there appears to be a general pattern to this. Groups with a majority of non-autistic people tend to come up with the largest numbers of explanations in these three categories: emotional, communicative and social/behavioural.

When given exactly the same behaviours, groups with a majority of autistic people tend to come up with the largest numbers of explanations in these three categories: functional, cognitive and sensory.

I would stress that this is merely a description of my experience and personal conclusions, not any sort of robust research. Nevertheless, I suspect that this apparent pattern may indicate that the differences in perspective between autistic and non-autistic people could (and, in my experience, does) lead to bias when non-autistic people attempt to analyse motivations/causes which may underlie the behaviour of an autistic person.

> Do you think you consider all the possible causes of an autistic person's behaviour before coming to any conclusions about why they are behaving in a particular way?
>
> What factors might influence your interpretation of an autistic person's behaviour?

For these reasons, in my view it is more ethically sound (and quite possibly more effective) to see 'challenging behaviour' in autistic people as merely one symptom of distress and to focus on identifying and alleviating the source(s) of distress.

To achieve this, I consider it vital to recognize autistic experiences of stress and to think in terms of overall stress management. To do this we need to be clear about what stress is. As Richard Mills says:

> According to the NHS, stress is the feeling of being under too much mental or emotional pressure. Pressure turns into stress when you feel unable to cope. The NHS description helps us to distinguish between stress, usually a result of external forces, and anxiety, which is more frequently found within the person and manifests in the form of worrying, and persistent thoughts. Too often the two are joined

together and, although related, they are different and the approaches to manage them will need to reflect this. (Mills 2016, p.1)

I have already discussed a significant part of what is needed in Chapter 4, under the heading 'Tackle environmental and other stressors'. The goal is to support autistic people to experience a world which is as comfortable, certain and predictable as possible.

When considering factors which might be causing an autistic person's distress (whether or not expressed through behaviour which may challenge others), we need to go beyond the widespread focus on 'triggers' and ABC charts (drawn from the behaviourist approach of Positive Behaviour Support (PBS) (see Caldwell 2014, Chapter 8, and Milton 2018 for detailed critique of PBS). In my experience, even when done reasonably well, excessive focus on 'triggers' can easily result in not being able to see the wood for the trees. So, rather than focusing on apparent immediate 'triggers', I would encourage a genuine collaboration with an autistic person to seek to identify and resolve or manage the underlying source(s) of distress.

Of course, many autistic people will be unable to communicate and may themselves be unable to identify the cause of their distress. As a result, it is often necessary to simply start from a checklist and consider the most likely possibilities. Unfortunately, such lists are often written by (undoubtedly well-meaning) professionals or family members working from a non-autistic perspective. In my view, it helps if your checklist has been written by autistic people! Here is one that was. Consider:

1. Abuse or mistreatment – are they currently experiencing abuse or mistreatment? Have they experienced trauma in the past (including experiences of detention, restraint – physical, chemical or psychological – or bullying)?

2. Medical issues – including undetected pain, depression and medication side effects.

3. Functional communication – what is being done to support them to develop functional communication in any form?

4. Autonomy – respect and getting needs met: is their communication (in whatever form) respected? Are they able

to get their needs met by non-aggressive means? Is their autonomy respected? Are they treated as younger than their chronological age (e.g. an adult being treated like a child)?

5. Autonomy – assumptions and trust: is their competence presumed? Are they trusted? Are people around them honest with them or do they lie (including to 'reassure' or avoid distress)?

6. Sensory needs – do they have access to sufficient sensory stimulation of the type(s) they need? Are they sufficiently protected from sources of sensory distress/overload?

7. Being allowed to say 'no' – are they allowed to say 'no' to non-essential things they dislike or are not interested in, for example discos, parties, social interaction or having their belongings touched/moved?

8. Coping with change – are they being expected to cope with too much change, too quickly and/or without sufficient preparation and support? Have they been given accurate, honest information?

9. Downtime and privacy – are they getting enough downtime (i.e. time when they are not expected to participate in activity or interaction)? Do they have sufficient personal privacy?

10. Emotional expression – is sadness, grief or anxiety being expressed as anger or irritability? (Adapted and summarized from Chavisory 2014)

Alongside preventing and minimizing causes of distress, it is also important to support autistic people to develop and use strategies to recognize and anticipate when our stress levels are increasing and manage our own needs both preventatively and responsively. Potentially useful self-management strategies include:

- Empowering the autistic person to meet their sensory needs. There are two main areas to think about: sensory protection (where someone experiences too much sensory input) and sensory stimulation (where someone experiences insufficient sensory input and/or finds one or more types of sensory stimulation calming or pleasurable). Exactly what is needed will vary from person to person. So, for example, empowering sensory protection could involve providing unrestricted access to:

- sunglasses, coloured lenses, coloured filters
- noise-cancelling headphones, ear defenders
- anything else the person finds helpful to reduce sensory distress.

Empowering sensory stimulation could include providing unrestricted access to:

- a trampoline
- open, outdoor space
- fidget toys
- items to spin
- a weighted vest or blanket
- anything else the person finds stress reducing or pleasurable.

Where entirely unrestricted access is not practicable, then access must at least be sufficiently regular and frequent to enable the person to meet their sensory needs effectively.

- Empowering the autistic person to meet their needs for certainty, predictability and information. Ways to do this could include:

  - Recognizing that repetition and familiarity may be comforting and pleasurable from an autistic person's perspective and respecting their autonomy rather than imposing change/variety for the benefit of support people or for the purpose of promoting 'normality'.[34]

  - Supporting the person to research an upcoming event online, such as visiting the website of the venue, finding photographs of past or similar events, obtaining information about transport options and timings.

- Supporting the person to request information from support workers/family/others (including providing non-verbal options for doing so) and respond positively to their requests for information (even where the request seems repetitive or unnecessary).

- Using timetables, schedules, planners, diaries (and ensuring unrestricted/constant access to these) and developing these to match the person's level of skill and understanding (for example, by teaching date/time/duration concepts (e.g. 'yesterday', 'tomorrow') and moving from a daily visual timetable to a week planner, introducing a diary and/or year planner, moving from pictures to written text where appropriate.

- Supporting the person to create systems and/or rules that work for them, including where these generate additional work for support people. Examples could include: 'only one new activity each week', 'a routine which involves specific times for planning and researching', or 'I prefer to go to the supermarket on a weekday during the daytime because it is not so busy then'.

- Making uncertainty or unpredictability more concrete and predictable, by:

  * Explaining why something is not certain at present, what the potential options are, when it will become certain and what it depends on, for example, rather than 'I don't know yet what we're doing this afternoon', say 'This afternoon we might play football in the park or a board game inside. If it isn't raining we'll play football, but if it rains we will stay indoors and play a board game. We will make a decision after lunch when we know what the weather is going to be like'.

  * Creating and/or identifying systems which are used when something goes wrong or something unexpected happens (see example below).

- Providing a non-verbal 'time out' card (including for those who use speech to communicate) and ensuring that all support people/family/other service users recognize and respond appropriately to a person using the card to withdraw from an activity or interaction and request time alone (or interaction-free time). Withdrawing from an interaction or activity that the autistic person is finding overwhelming is a common autistic need and is likely to enable the person to manage their own stress levels. However, in non-autistic social environments, it is often extremely difficult to communicate a wish to withdraw and to be allowed to do so without either a great deal of communication and interaction or this being interpreted as 'rude'.

- Considering the use of an emotion management scale (such as a five-point scale where five is 'overload') to support the autistic person in recognizing and communicating their emotions/level of distress.

- Planning recovery time. Over time, it is possible for an autistic adult to develop a good understanding of their overall resources and capacity for undertaking activities/interactions/ situations they find stressful. It is important to acknowledge and accept that for some autistic people the level of stress/ effort/demands involved in undertaking some activities are such that this may limit the overall quantity of what they can manage in any given day/week/year. For some autistic people, a healthy, good quality of life may well look more restricted and less productive than a 'normal' non-autistic life. This is OK. It is vital that services, commissioners and regulators recognize that a constantly 'busy' schedule of 'normal' activities is not necessarily healthy and that high-quality support includes providing downtime/recovery time (e.g. time free from interaction, time alone, time spent engaging in pleasurable, relaxing activity – including 'stimming' or 'repetitive' behaviours). So, for example, if an autistic person did their shopping in a busy supermarket this morning, it might be healthy and preferable for them to spend their afternoon alone in their bedroom playing a computer game, rather than being 'included' in a trip to a bowling alley!

- Providing unrestricted and communication-free access to safe spaces and ensuring that an autistic person has a safe space they can retreat to (whether this is a small tent, the corner of a room, their bedroom or their entire home). The safe space should be defined and designed by the autistic person themselves and must be free from sources of sensory distress, free from intrusion from others/demands to communicate and (unless desired by the autistic person themselves) not shared with any other person.

EXAMPLE

Day centre staff noticed that two of their service users (who were autistic) tended to become distressed when there was a substitution of staff members due to illness. Initially, they thought that nothing could be done about this since staff illness is inherently unpredictable. However, after receiving some advice, they created a wall display with two large squares labelled 'on-duty' and 'off-duty' and developed a routine of moving staff photos between the squares each day. The next time a staff member was off ill, they involved the two service users in removing that person's photo from the on-duty square, placing it in the off-duty square and replacing it with the photo of the substitute staff member.

Initially, this made no noticeable difference, but, over time, one of the service users began to take the lead in going to the display and moving photos as soon as anything was said about a staff member being unwell. Both individuals seemed less distressed when changes occurred. The service developed and extended the system, using it for planned absences such as holidays and to introduce new staff.

What interpretations do you think may have been previously suggested for distressed behaviour of the two service users?

How do you think the two service users may have felt before and after this change of practice?

Can you think of any situations where a similar approach might be helpful in your practice?

9.4 The wider context: preventing the breakdown of community placements and ending the inappropriate use of inpatient settings

Placement breakdown and the use of inappropriate inpatient settings are issues which affect a wide range of individuals who have learning disabilities and/or autism and/or mental health conditions. Reliable national statistics for autism specifically have only become available very recently and suggest that at least 38% of all people covered by the Transforming Care programme were autistic (both with and without a learning disability) and that, by the end of the Transforming Care programme, the numbers of autistic people in inpatient settings had risen rather than reduced (National Autistic Society 2018). Anecdotal evidence and the findings of some reviews suggest that even this is likely to be an under-estimate. For example, a recent interim report published by the CQC into the use of restraint, prolonged seclusion and segregation within inpatient settings for young people with a mental health problem, a learning disability or autism (Care Quality Commission 2019, p.18) found a substantial majority were autistic: 'Thirty-one of the 39 (79%) people in segregation we had visited by the time of this report have autism, often in association with other conditions.'

This was substantially higher than the 45% identified as autistic in data submitted by the care providers. A recent Scottish report also identifies 'that coexisting autism is a significant factor', concluding that 'those who were autistic were more likely to have challenging behaviour, more likely to be placed out-of-area in crisis, and likely to be in more expensive placements' (MacDonald 2018, p.49). Overall, the data clearly illustrates that autistic people are at particular risk of entering inpatient settings.

In many (I would argue almost *all*) cases, this is not because inpatient care is genuinely the appropriate form of care and support the person needs. Individuals (children or adults) who behave in ways which challenge services experience high levels of placement breakdown and risk ending up in inappropriate (and extremely expensive) inpatient 'care' simply because a suitable community-based care option cannot be identified (despite the cost-effectiveness of community-based care). As the Care Quality Commission (2019, p.17) puts it:

We heard stories of where the person's non-hospital, residential community placement had broken down because of a sudden or escalating challenging situation which caused staff working with the person or the family to conclude that they could no longer meet the person's needs. The person had ended up in hospital because there was nowhere else for them to go.

Inpatient settings are not an appropriate way of 'treating' behaviour which may challenge (Iemmi *et al.* 2017; National Autistic Taskforce 2019). Once admitted, the average length of stay is almost five and a half years (National Autistic Society 2018). The environment which such inpatient settings provide is often highly unsuitable for autistic people:

> Several of the wards did not have a built environment that was suitable for people with complex needs, especially for people with autism. They were noisy and had a layout that did not achieve the necessary balance between ensuring safety while allowing people access to quiet, personal space when they needed it. (Care Quality Commission 2019, p.18)

'Treatment' often consists of inappropriate medication with anti-psychotic medications (Care Quality Commission 2016b), an issue highlighted by the 'Stopping Over Medication of People with a learning disability, autism or both with psychotropic medicines' (STOMP) campaign (NHS England 2016). 'Care' is often provided by unqualified staff who have received little or no training in supporting autistic people:

> We found that several of the hospitals that we have visited did not employ staff with the necessary skills to work with people with autism who also have complex needs and challenging behaviour.
>
> In addition, many of the staff we saw, including those working directly with the people in segregation, were unqualified healthcare or nursing assistants. Many hospitals used agency staff to fill a substantial number of shifts.
>
> Some of the hospitals provided their staff with little or no training in autism. Training may amount to a brief module at induction or a basic package delivered through e-learning. This basic level of training would not fully equip staff with the skills necessary

to anticipate, deescalate or understand and interpret individual behaviours: skills essential to the care of this group of people with very complex needs. (Care Quality Commission 2019, p.19)

The medical focus of such settings encourages and perpetuates the medicalization of autistic people's 'behaviour' when, in almost all cases, what are not being provided are the basics of:

- a suitable environment

- appropriate adaptations (such as for communication and to create predictability)

- an adequate standard of care and support by staff who have a good understanding of autism and are able to empathize with an autistic perspective (National Autistic Taskforce 2019).

Following the failure of Transforming Care to actually deliver real change, it may well be that the only structural change capable of delivering a significant cultural shift away from institutional care would be for autism (and learning disability) to be removed from the definition of 'mental disorder' in the Mental Health Act – a change that would remove the basis on which these individuals are detained.

Whilst that might force rapid creation of community-based options, it would not address the basic reality that a good deal of the 'care' provided to autistic people whose behaviour may challenge, whether in institutions or in the community, is provided by poorly paid, over-worked staff, who have rarely had access to adequate practical training on autism and in environments which are not designed to suit the needs of autistic people. It is hardly surprising if people receiving such 'care' become distressed and behave in ways which others find challenging.

On a more positive note, however, there is a great deal social workers can do to contribute to improving the situation: by asking good questions; through robust professional challenge; and by seeking to commission services on the basis of the quality of the care they provide. In April 2019, the National Autistic Taskforce published *An Independent Guide to Quality Care for Autistic People* which set out, for the first time from an autistic perspective, what good quality care, particularly for those with the most 'complex' and 'challenging' needs, looks like.

Reproduced below are the key recommendations, a good practice example and the concluding comments from the *Guide*'s section on supporting autistic people whose behaviour may challenge:

KEY RECOMMENDATIONS FOR CARE PROVIDERS

- Treat the use of any physical intervention, pharmaceutical control of behaviour or any other forms of restraint as failures and seek to create a service free from physical interventions and pharmaceutical control of behaviour.

- Don't blame autism. 'Challenging' behaviours are not an inevitable consequence of autism.

- Don't label people as 'complex'; seek to understand and empathize with their perspective.

- Do not remove choice and control from an autistic person.

- Challenge proposals/decisions to remove an autistic person from their local community.

- Modify the environment to meet needs; look for underlying causes not just triggers.

- Work with, not against, the autistic person – supporting them to manage stress and recover from distress.

- Avoid focusing on behaviour 'management' at the expense of meeting needs.

- Accept and accommodate autistic behaviours that do not infringe the rights of others.

- Support autistic people to find practical ways to meet their needs which minimize overall harm to themselves and respect the rights of others.

- Recognize when service policies, placement environments or particular staff are not the right match for an individual.

- Identify when stretched public resources are leading to short-term decisions which are unlikely to be cost-effective in the long term.

- Identify when behaviour is related to an unmet need and meet the need.

Reproduced with kind permission from the
National Autistic Taskforce

GOOD PRACTICE EXAMPLE

St Clement's School is a Special School serving a rural catchment area in Highland, Scotland. Pupils range from 3 to 19 years and have a diverse range of needs. A substantial majority are autistic and many have complex needs. Under headteacher Toni Macartney, the school has undergone an improvement process which included rapid and sustained reduction in the use of restraint to zero.

At the start of the process the school needed to improve in a number of areas, particularly in the provision offered to autistic pupils, a view endorsed by Education Scotland inspectors. Highlighted weaknesses included:

- some pupils 'with autism spectrum disorders feel anxious during the day as their needs are not being well met'

- 'For some pupils with autism spectrum disorder, staff do not address barriers or inhibitors to learning and therefore focus on resulting behaviours'.

Working with inspectors, the school set a goal to:

'identify learning needs accurately and implement appropriate strategies to overcome barriers to learning, especially for children and young people with autism spectrum disorders'.

The whole school community (staff, pupils and parents) were engaged with an autism knowledge and development programme, which focused on supporting pupils to meet their communication, structure and sensory needs appropriately, reducing stress and distress. The school aims to maintain a zero restraints record.

✳ ✳ ✳

A good service for autistic people is one where staff try to put themselves in an autistic person's shoes, get to know them as individuals and maintain relationships with them based on trust and respect. A good service for autistic people works with them to modify their environment to meet their needs and minimize distress. A good service for autistic people offers regular opportunities for 'quiet' or downtime (but does not use this punitively) and offers regular opportunities to meet sensory stimulation needs.

Good service commissioning for autistic people is organized locally for one person at a time. Good service commission for autistic people requires working together for better long-term outcomes and proactively resists short-term decision making driven by the agendas and budgets of individual bodies.

Ever-tightening budgets and ever-present performance targets have a tendency to encourage short-termism and narrow horizons. The idea of spending now to save later or to save elsewhere – or indeed both (what is sometimes called 'diagonal accounting') – may be challenging for policy makers but is exactly the strategic approach needed to improve the life-chances and wellbeing of autistic people over the life-course.

Transformational change involves a change of attitude and culture, a new belief in what is possible, resulting in significant changes in structures and systems. This type of change is what is required to address this problem; it will include a change in relationships and a shift in mindsets from all involved.

A good service for autistic people is located in the area in which they live and have connections.

Good service commissioning for autistic people recognizes the cost-effectiveness of good quality community-based support and does not allow short-term budgetary constraints to dictate decisions which are not in the long-term interests of autistic people and their local communities.

Extract from National Autistic Taskforce
(2019, pp.34–35)

It is likely that practitioners will continue to struggle with a lack of pre-existing, appropriate community placements available to be commissioned. Rather than continuing to wait for such services to be developed, I would strongly encourage creative use of the flexibilities offered by direct payments, individual service funds and support brokerage to enable the development of bespoke care packages. Directly employing individual Personal Assistants (PAs) and commissioning support with the administrative responsibilities of employing them is, in my experience, an option which can deliver high-quality, stable, consistent support over the long term. In addition to flexibility, directly employing PAs puts the autistic person in control of their own support to a far greater degree than is possible when commissioning care providers. To ensure packages are successful and sustainable in all situations (including those where an autistic person behaves in ways which may challenge), a robust direct payment package requires:

- fully funded support brokerage to develop and initially set up the package, including: care planning; initial recruitment incorporating developing bespoke job descriptions and advertisements; ongoing support with employment paperwork and procedures such as contracts, induction and supervision

- where an individual is unable to manage a direct payment themselves, fully funded options for a competent, independent person to manage the direct payment (rather than reliance on family members)

- funding hourly rates at a level which enables recruitment and long-term retention of PAs with suitable skills and experience

- funding hourly rates at a level which allows for additional costs incurred as a result of holiday, sickness, parental leave, pension and redundancy to enable conditions of employment compatible with long-term retention

- fully funded administrative support with recruitment, HR issues and payroll

- funding for training/development of PAs

- effective planning for crisis situations

- where required, such as where a service user has fluctuating capacity and needs a PA to offer them advice and direction at times when they struggle to act in accordance with their needs or settled wishes, support (for both the person and their PA) to establish agreements about boundaries and supervision (for the PA), to enable a PA to provide this challenge, despite the service user being their employer.

The costs to local authorities of providing such packages would undoubtedly be higher than the current costs of direct payments and, possibly, greater than the typical cost of a mainstream care agency. However, it is important to consider the likely cost-effectiveness of stable community-based support in terms of (at least):

- decreasing the risk of inpatient admissions

- improved access to healthcare and, potentially, improved health

- decreasing strain on informal carers.

9.5 Crisis planning

The CQC identify placement breakdown crises as frequent precursors to admission to inappropriate inpatient settings: 'Moves were often triggered by a breakdown of the existing placement. The last such crisis had been the immediate cause of admission to hospital – which was seen as the only available option' (Care Quality Commission 2019, p.6).

As I mentioned above, good crisis planning is a vital component of keeping autistic people out of inappropriate institutional settings. Again, though, practitioners are likely to encounter a lack of pre-existing services or options available to make such plans robust and fit for purpose. In the mental health field, crisis houses across the UK provide an alternative to hospital admission (Obuaya, Stanton and Baggaley 2013). Mental health crisis houses are unlikely to provide a suitable alternative to hospital for autistic people who do not have a mental illness, but who present with behaviour which may challenge and whose current situation has broken down. However, I believe that a similar model could be developed to provide a refuge for autistic people in crisis. The purpose of a crisis house would be to provide a temporary 'safe space' whilst either: additional support or other changes are made to the previous placement/situation to make it more suitable; or a new long-term placement/situation is identified.

An ideal autistic crisis house would be autistic space, that is, space which is created and controlled by autistic people. It would provide:

- an absence of pressure and interaction

- structure and predictability (a simple, clear, unchanging routine)

- a low-arousal sensory environment

- access to sensory stimulation such as outdoor space, sensory room, etc.

- access to a range of options, adaptations and support for communication

- access to information in accessible formats (e.g. about the crisis house and about placement options).

At present, this may seem like an unrealistic dream. But I believe a dedicated autistic crisis house could be effective in preventing hospital admissions and I would encourage social workers to take a lead in promoting the idea in their area.

9.6 Chapter summary and key points

- Recognize behaviour which may challenge as indicating distress and challenge assumptions that such 'behaviours' are an inevitable consequence of autism.

- Consider whether the behaviour infringes someone else's human rights or is merely unusual (and should be accommodated).

- Ensure carers recognize the fight–freeze–flight response and that appropriate responses, focusing on reducing demands and supporting the autistic person to feel safe, are planned for and implemented in practice.

- Be wary of the likelihood of bias in non-autistic interpretations of an autistic person's behaviour.

- Focus behaviour support on the prevention of distress, working with the autistic person and using their or an autistic-written checklist to try to identify and eliminate causes of distress.

- Empower self-management strategies.

- Admission to hospital is not an appropriate way to 'treat' behaviour which may challenge.

- Identify, commission or create appropriate, bespoke community care packages, including the use of direct payments, individual service funds and support brokerage where these may be helpful.

- Plan for crises to prevent hospital admission, including considering the development of autistic-led crisis houses.

Recommended resources

Bradley, E. and Caldwell, P. (2013) 'Mental health and autism: Promoting Autism FaVourable Environments (PAVE).' *Journal on Developmental Disabilities 19*, 1, 8–23.

Mills, R. and McCreadie, M. (2018) *SYNERGY: Knowing me – knowing me. Changing the story around 'behaviours of concern'. Promoting self-awareness, self-control and a positive narrative.* Accessed on 14/10/19 at www.atautism.org/wp-content/uploads/2018/06/Knowing-me-knowing-me-June-18-Final-version.pdf.

Milton, D., Mills, R. with Jones, S. (2016) *Ten rules for ensuring people with learning disabilities and those who are on the autism spectrum develop 'challenging behaviour'... and maybe what to do about it.* Shoreham-by-Sea: Pavilion.

National Autistic Society (n.d.) SPELL. Accessed on 6/12/19 at www.autism.org.uk/about/strategies/spell.aspx.

References

Aitken, K.J. (2012) *Sleep Difficulties and Autism Spectrum Disorders: A Guide for Parents and Professionals*. London: Jessica Kingsley Publishers.

All Party Parliamentary Group on Autism (2017) *Autism and Education in England*. London: APPGA/NAS. Accessed on 10/8/19 at www.autism.org.uk/get-involved/campaign/appga/highlights.aspx.

Allely, C. (2018) 'A systematic PRISMA review of individuals with autism spectrum disorder in secure psychiatric care: prevalence, treatment, risk assessment and other clinical considerations.' *Journal of Criminal Psychology 8*, 1, 58–79.

Ambitious about Autism (2018) 'Exclusions of pupils with autism rocket in England, new data shows.' London: Ambitious about Autism. Accessed on 26/4/19 at www.ambitiousaboutautism.org.uk/understanding-autism/exclusions-of-pupils-with-autism-rocket-in-england-new-data-shows.

American Psychiatric Association (2013) 'Neurodevelopmental Disorders.' In *Diagnostic and Statistical Manual of Mental Disorders (5th edition)*. Accessed on 26/4/19 at https://doi.org/10.1176/appi.books.9780890425596.dsm01.

Anderson, K.A., Shattuck, P.T, Cooper, B.P., Roux, A.M. and Wagner, M. (2014) 'Prevalence and correlates of postsecondary residential status among young adults with an autism spectrum disorder.' *Autism 18*, 5, 562–570.

Anderson, K.A., Sosnowy, C., Kuo, A. and Shattuck, P.T. (2018) 'Transition of individuals with autism to adulthood: a review of qualitative studies.' *Pediatrics* 141 (Supplement 4): S318–S327.

Attwood, T., Henault, I. and Dubin, N. (2014) *The Autism Spectrum, Sexuality and the Law*. London: Jessica Kingsley Publishers.

Autism Injustice (2019). 'Kat's Story.' Accessed on 25/4/19 at http://autisminjustice.org/Stories/kat's-story.html.

Autism Rights Group Highland (2018) *Highland One Stop Shop: user evaluation*. Accessed on 7/10/19 at http://arghighland.co.uk/pdf/HOSSsurveyreport.pdf.

Baeza-Velasco, C., Cohen, D., Hamonet, C., Vlamynck, E. *et al*. (2018) 'Autism, joint hypermobility-related disorders and pain.' *Frontiers in Psychiatry 9*, 656.

Baron-Cohen, S. (2009) 'Autism: the empathizing-systemizing (E-S) theory.' *Annals of the New York Academy of Sciences* 1156: 68–80. DOI 10.1111/j.1749-6632.2009.04467.x.

Bodner, K.E., Engelhardt, D.E., Minshew, N.J. and Williams, D.L. (2015) 'Making inferences: comprehension of physical causality, intentionality, and emotions in discourse by high-functioning older children, adolescents, and adults with autism.' *Journal of Autism and Developmental Disorders 45*, 9, 2721–2733.

Bogdashina, O. (2003) *Sensory Perceptual Issues in Autism and Asperger Syndrome*. London: Jessica Kingsley Publishers.

Bradley, E. and Caldwell, P. (2013) 'Mental health and autism: Promoting Autism FaVourable Environments (PAVE).' *Journal on Developmental Disabilities 19*, 1, 8–23.

British Association of Social Workers (2012) *The Code of Ethics for Social Work*. Birmingham: British Association of Social Workers. Accessed on 4/10/19 at www.basw.co.uk/about-basw/code-ethics.

Brook, K. (2017) *Advice for Professionals on how to Support Autistic Parents Network Autism*. London: National Autistic Society. Accessed on 4/10/19 at https://network.autism.org.uk/sites/default/files/ckfinder/files/Supporting%20autistic%20parents(1).pdf.

Brook, K. (2019) 'Do autistic parents play differently? Do we need new assessments? How do existing frameworks for analysing interaction relate to the way autistic parents play with their children? Research in progress.' University of Edinburgh. Accessed on 4/10/19 at www.autistica.org.uk/our-research/research-projects/autistic-parents-interactions.

Brown, R., Barber, P. and Martin, D. (2015) *The Mental Capacity Act 2005: A Guide for Practice*. London: Sage.

Buckle, K.L. (2017) Remark made in person during a meeting of the Autistic Advisory Panel of the National Autism Project.

Buckle, K.L. (2019) 'Initiation impairments in autistic people.' *Autistica Discover Conference*. University of Reading.

Butler-Cole QC, V. Edwards, S., Allen, N., Scott, K. *et al.* (2019) *Mental Capacity Guidance Note: A Brief Guide to Carrying Out Capacity Assessments*. London: 39 Essex Chambers. Accessed on 4/10/19 at www.39essex.com/mental-capacity-guidance-note-brief-guide-carrying-capacity-assessments.

Caldwell, P. (2014) *The Anger Box*. Hove: Pavillion.

Camm-Crosbie, L., Bradley, L., Shaw, R., Baron-Cohen, S. and Cassidy, S. (2018) '"People like me don't get support": autistic adults' experiences of support and treatment for mental health difficulties, self-injury and suicidality.' *Autism 23*, 6, 1431–1441.

Care Quality Commission (2016a) *The State of Health Care and Adult Social Care in England 2015/16: The Deprivation of Liberty Safeguards*. London: Care Quality Commission.

Care Quality Commission (2016b) *Survey of Medication for Detained Patients with a Learning Disability*. London: Care Quality Commission.

Care Quality Commission (2019) *Review of Restraint, Prolonged Seclusion and Segregation for People with a Mental Health Problem, A Learning Disability or Autism: Interim Report*. Newcastle upon Tyne: Care Quality Commission.

Cassidy, S., Hannant, P., Tavassoli, T., Allison, C., Smith, P. and Baron-Cohen, S. (2016) 'Dyspraxia and autistic traits in adults with and without autism spectrum conditions.' *Molecular Autism 7*, 48.

Cassidy, S. and Rodgers, J. (2017) 'Understanding and prevention of suicide in autism.' *The Lancet 4*, 6. Accessed on 18/10/19 at www.thelancet.com/journals/lanpsy/article/PIIS2215-0366(17)30162-1/fulltext.

Cassidy, S., Bradley, L., Shaw, R. and Baron-Cohen, S. (2018) 'Risk markers for suicidality in autistic adults.' *Molecular Autism 9*, 1, 42.

Chavisory (2014) 'A checklist for identifying sources of aggression.' Accessed on 3/8/19 at https://wearelikeyourchild.blogspot.com/2014/05/a-checklist-for-identifying-sources-of.html.

Council for Disabled Children (2009) *The Use of Eligibility Criteria in Social Care Services for Disabled Children*. London: National Children's Bureau. Accessed on 4/10/19 at https://councilfordisabledchildren.org.uk › eligibility_criteria_statement.

Courchesne, V., Meilleur, A.S., Poulin-Lord, M., Dawson, M. and Soulières, I. (2015) 'Autistic children at risk of being underestimated: school-based pilot study of a strength-informed assessment.' *Molecular Autism 6*, 12.

Craig, F., Margari, F., Legrottaglie, A.R. Palumbi, R., de Giambattista, C. and Margari, L. (2016) 'A review of executive function deficits in autism spectrum disorder and attention-deficit/hyperactivity disorder.' *Neuropsychiatric Disease and Treatment 12*, 1191–1202.

Cusack, J., Shaw, S., Spiers, J. and Sterry, R. (2018) *Personal Tragedies, Public Crisis.* London: Autistica. Accessed on 4/10/19 at www.autistica.org.uk/downloads/files/Personal-tragedies-public-crisis-ONLINE.pdf#asset:1499.

D'Astous, V., Manthorpe, J., Lowton, K. and Glaser, K. (2014) 'Retracing the historical social care context of autism: a narrative overview.' *British Journal of Social Work.* DOI: 10.1093/bjsw/bcu131.

Dawson, M., Soulieres, I., Gernsbacher, A. and Mottron, L (2007) 'The level and nature of autistic intelligence.' *Psychological Science 18*, 8, 657–662.

De Martino, B., Harrison, A., Knafo, S., Bird, G. and Dolan, D. (2008) 'Explaining enhanced logical consistency during decision making in autism.' *The Journal of Neuroscience 28*, 42, 10746–10750.

Dekker, M. (2017) *Cure vs Acceptance.* Autism without violence conference. Wroclaw, Poland. Accessed on 4/10/19 at www.inlv.org/slides/Leczenie,%20czy%20akceptacja.pdf.

Department for Education (2015) *Special Educational Needs and Disability Code of Practice: 0 to 25 Years.* London: Department for Education.

Department for Education (2018) *Special Educational Needs in England: January 2018.* London: Department of Education.

Department of Health (2014) *Care and Support Statutory Guidance.* London: Department of Health. Accessed on 18/10/19 at www.gov.uk/government/publications/care-act-statutory-guidance/care-and-support-statutory-guidance.

Department of Health (2015) *Statutory Guidance for Local Authorities and NHS Organisations to Support Implementation of the Adult Autism Strategy.* London: Department of Health.

Department of Health (2016) *National Framework for Children and Young People's Continuing Care.* Leeds: Department of Health.

Devnani, P.A. and Hegde, A.U. (2015) 'Autism and sleep disorders.' *Journal of Pediatric Neurosciences 10*, 4, 304–307.

Disability Law Service (2019) *Autistic Children and Care Assessments: The Problem with Local Authority Eligibility Criteria.* Accessed on 19/4/19 at https://dls.org.uk/autistic-children-and-care-assessments.

Disabled Children's Partnership (2018) *Changes in Quality of Health and Social Care Services for Disabled Children and Their Families.* London: Disabled Children's Partnership.

Doherty, M., O'Sullivan, J. and Neilson, S. (2020) 'Barriers to healthcare for autistic adults; consequences and policy implications. A cross-sectional study.' Accessed on 21/4/20 at https://doi.org/10.1101/2020.04.01.20050336.

Donnellan, A.M., Hill, D.A. and Leary, M.R. (2013) 'Rethinking autism: implications of sensory and movement differences for understanding and support.' *Frontiers in Integrative Neuroscience 6*, 124.

Dovidio, J.F., Kawakami, K., Johnson, C., Johnson, B. and Howard, A. (1997) 'On the nature of prejudice: automatic and controlled processes.' *Journal of Experimental Social Psychology 33*, 5, 510–540.

Dowling, S., Kelly, B. and Winter, K. (2012) *Disabled Children and Young People who are Looked After: A Literature Review.* Belfast: Queen's University Belfast. Accessed on 4/10/19 at https://pure.qub.ac.uk/portal/files/10445548/Literature_Review_Disabled_Children_and_Young_People_who_are_Looked_After.pdf.

Dubin, N.I. (2014) 'Doctoral degree.' In T. Attwood, Henault T. and N. Dubin. *The Autism Spectrum, Sexuality and the Law.* London: Jessica Kingsley Publishers.

Dugdale, D. and Symonds, J. (2017) *Fathers with Learning Disabilities and Their Experiences of Adult Social Care Services.* Bristol: University of Bristol. Accessed on 4/10/19 at www.sscr.nihr.ac.uk/PDF/Findings/RF76.pdf.

Ecker, C., Bookheimer, S. and Murphy, D. (2015) 'Neuroimaging in autism spectrum disorder: brain structure and function across the lifespan.' *Lancet Neurology, 14*, 11, 1121–1135.

Emerson, E. and Baines, S. (2010) *The Estimated Prevalence of Autism among Adults with Learning Disabilities in England.* Learning Disabilities Observatory, NHS Digital. Accessed on 4/10/19 at www.wecommunities.org/MyNurChat/archive/LDdownloads/vid_8731_1HAL2010-05Autism.pdf.

Finkelhor, D. (2009) 'The prevention of childhood sexual abuse [online].' *The Future of Children 19*, 2, 169–194.

Flood, A. and Sharp, A. (2019) 'The Coventry Grid for adults: a tool to guide clinicians in differentiating complex trauma and autism.' *Good Autism Practice 20*, 1, 76–87.

Ford, T., Vostanis, P., Meltzer, H. and Goodman, R. (2007) 'Psychiatric disorder among British children looked after by local authorities: comparison with children living in private households.' *British Journal of Psychiatry 190*, 4, 319–325.

Fortuna, R., Robinson, L., Smith, T., Meccarello, J. *et al.* (2016) 'Health conditions and functional status in adults with autism: a cross-sectional evaluation.' *Journal of General Internal Medicine 31*, 1, 77–84.

Fuld, S. (2018) 'Autism spectrum disorder: the impact of stressful and traumatic life events and implications for clinical practice.' *Clinical Social Work Journal 46*, 3, 210–219.

Goodall, C. (2018) 'Mainstream is not for all: the educational experiences of autistic young people.' *Disability & Society 33*, 10, 1661–1665.

Green, A.E., Kenworthy, L., Mosner, M.K., Gallagher, N.M. *et al.* (2014) 'Abstract analogical reasoning in high-functioning children with autism spectrum disorders.' *Autism Research 7*, 6, 677–686.

Green, S.A. and Carter, A.S. (2014) 'Predictors and course of daily living skills development in toddlers with autism spectrum disorders.' *Journal of Autism and Developmental Disorders 44*, 2, 256–263.

Gregory, J. and Bryan, K. (2011) 'Speech and language therapy intervention with a group of persistent and prolific young offenders in a non-custodial setting with previously undiagnosed speech, language and communication difficulties.' *International Journal of Language and Communication Disorders 46*, 2, 202–215.

Gwillim, P. (2009) *Police awareness of Autism and how to deal with the criminal justice system.* Autscape conference, London. Accessed on 4/10/19 at www.autscape.org/2009/presentations#police-autism.

Halpern, D. (2005) *Social Capital.* Cambridge: Polity Press.

Happé, F. and Baron-Cohen, S. (2014) 'Remembering Lorna Wing (1928–2014).' Accessed on 22/4/19 at www.spectrumnews.org/opinion/remembering-lorna-wing-1928-2014.

Happé, F.G. (1994) 'Wechsler IQ profile and theory of mind in autism: a research note.' *Journal of Child Psychology and Psychiatry 35*, 8, 1461–1471.

Harbottle, C., Jones, M.R. and Thompson, L.M. (2014) 'From reactionary to activist: a model that works.' *The Journal of Adult Protection 16*, 2, 113–119.

Harris, J. (2016) '"All my life suddenly made sense": how it feels to be diagnosed with autism late in life.' *The Guardian,* 19 November. Accessed on 1/10/19 at www.theguardian.com/society/2016/nov/19/autism-diagnosis-late-in-life-asperger-syndrome-john-harris.

Hartman, D. (2014) *Sexuality and Relationship Education for Children and Adolescents with Autism Spectrum Disorders.* London: Jessica Kingsley Publishers.

Haruvi-Lamdan, N., Horesh, D. and Golan, O. (2018) 'PTSD and autism spectrum disorder: co-morbidity, gaps in research, and potential shared mechanisms.' *Psychological Trauma 10*, 3, 290–299.

Health Education England (2019) *Core Capabilities Framework for Supporting Autistic People.* London: Department of Health and Social Care. Accessed on 6/12/19 at www.skillsforhealth.org.uk/learningdisabilityandautismframeworks.

Helen Sanderson Associates (2019) *What's working/not working*. Accessed on 9/9/19 at www.helensandersonassociates.co.uk/wp-content/uploads/2015/02/workingnotworking.pdf.

Hingsburger, D. and Tough, S. (2002) 'Healthy sexuality: attitudes, systems, and policies.' *Research and Practice for Persons with Severe Disabilities 27*, 1, 8–17.

HM Government (2018) *Working Together to Safeguard Children*. London: HM Government. Accessed on 8/8/19 at https://assets.publishing.service.gov.uk/government/uploads/system/uploads/attachment_data/file/779401/Working_Together_to_Safeguard-Children.pdf.

Holler, J., Kendrick, K., Casillas, M. and Levinson, S. (2015) 'Editorial: turn-taking in human communicative interaction.' *Frontiers in Psychology 6*, 1919.

Hull, L., Mandy, W., Lai, M.C., Baron-Cohen, S. *et al.* (2019) 'Development and validation of the Camouflaging Autistic Traits Questionnaire (CAT-Q).' *Journal of Autism and Developmental Disorders 49*, 3, 819–833.

Iemmi, V., Knapp, M. and Ragan, I. (2017) *The Autism Dividend*. London: National Autism Project. Accessed on 4/10/19 at http://nationalautismproject.org.uk/wp-content/uploads/2017/01/autism-dividend-report.pdf.

Jones, L., Bellis, M.A., Wood, S., Hughes, K. *et al.* (2012) 'Prevalence and risk of violence against children with disabilities: a systematic review and meta-analysis of observational studies.' *The Lancet 380*, 9845, 899–907.

Justice for LB (2018) *Justice for LB Toolkit*. Accessed on 9/8/19 at www.advocacyfocus.org.uk/justiceforlb.

Kenyon, L. (2015) 'Managing autism in the workplace.' *Occupational Health 67*, June, 3.

King, C. and Murphy, G.H. (2014) 'A systematic review of people with autism spectrum disorder and the criminal justice system.' *Journal of Autism and Developmental Disorders 44*, 11, 2717–2733.

Lakoff, G. and Johnson, M. (1980) *Metaphors We Live By*. Chicago, IL: University of Chicago.

Lawson, W. (2015) *Older Adults and Autism Spectrum Conditions*. London: Jessica Kingsley Publishers.

Leekam, S.R., Libby, S.J., Wing, L., Gould, L. and Taylor, C. (2002) 'The Diagnostic Interview for Social and Communication Disorders: algorithms for ICD-10 childhood autism and Wing and Gould autistic spectrum disorder.' *Journal of Child Psychology and Psychiatry, and Allied Disciplines 43*, 3, 327–342.

Leitner, Y. (2014) 'The co-occurrence of autism and attention deficit hyperactivity disorder in children – what do we know?' *Frontiers in Human Neuroscience 8*, 268–268.

Lenehan, D.C. (2017) *These Are Our Children*. London: Council for Disabled Children. Accessed on 4/10/19 at www.ncb.org.uk/sites/default/files/field/attachment/These%20are%20Our%20CHildren_Lenehan_Review_Report.pdf.

Lord, C., Rutter, M., DiLavore, P.C., Risi, S. *et al.* (2012) *Autism Diagnostic Observation Schedule, Second Edition: ADOS-2*. London: Pearson.

Lorenz, T. and Heinitz, K. (2014) 'Aspergers – different, not less: occupational strengths and job interests of individuals with Asperger's syndrome.' *PLoS ONE 9*, 6.

Luke, L., Clare, I., Ring, H., Redley, M. and Watson, P. (2012) 'Decision-making difficulties experienced by adults with autism spectrum conditions.' *Autism 16*, 6, 612–621.

MacDonald, A. (2018) *Coming Home: A Report on Out-of-Area Placements and Delayed Discharge for People with Learning Disabilities and Complex Needs*. Scottish Government. Accessed on 4/10/19 at www.gov.scot/publications/coming-home-complex-care-needs-out-area-placements-report-2018/pages/6.

Maguire, M. (2010) *Not a Marginal Issue: Mental Health and the Criminal Justice System in Northern Ireland*. Criminal Justice Inspection Northern Ireland. Accessed on 4/10/19 at www.cjini.org/CJNI/files/24/24d6cd45-20bb-4f81-9e34-81ea59594650.pdf.

Mandelstam, M. (2017) *Care Act 2014: An A–Z of Law and Practice*. London: Jessica Kingsley Publishers.

Mills, R. (2016) 'Reflections on Stress and Autism.' *Network Autism*. London: National Autistic Society. Accessed on 3/8/19 at https://network.autism.org.uk/sites/default/files/ckfinder/files/Stress%20article%20Final(2).pdf.

Mills, R. and McCreadie, M. (2018) *SYNERGY: Knowing me – knowing me. Changing the story around 'behaviours of concern'. Promoting self-awareness, self-control and a positive narrative*. Accessed on 14/10/19 at www.atautism.org/wp-content/uploads/2018/06/Knowing-me-knowing-me-June-18-Final-version.pdf.

Milton, D. (2012) 'On the ontological status of autism: the "double empathy problem".' *Disability & Society 27*, 6, 883–887.

Milton, D. (2013) *'Nature's answer to over-conformity': deconstructing Pathological Demand Avoidance*. University of Kent. Accessed on 8/10/19 at https://kar.kent.ac.uk/62694.

Milton, D. (2018) 'A critique of the use of Applied Behavioural Analysis (ABA): on behalf of the Neurodiversity Manifesto Steering Group.' University of Kent. Accessed on 4/10/19 at https://kar.kent.ac.uk/69268/1/Applied%20behaviour%20analysis.pdf.

Milton, D. (2019) 'Difference versus Disability: implications of characterisation of autism for education and support.' In R. Jordan, J.M. Roberts and K. Hume (eds) *The Sage Handbook of Autism and Education*. London, Sage.

Milton, D., Mills, R. with Jones, S. (2016) *Ten rules for ensuring people with learning disabilities and those who are on the autism spectrum develop 'challenging behaviour' ... and maybe what to do about it*. Shoreham-by-Sea: Pavilion.

Moran, H. (2010) 'Clinical observations of the differences between children on the autism spectrum and those with attachment problems: the Coventry Grid.' *Good Autism Practice 11*, 2, 44–57.

Muggleton, J. (2018) 'Autism and CBT.' *Network Autism*. London: National Autistic Society.

Murray, D. (2013) 'Art...a positive necessity of life.' *Autonomy, the Critical Journal of Interdisciplinary Autism Studies 1*, 2.

Murray, D., Lesser, M. and Lawson, W. (2005) 'Attention, monotropism and the diagnostic criteria for autism.' *Autism 9*, 2, 139–156.

National Autistic Society (2006) *B is for Bullied*. Network Autism. Accessed on 4/10/19 at https://network.autism.org.uk/sites/default/files/ckfinder/files/B_is_for_bullied%5B1%5D.pdf.

National Autistic Society (2016) *The Autism Employment Gap*. London: National Autistic Society. Accessed on 8/8/19 at www.autism.org.uk/get-involved/media-centre/news/2016-10-27-employment-gap.aspx.

National Autistic Society (2018) *Beyond Transforming Care. What Needs to Change?* London: National Autistic Society. Accessed on 6/8/19 at www.autism.org.uk/get-involved/media-centre/news/2018-12-06-beyond-transforming-care.aspx.

National Autistic Taskforce (2019) *An Independent Guide to Quality Care for Autistic People*. London: National Autistic Taskforce. Accessed on 4/10/19 at https://nationalautistictaskforce.org.uk/an-independent-guide-to-quality-care-for-autistic-people.

National Institute for Health and Care Excellence (NICE) (2012) *Autism spectrum disorder in adults: diagnosis and management*. Clinical guideline [CG142]. London: NICE.

NHS Digital (2012) *Estimating the Prevalence of Autism Spectrum Conditions in Adults – Extending the 2007 Adult Psychiatric Morbidity Survey*. National Statistics.

NHS England (2016) *Stopping over medication of people with a learning disability, autism or both (STOMP)*. Accessed on 6/9/19 at www.england.nhs.uk/learning-disabilities/improving-health/stomp.

Niemczyk, J., Wagner, C. and von Gontard, A. (2018) 'Incontinence in autism spectrum disorder: a systematic review.' *European Child and Adolescent Psychiatry 27*, 12, 1523–1537.

O'Regan, D. (2014) 'Diagnosing autism spectrum disorders in older adults.' *CME Journal Geriatric Medicine 33*, 46–51.

Obuaya, C., Stanton, E. and Baggaley, M. (2013) 'Is there a crisis about crisis houses?' *Journal of the Royal Society of Medicine 106*, 8, 300–302.

Office of the Public Guardian (2007) *Mental Capacity Act Code of Practice*. Accessed on 14/10/19 at www.gov.uk/government/publications/mental-capacity-act-code-of-practice.

Perraudin, F. (2019) 'Councils spend millions on agency social workers amid recruiting crisis.' *The Guardian,* 7 April. Accessed on 9/8/19 at www.theguardian.com/society/2019/apr/07/social-work-recruiting-woes-see-councils-pay-millions-to-agencies.

Poquérusse, J., Pastore, L., Dellantonio, S. and Esposito, G. (2018) 'Alexithymia and autism spectrum disorder: a complex relationship.' *Frontiers in Psychology 9*, 1196–1196.

Ramachandran, V. (2011) *The Tell-Tale Brain*. London: William Heinemann.

Rees, K. (2017) *Safeguarding Adult Review – Mr. C – Overview Report*. Hampshire Safeguarding Adults Board. Accessed on 4/10/19 at www.hampshiresab.org.uk/wp-content/uploads/HSAB-Mr-C-SAR.pdf.

Research Autism (2019) *Conditions and Syndromes Related to or Commonly Occurring Alongside Autism*. Accessed on 1/10/19 at www.researchautism.net/autism-issues/conditions-related-to-autism.

Rose, D.R., Yang, H., Serena, G., Sturgeon, C. *et al.* (2018) 'Differential immune responses and microbiota profiles in children with autism spectrum disorders and co-morbid gastrointestinal symptoms.' *Brain, Behavior, and Immunity 70*, 354–368.

Rutgers, A., van IJzendoorn, M., Bakermans-Kranenburg, M., Swinkels, S. *et al.* (2007) 'Autism, attachment and parenting: a comparison of children with autism spectrum disorder, mental retardation, language disorder, and non-clinical children.' *Journal of Abnormal Child Psychology 35*, 5, 859–870.

Rydzewska, E., Hughes-McCormack, L.A., Gillberg, C., Henderson, A. *et al.* (2018) 'Prevalence of long-term health conditions in adults with autism: observational study of a whole country population.' *British Medical Journal Open 8*, 8. Accessed on 18/10/19 at http://dx.doi.org/10.1136/bmjopen-2018-023945.

Saeki, M. and Powell, A. (2008) *Social Care: Assessment of need for adults with an autism spectrum disorder*. London: National Autistic Society. Accessed on 4/10/19 at www.autism.org.uk/professionals/training-consultancy/good-practice-guides/assessments.aspx.

Scheuffgen, K., Happe, F., Anderson, M. and Frith, U. (2000) 'High "intelligence," low "IQ"? Speed of processing and measured IQ in children with autism.' *Developmental Psychopathology 12*, 1, 83–90.

Scottish Transitions Forum (2017) *Principles of Good Transitions 3*. Dalkeith: Scottish Transitions Forum. Accessed on 4/10/19 at https://scottishtransitions.org.uk/summary-download.

Select Committee on the Mental Capacity Act 2005 (2014) *Mental Capacity Act 2005: post-legislative scrutiny*. London: HMSO. Accessed on 14/10/19 at https://publications.parliament.uk/pa/ld201314/ldselect/ldmentalcap/139/139.pdf.

Shah, A.D. (2019) *Catatonia, Shutdown and Breakdown in Autism: A Psycho-Ecological Approach*. London: Jessica Kingsley Publishers.

Shea, E. (2015) 'Supporting autistic people with eating difficulties.' *Network Autism*. Accessed on 4/10/19 at https://network.autism.org.uk/sites/default/files/ckfinder/files/Eating%20difficulty%20article.docx.pdf.

Shifrer, D. (2013) 'Stigma of a label: educational expectations for high school students labeled with learning disabilities.' *Journal of Health and Social Behavior 54*, 4, 462–480.

Silberman, S. (2015) *Neurotribes*. London: Allen & Unwin.

Stobart, A. (n.d.) *Transition Toolkit*. London: Autism Education Trust. Accessed on 10/8/19 at http://dspl7.org.uk/data/documents/Transition-Toolkit.pdf

Taylor, J.L., Henninger, N.A. and Mailick, M.R. (2015) 'Longitudinal patterns of employment and postsecondary education for adults with autism and average-range IQ.' *Autism: The International Journal of Research and Practice 19*, 7, 785–793.

The Advocate's Gateway (2016) 'Planning to question someone with an autistic spectrum disorder including Asperger Syndrome.' *Toolkit 3*. Accessed on 11/6/17 at www.theadvocatesgateway.org/images/toolkits/3-planning-to-question-someone-with-an-autism-spectrum-disorder-including-asperger-syndrome-2016.pdf.

Think Local Act Personal (2019) *Personalised Care and Support Planning*. Accessed on 9/8/19 at www.thinklocalactpersonal.org.uk/personalised-care-and-support-planning-tool.

Thoburn, J., Norford, E. and Rashid, S. (2000) *Permanent Family Placement for Children of Minority Ethnic Origin*. London: Jessica Kingsley Publishers.

Thomas, S., Hovinga, M.E., Rai, D. and Lee, B.K. (2017) 'Brief report: prevalence of co-occurring epilepsy and autism spectrum disorder: The U.S. National Survey of Children's Health 2011–2012.' *Journal of Autism and Developmental Disorders 47*, 1, 224–229.

Tostrud, E. (2016) 'Autism spectrum disorder and professional job interviews.' *UW-Stout Journal of Student Research 50–60*. Accessed on 18/10/19 at http://digital.library.wisc.edu/1793/77634.

Treffert, D.A. (2011) 'Hyperlexia: reading precociousness or savant skill? Distinguishing autistic-like behaviors from Autistic Disorder.' *Wisconsin Medical Journal 110*, 6.

Van Der Miesen, A., Hurley, H. and De Vries, A. (2016) 'Gender dysphoria and autism spectrum disorder: a narrative review.' *International Review of Psychiatry 28*, 1, 70–80.

Vicker, B. (n.d.) *Social Communication and Language Characteristics Associated with High Functioning, Verbal Children and Adults with ASD*. Indiana Resource Center for Autism. Accessed on 10/8/19 at www.iidc.indiana.edu/pages/Social-Communication-and-Language-Characteristics-Associated-with-High-Functioning-Verbal-Children-and-Adults-with-ASD.

Waddell, G. and Burton, A. (2006) *Is work good for your health and wellbeing?* Norwich: The Stationery Office.

Waddington, E.M. and Reed, P. (2017) 'Comparison of the effects of mainstream and special school on National Curriculum outcomes in children with autism spectrum disorder: an archive-based analysis.' *Journal of Research in Special Educational Needs 17*, 2, 132–142.

Westminster Commission on Autism (2016) *A Spectrum of Obstacles – An Inquiry into Access to Healthcare for Autistic People*. London: Westminster Commission on Autism. Accessed on 10/8/19 at https://westminsterautismcommission.files.wordpress.com/2016/03/ar1011_ncg-autism-report-july-2016.pdf.

Williams, D. (2002) *Exposure Anxiety – The Invisible Cage*. London: Jessica Kingsley Publishers.

Wilson, K., Ruch, G., Lymbery, M. and Cooper, A. (2011) *Social Work: An Introduction to Contemporary Practice*. Harlow: Pearson.

Wirral Autistic Society (2015) *Mate Crime in Merseyside*. Accessed on 28/4/17 at http://www.autismtogether.co.uk/wp-content/uploads/2015/07/WAS-mate-crime-report-June-2015.pdf.

Woods, R. (2017) 'Exploring how the social model of disability can be re-invigorated for autism: in response to Jonathan Levitt.' *Disability & Society 32*, 7, 1090–1095.

Working Together with Parents Network (2014) *Good Practice Guidance on Working with Parents with a Learning Disability*. Accessed on 15/5/19 at www.bristol.ac.uk/sps/wtpn.

World Health Organization (2018) *International classification of diseases for mortality and morbidity statistics* (11th Revision). Accessed on 4/10/19 at https://icd.who.int/browse11/l-m/en.

Wright, J. (2015) 'The missing generation.' *Spectrum News*. Accessed on 4/10/19 at www.spectrumnews.org/features/deep-dive/the-missing-generation.

Xie, S., Karlsson, H., Dalman, C., Widman, L. *et al.* (2019) 'Family history of mental and neurological disorders and risk of autism.' *JAMA Network Open 2*, 3. Accessed on 18/10/19 at https://jamanetwork.com/journals/jamanetworkopen/fullarticle/2726710.

Zerbo, O., Leong, A., Barcellos, L., Bernal, P. *et al.* (2015) 'Immune mediated conditions in autism spectrum disorders.' *Brain, Behaviour and Immunity 46*, 232–236.

Statutes and statutory instruments

Care Act 2014

Children Act 1989

Mental Capacity Act 2005

The Advocacy Services and Representations Procedure (Children) (Amendment) Regulations 2004

The Care and Support (Assessment) Regulations 2014

The Care and Support (Direct Payments) Regulations 2014

The Care and Support (Eligibility Criteria) Regulations 2015

The Special Educational Needs and Disability Regulations 2014

Cases (England and Wales)

A Local Authority v G (Parent with Learning Disability) [2017] EWFC B94

LBX v K & Ors [2013] EWHC 3230 (Fam)

R (on the application of Luke Davey) v Oxfordshire County Council & Ors [2017] EWCA Civ 1308

R (on the application of JF by his litigation friend KF v LB Merton [2017] EWHC 1519 (Admin)

The Government Legal Service v Brookes [2017] UKEAT/0302/16/RN

WBC (Local Authority) v Z (by her litigation friend the Official Solicitor) & Ors [2016] EWCOP 4

Endnotes

1 Mental capacity assessments will be discussed in Chapter 6.

2 Reg. 5 The Care and Support (Assessment) Regulations 2014; Para. 6.86 *Care and Support Statutory Guidance* (Department of Health 2014); Para. 9.26 *Special Educational Needs and Disability Code of Practice: 0 to 25 Years* (Department for Education 2015); Para. 1.49 *Working Together to Safeguard Children* (HM Government 2018).

3 However, it is important to note that, while there must be significant engagement with the adult's own views, the final decisions about whether an adult's needs for care and support meet the eligibility criteria and what is needed to meet those needs are decisions for the local authority. See ss.13 and 24 Care Act 2014.

4 Similarly, final decisions about whether to issue, and the contents of, an EHCP are for the local authority. See ss.36 and 37 Children & Families Act 2014.

5 A 'first–then' frame is simply a line drawing of two boxes in which the left box is labelled 'First' and the right box is labelled 'Then'. Activities, sequential events or causes and effects can then be placed into each box using a form of representation that the person understands, whether that is physical objects, photographs, symbols or written text.

6 Toby may or may not understand the concept of consent in sexual relationships. In this example, Tuxcia is merely exploring the issue with him and is not undertaking an assessment of Toby's mental capacity to make any decision. Capacity assessment will be discussed in Chapter 6.

7 Reg. 2 The Care and Support (Eligibility Criteria) Regulations 2015.

8 Which might then need to be explored further to distinguish between needs resulting from a physical or cognitive impairment and those resulting from a mental health need.

9 The Care Act 2014 and the Children and Families Act 2014 were designed to work together seamlessly and support a transition process from age 13/14 to 25.

10 The Autism Strategy has now been extended to include children. See also s.9 Care Act, which requires local authorities to assess an adult's social care needs where it appears that 'they may have needs for care and support', and s.58 Care Act requiring transition assessments for children who are 'likely to have needs for care and support after becoming 18'.

11 Around 60% of autistic people do not have a learning disability.

12 s.22 Care Act 2014 prohibits local authorities from providing any service required to be provided under the NHS Act 2006, unless doing so would be merely incidental or ancillary to meeting needs under the Care Act. This is often (and wrongly) interpreted as meaning that local authorities are under no obligation to meet needs which are in any way related to healthcare needs. In fact the Care Act eligibility criteria include 'making use of necessary facilities or services in the local community' and the statutory guidance is extremely clear that 'Local authorities do not have responsibility for the provision of NHS services such as patient transport, *however they should consider needs for support when the adult is attending healthcare appointments*' (Para. 6.106). This is consistent with the case law on the intersection between Continuing Health Care and social care, which demonstrates that the prohibition in s.22 Care Act (which replicates the prior legal situation) merely prohibits a local authority from meeting primary health needs that should result in eligibility for CHC (see Mandelstam 2017, pp.114–115 for a summary of the case law).

13 'Duty of care' requires carers not to act negligently rather than to eliminate all risk.

14 Which I define as the ability to communicate basic needs.

15 An annual UK-based conference run by and for autistic people. See www.autscape.org.

16 s.67 and 68 Care Act 2014; s.37–39 and Sch. AA1 Mental Capacity Act 2005 (as amended); SEND Code of Practice Paras. 8.18, 9.29; Children Act 1989 s.26A (as amended); and The Advocacy Services and Representations

Procedure (Children) (Amendment) Regulations 2004.

17 Note that, whilst the UNCRPD has been ratified by the UK, it is not binding in UK law. Nevertheless, these principles represent good practice.

18 See *R (on the application of Luke Davey) v Oxfordshire County Council & Ors [2017] and R (on the application of JF by his litigation friend KF v LB Merton [2017].*

19 The title of a 2005 Channel 4 documentary about the education of a group of autistic children.

20 Up until the 1970s, autism was widely blamed on poor parenting (and particularly on the mother–child relationship). As a result, parents can be hyper-sensitive to the possibility of being blamed for an autistic child's behaviour.

21 By the Care Act 2014 and Children and Families Act 2014.

22 Similar issues may recur later in other transitions such as moving home, entering/leaving residential placements (including in old age) and as a consequence of relationship formation/breakdown or bereavement.

23 Currently under review. See https://www.theyworkforyou.com/sp/?id=2019-03-19.6.0.

24 A person's capacity to make the decision cannot be lawfully assessed until they have this full information (see *CC v KK & STCC [2012] EWCOP 2136*).

25 Specific steps that can be taken to support autistic people with decision making are set out in Chapter 7.

26 It is important to note that it is also the case that their capacity to make the decision cannot be lawfully assessed until they have this full information (see *CC v KK & STCC [2012] EWCOP 2136*).

27 This can also pose issues in effectively consulting autistic service users about potential change. Some will be able to understand the hypothetical and contingent nature of options at a consultation stage, but others may not. It is therefore important to consider the ethical implications of presenting (and then potentially 'snatching away') a hypothetical option where a person may not understand that the option may not be actually available to them as a choice.

28 The Care Act 2014 (s.42) requires local authorities to carry out an adult safeguarding enquiry only where the adult is unable to protect himself or herself against the abuse or neglect or the risk of it.

29 The use of Registered Intermediaries to facilitate the communication of vulnerable victims and witnesses in the criminal justice system is slowly growing and should help to reduce this.

30 See Sexual Offences Act 2003 s.30–44.

31 Antecedent–Behaviour–Consequences.

32 Self-injurious behaviour is defined as repetitive (and sometimes rhythmic) behaviours (which may be compulsive and/or non-volitional) which cause significant physical harm to the person. Examples might include: eye poking, self-biting, head banging and skin picking. I use 'self-injurious behaviour' as distinct from 'self-harm' – which I define as deliberate infliction of harm and/or pain related to mental health, examples of which might include: cutting/scratching the skin, burning with cigarettes, taking overdoses, etc. These are not hard and fast distinctions. Both may occur in autism (and in the same individual) and there is some overlap, but, on the whole, the two categories occur in two distinctly different populations and may have distinctly different underlying causation.

33 However, the use of restraint should *never* be routine, regular or commonplace. Careful consideration needs to be given to overall policies on the use of restraint to ensure that any use of restraint is seen as a failure and that restraint is only permissible at all on the same basis that it would be permissible to restrain a non-disabled person, i.e. where a less restrictive option is not possible and the level of force and length of restraint (including consideration of the emotional/psychological harm) is less than the harm that would have occurred otherwise. To identify the level of justification necessary to justify restraint, compare the situation with whether a defence of 'self-defence' (or the defence of others) would provide a defence in criminal law to a charge of assault. All services should seek to eliminate the use of restraint entirely by focusing on prevention of distress and alternative coping strategies (see below in this chapter, for example).

34 However, this must be balanced with avoiding restricting an autistic person's life totally to within their current comfort zone. Without imposing change/variety purely for the sake of others (or to promote normality), it is appropriate to encourage new experiences that they might like based on their preferences.

Subject Index

Author Index